MONEY IN THE PRE-INDUSTRIAL WORLD: BULLION, DEBASEMENTS AND COIN SUBSTITUTES

T0330900

FINANCIAL HISTORY

Series Editor: *Robert E. Wright*

FORTHCOMING TITLES

MONEY IN THE PRE-INDUSTRIAL WORLD: BULLION, DEBASEMENTS AND COIN SUBSTITUTES

EDITED BY

John H. Munro

Routledge
Taylor & Francis Group

LONDON AND NEW YORK

First published 2012 by Pickering & Chatto (Publishers) Limited

Published 2016 by Routledge
2 Park Square, Milton Park, Abingdon, Oxfordshire OX14 4RN
711 Third Avenue, New York, NY 10017, USA

First issued in paperback 2015

Routledge is an imprint of the Taylor & Francis Group, an informa business

BRITISH LIBRARY CATALOGUING IN PUBLICATION DATA

Money in the pre-industrial world: bullion, debasements and coin substitutes.
– (Financial history) 1. Money – History. 2. Monetary policy – History. 3.
Coinage – History.
I. Series II. Munro, John H. A.
332.4'9-dc23

ISBN-13: 978-1-138-66171-4 (pbk)
ISBN-13: 978-1-8489-3230-2 (hbk)
Typeset by Pickering & Chatto (Publishers) Limited

CONTENTS

LIST OF FIGURES AND TABLES

LIST OF CONTRIBUTORS

John S. Deyell	Independent Scholar Ottawa, Canada
Arturo Giraldez	Professor, School of International Studies, University of the Pacific, California, USA
Kenneth W. Harl	Professor of Classical and Byzantine History Tulane University, USA
Renate Pieper	Professor of Economic and Social History Karl-Franzens Universität Graz, Austria
Nicholas J. Mayhew	Professor of Numismatics and Monetary History Ashmolean Museum, University of Oxford, UK
John H. Munro	Professor Emeritus of Economics University of Toronto, Canada
José Antonio Mateos Royo	Lecturer in Economic History University of Zaragoza, Spain
Peter Spufford	Professor Emeritus of European History University of Cambridge, UK
Alan Stahl	Curator of Numismatics Princeton University, USA
Herman Van der Wee	Professor Emeritus of Social and Economic History Katholieke Universiteit Leuven, Belgium

INTRODUCTION

John H. Munro

'Money makes the world go around' is a commonplace, admittedly trite expression, yet one that has profound importance for the evolution of the global economy, well beyond the Industrial Revolution era that marks the temporal terminus of this collection of ten essays.[1] Understanding how market-based economies functioned from even ancient times to the present is impossible without considering the role of money. Thus the ten authors of essays in this volume do not accept the Classical School of Economics' view that money is 'neutral', in terms of its impact on economic change – a view that has led some economists to ignore the role of money. Often allied with that view is a disdain for so-called 'monetarism'. But, to cite the famous Nobel Prize-winning Italian economist Franco Modigliani (1918–2003): if 'monetarism' simply means that 'money matters', so that monetary changes are not merely passive, neutral phenomena, but have some active role of their own, then 'we are all monetarists'. The authors of this volume all agree that 'money matters' and support as well the famous corresponding observation of Marc Bloch (1886–1944): that monetary phenomena may be compared to peculiar 'seismographs that not only register earth tremors, but sometimes bring them about'.[2] All ten chapters in this volume focus, to one degree or another, on three inter-related themes: bullion (uncoined precious metals), coinages (precious-metal commodity moneys) and their debasements, and substitutes for precious-metal moneys.

But what is meant by 'money' in this volume? We may begin with the catechism presented in so many introductory economics courses: on the four functions of money. The first and most important is in serving as a medium of exchange. For Aristotle, medieval scholastics and for many in the Classical School, this was and is the only true function of money. But the other three roles of money are also vitally important: as a 'money of account', or standard of value used in reckoning prices, costs and values; as a store of value (i.e. if the purchasing power of money remains stable); and as a standard of deferred payment (money in the form of a wide variety of credit instruments). First, we must understand the difference between bullion and coin; and, second, we must understand the link between coined money and moneys of account. Only then can we appreciate why debasement is so important in monetary history, and why it helped create the conditions for producing substitute moneys.

Bullion in International Trade

The term 'bullion' means any form of precious metal that is not in the form of legal tender coins, and any such precious metal that was destined to be minted into such coin, rather than directed to industrial or artistic purposes. Certainly a considerable amount of international trade was conducted in bullion rather than in coin. In late medieval Europe, however, from the onset of the widespread *guerres monétaires,* wars of highly competitive coinage debasements, most princely governments – thus notably excepting the Italian city-states – imposed bans on any trade in or on the export of 'bullion' and on the circulation of most foreign coins (usually excluding Italian gold florins and ducats). The objective of these bans was to force foreign coin and bullion in to the domestic ruler's mints: both to promote their own debasements and to defend themselves from neighbours' debasements. The penalties of fines and confiscations for violating these bans (or the cost of acquiring export licences) thus raised the transaction costs of dealing in bullion and demonetized foreign coin. Most west European states did permit the export of legal tender coins (domestic and foreign), with the significant exception of England, whose Parliament banned the export of all forms of precious metals (gold and silver, bullion and coin) from January 1364 to May 1663.[3]

Several studies in this volume – especially those by Herman Van der Wee, Nicholas Mayhew, Renate Pieper, Arturo Giraldez, and John Deyell – examine the importance of bullion payments in early-modern international trade, especially from the mid-sixteenth century, when a veritable flood of Spanish American silver vastly expanded western Europe's ability to finance a new global commerce, especially with 'the East': the Baltic and Russia, the Levant, southern and eastern Asia. Most of these regions had a limited demand for European manufactures and raw materials, except for silver and copper, especially because the long, peril-ridden maritime voyages, with high transaction costs, made most such goods prohibitively expensive (except in the nearby Levant). Normally, silver prevailed over gold, because these regions generally maintained a bimetallic ratio more favourable for that metal; and silver was also a useful ballast for half-empty outbound European ships.

**Table I.1: Gold and Silver Exports of the East India Company to Asia in kilograms of
pure metal, in Pound Sterling values, in decennial means, 1660–9 to 1710–19.**

Decade	Silver kg	Silver value in £ sterling	Gold kg	Gold Value in £ sterling	Total Treasure in £ sterling	Silver %	Gold %
1660–9	5,729.600	51,445.568	175.140	22,576.832	74,022.400	69.50	30.50
1670–9	11,364.000	102,063.850	1,015.300	132,027.550	234,091.400	43.60	56.40
1680–9	29,276.000	262,839.775	929.070	120,867.926	383,707.700	68.50	31.50
1690–9	18,179.000	163,230.172	24.690	3,331.228	166,561.400	98.00	2.00
1700–9	36,294.300	325,887.606	79.540	11,121.294	337,008.900	96.70	3.30
1710–19	41,133.600	369,189.591	14.970	2,228.509	371,418.100	99.40	0.60
TOTAL	141,976.500	1,274,656.563	2,238.710	292,153.337	1,566,809.900	81.35	18.65

Source: K. N. Chaudhuri, 'Treasure and Trade Balances: the East India Company's Export
Trade, 1660–1720', *Economic History Review*, 2nd ser., 21 (December 1968), Table 1,
pp. 497–8.

But were the precious metals so exported actually in the form of bullion or coin?
For there is much evidence that the Spanish and many other Europeans used
virtually fine silver *peso* coins minted in Mexico (New Spain); and, from the
early seventeenth century, the Dutch East India Company and other merchants
used high-denomination silver coins known as *negotiepenningen* (or *rixdollars* –
chiefly *Rijksdaalders, Leeuwendaalders, Rijders,* and silver *Dukaats*).

In seventeenth-century England, its East India Company had been forced to
evade the long-standing export ban on bullion and specie, until the Company
finally exerted enough pressure to convince Parliament, in May 1663, to repeal
most of the restrictions, thereby permitting the free export of 'all sortes of Forreigne Coyne or Bullion of Gold and Silver'.[4] But this statute still retained the ban
on exporting English coin, a ban that was not repealed until July 1819.[5] What
then did the East India Company export between 1663 and 1819: 'all sortes of
Forreigne Coyne' (e.g. Spanish and Dutch), or actual bullion? That question
remains to be answered. But Nicholas Mayhew's fascinating essay on 'Silver in
England, 1600–1800' demonstrates a third use of bullion from the goldsmiths'
accounts: as manufactured plate (and other jewellery), which could be readily
converted into either coinage or an export commodity. Indeed, in some years, the
goldsmiths' output of hallmarked silver in Troy lb (373.242 g) exceeded either the
Tower Mint's outputs or the silver exports of the East India Company.

Bullion and Precious Metal Coins

What is the real difference between bullion and coin? In this volume, the term
'coin' usually means a non-fiat commodity-money that is minted from precious
metals, gold and silver. In Europe, as opposed to the ancient, subsequent Islamic
worlds, and India, for example, such coins always contained at least some precious metal – even the very low denomination, base or petty coins known as

monnaies noires – until about the mid-sixteenth century. Even though the silver contents were so meagre in base coins, their presence was necessary to convince the public that such coins were still legitimate forms of money.

Coins minted from these two precious metals had two obvious advantages over bullion. First, they enjoyed the unique status of legal tender, denied to bullion, including the freedom to export them – with that notable exception of late medieval, early-modern England. Second, their use provided a significant saving in transaction costs in obviating the error-prone tasks of weighing the precious metals, assaying their exact fineness and assigning market values. So long as the issuing authority – prince or city – could retain respect for its own coins, those coins would circulate by 'tale' – i.e. by counting alone, at 'face value'. By enjoying these two advantages coins normally commanded an *agio* or premium over bullion, one that equalled the sum of minting fees: the mint-master's *brassage* and the ruler's *seigniorage* (coinage tax).

The Relationship between Precious-Metal Coins and Moneys of Account

The values of legal-tender coins can be understood only by examining the link between coins and the region's money of account systems. In western Europe from late Carolingian times, the most widespread system was the familiar one of pounds, shillings, and pence. Originally, the pound money of account equalled the value of a pound weight of fine silver. For accounting purposes, that notional pound (*libra, livre, lira*) was subdivided into 20 shillings (based on the Roman gold *solidus*), which in turn were subdivided into 12 pence (based on the Roman silver *denarius*): hence the standard notation of £, s, and d. The only coins struck in Carolingian times, however, were silver pennies (and subdivisions), so that the pound weight of fine silver was initially coined into 240 pennies. Not until the early thirteenth century were higher denomination European silver coins struck – some but not all worth a shilling (= 12d). From then to the French Revolution (in Great Britain to 1972), the 'pound' moneys of account were always equal to 240 currently circulating silver pennies in countries using this system.[6]

Coinage Debasement and European Moneys of Account

In medieval western Europe, however, the initially firm relationship between the pound weight of fine silver and the pound money of account soon broke down for one simple, universal reason: debasement. That term simply means a diminution in the quantity of fine precious metal represented in the unit of money of account. Such a change was undertaken by one or more of the following three techniques: (1) by reducing the weight of the coin, so that more coins were struck from the mint-weight; (2) by lowering the fineness of the coin, simply by adding more base metal, almost always copper (hence the very term 'debasement'); and (3) by increasing the coin's official money of account value. Whatever the combination of methods, the corresponding automatic result was an increase in the money of account value of the mint-weight of commercially fine metal: i.e. a greater number and nominal value of coins so struck.[7]

That third technique was virtually never applied to the penny itself, but only to some higher denomination silver coins and more especially to gold coins. If the ruler refused to debase higher-valued coins to the same degree, or failed to increase sufficiently their money of account values, then the market would have dictated an appropriate increase, relative to the penny's debasement.[8] The problem was the more acute with gold, whose coinage issues were first resumed in the West, in 1252, with the Florentine florin and the Genoese genovino. The next European gold coin issued was the French *écu* (shield), issued as part of Louis IX's monetary reform of August 1266; somewhat surprisingly, the Venetian ducat was first issued only in 1284–5. Other northern European realms did not issue their own gold coins until the 1330s and 1340s. The ensuing European monetary regimes were not really bimetallic: for the chief medium of exchange in most domestic economies was the silver coinage, while the gold coins were primarily reserved for regional and international trade (and 'priced' in terms of the silver-based moneys of account). For this reason, the majority of debasements in medieval Europe were of local silver coinages, since so many rulers were reluctant to damage their prestige abroad by tampering with their gold coins, as a symbol of their sovereignty, especially those that served internationally as 'dollars of the Middle Ages' – the Italian florins and ducats. Alan Stahl's chapter thus focuses on the assiduous determination of the Venetian governments to maintain the full purity of the gold ducat, in fineness, if not always in weight (from the sixteenth century), throughout the ensuing medieval and early modern eras (to 1797, having long been known as the *zecchino*, from *zecca* = mint).

The Florentine *florin*, last issued far earlier, in 1532, was not quite so successful in maintaining that pristine purity, though the changes were relatively minor compared to those in other, far less renowned European gold coins. Both Florence and Venice, while using gold-based moneys of account for international trade and finance, allowed the market to determine the exchange values of these gold coins, in terms of the silver-based *piccioli* (or *piccoli*) moneys of account. For the far better documented gold florin, we know that its market value in terms of the *lira di piccioli* rose from the initial £1 0s 0d in 1252, to £2 18s 8d in 1306, to its final value of £7 10s 0d in 1531–2: an overall increase of 650 per cent. That increase reflected, of course, not the physical debasement of gold but rather of the Florentine silver *denari*, *quattrini* and *soldi* coins. One might well say that the market imposed a corresponding 'debasement' on the florin, in terms of its money of account value, to correspond with the silver debasements.

In other European realms, their less prestigious gold coins often did undergo debasements: in both physical alterations and increased silver-based money of account values. Very often princes undertook such debasements by issuing entirely new gold coins, attempting to establish a new money of account value for such effectively debased coins in order to keep the mint's bimetallic ratio in line with the market ratios. If these princes failed to do so properly, the market would respond – in a manner so well described in Peter Spufford's chapter on Burgundian-Habsburg coinage debasements. The market would also respond, not just in raising the money of account value of the gold coins but also in promoting their export, if they remained undervalued, in accordance with Gresham's Law: that 'cheap' money drives out 'dear'.

The Motives for Coinage Debasements

Much of the economic history literature treats coinage debasements with ill-concealed disdain: for both the princes' ulterior motives and the often dire consequences for the public. Peter Spufford's long chapter on the 'Scourge of Debasement', in his magisterial *Money and its Use in Medieval Europe* (1988), presents a sound case for contending that the overall impacts of medieval European debasements were very harmful.[9] Those negative views are not always justified, everywhere, at all times, especially not in early-modern Europe. For debasements had not one but two powerful motives: aggressive and defensive, with very different consequences.

We begin with the first: the aggressive motives. As noted earlier, one of the costs that a merchant had to pay in having his bullion minted into legal-tender coin was the ruler's tax known as seigniorage. When so many rulers found that their fiscal resources were limited or constrained, they often had no recourse but to exploit their mints to produce greater seigniorage revenues (as explained in Chapter 1). That was especially true in times of war. Who can deny that a ruler's chief obligation was the defence of his realm, for most warfare was viewed in such terms (even by most aggressors)? It is hardly necessary to prove that the mint-seigniorage provided the major role in financing warfare: only that such revenues were important *at the margin*, when the ruler's ability to raise funds quickly from taxes or feudal dues was severely limited. The significance of coinage debasements for such fiscal purposes in financing warfare and defence is also well demonstrated and documented in Harl's Chapter 2 on third-century imperial Rome, in Spufford's Chapter 4 on the late fifteenth-century Netherlands, and in Mateos Royo's Chapter 7 on seventeenth-century Aragon.

These fiscal motives may also have been present in the chronic, long-term silver-coinage debasements in late-medieval India, particularly in the Delhi sultanate (if not in Bengal), from *c.* 1340 to *c.* 1500, as discussed in John Deyell's essay. But possibly there, and more certainly in late-medieval, early-modern Europe, an opposite motive often prevailed: defensive debasements to protect the ruler's mints and his realm's coinages. Such debasements had three major aspects, of roughly equal importance, in most countries. The first was, obviously, defence against aggressive debasements from mints in adjacent lands, for such debasements proved to be the most successful in attracting foreign bullion when debased coins so issued could be spent abroad: coins that were often imitations or direct counterfeits of a neighbouring realm's own coins that again circulated by tale.[10] A second related defensive reason was to counteract a form of internal and private criminal debasement: i.e. the clipping, filing and 'sweating' of coins. But the third reason was simply to remedy the silver losses from normal wear and tear in high-velocity coin circulations (i.e. of low denomination silver coins).

When the domestic coin circulation had suffered considerable deterioration from all these causes, the ruler's coin would lose the public's confidence and thus its premium or *agio* over bullion. Merchants would, consequently, no longer deliver bullion to the mint, and would cull recently, properly minted and thus overvalued silver coins and sell them along with bullion for export, usually to offending foreign mints. This form of Gresham's Law was frequently cited in so many late medieval monetary ordinances as a justification for a defensive debasement. Clearly such a debasement was absolutely necessary, under such circumstances, to restore the *agio* on coinage in order to reactivate the mints and to protect the realm against further exports of precious metals. That necessarily meant a newly issued coinage whose precious metal content was reduced to match the level of currently circulating coinage. In many instances, however, a legitimate defensive justification was used to disguise a new round of aggressive debasements: undoubtedly on the grounds that the best defence was offence, especially if it proved to be profitable.[11] We may readily detect the difference simply by comparing the seigniorage rates: high with aggressive debasements, low with defensive debasements.

The Special Case of Early-Modern Spain: Castile and Aragon

In early-modern Europe, the Iberian peninsula provided a remarkable exception to the otherwise almost universal pattern of silver-coinage debasements. The principal reason, explored further in the chapters by José Mateos Royo, Renate Pieper and Arturo Giraldez, is that the kings of Aragon (1372) and Castile (1474, 1497) had surrendered both their right to alter the coinage without parliament's consent, and their prerogative to collect more than the customary mint fees.[12] Indeed, the Castilian and Aragonese silver and gold coinages remained unaltered from 1497 to 1686. That monetary restriction did not apply, however, to the largely copper *vellón* or billon coinages. In 1599, Philip III issued the kingdom's first issues of purely copper *vellón* coins, subsequently debasing them, by weight.[13] The results, as Mateos Royo so well demonstrates, was a classic demonstration of Gresham's Law in both Spanish kingdoms. Because the gold and true silver coinages remained unchanged, market transactions brought about two changes: first, an increased premium value on the high-value coins, and, second, in so far as such coins remained undervalued, their increased export to France and other realms. At the same time, both Castile and Aragon were inundated with influxes of foreign debased silver and billon coins (some from Valencia and Catalonia, outside the crown's jurisdiction), promoting a relative shift, in domestic circulation, to worn and impaired coins, further aggravating the Spanish monetary plight, which, in Aragon itself, was worsened by rising balance of payments deficits. The appeals of seventeenth-century mercantilist-minded Aragonese *arbitrists* for rational, purely defensive debasements of the silver, and for various state measures to address the balance of payments deficits were, in the face of trenchant traditionalist opposition, largely in vain (especially before the Castilian coin adjustments of 1686).

The Dutch Reaction to the Circulation of Foreign Debased Coin: the Wissebank and its 'Bank Money'

In the early seventeenth century, the young Dutch Republic was similarly being inundated by an influx of debased, counterfeit, and defective foreign coins, all the more so since Dutch trade was attracting merchants and their heterogeneous coinages from all over western Europe to Amsterdam. But as Herman Van der Wee demonstrates in his Chapter 5, the newly civic-founded Wisselbank (1609) adopted a far more effective and economically progressive solution: a coin substitute in the form of 'bank money', expressed in the bank deposit accounts and ledgers as money of account Dutch guilders (*gulden* or *florins*), each of which represented a fixed, unvarying amount of fine silver. All merchants were required to surrender all foreign coins (and suspect domestic coins) to the Wisselbank to be deposited (after being weighed and assayed) in bank accounts as such fixed-value guilders, while the Wisselbank delivered those coins to the mint for recoinage into perfectly stable *gulden* (guilders) and the aforesaid, high-value *negotiepennigen*. Merchants were also required to redeem acceptance bills (bills of exchange) at the Wisselbank, above a modest minimum. The overall result was that most merchants, domestic and foreign, while still permitted to make withdrawals in good coin, were strongly encouraged to conduct domestic commercial and financial transactions instead in bank money (bank account transfers). In doing so, they reduced transaction costs in trade, and, more important, reserved relatively scarce supplies of silver *negotiepennigen* for their most profitable use: in exports to the Baltic, Russia, the Levant, southern and eastern Asia. Late medieval private Italian banks had, to be sure, pioneered the system of *moneta di banco,* but not with the far-reaching beneficial economic consequences produced by Amsterdam's public Wisselbank in early-modern Europe.

The increasing role of copper as a substitute for silver coins

As indicated earlier, the most widespread seventeenth-century substitute for precious metal coins was copper – a genuine monetary metal of great historic importance: not just for debasements, but for the effective circulation of good-quality gold and silver coins, since copper supplied the necessary hardening agent to counteract both wear and tear and chemical erosion. A transition to purely copper coins was thus both natural and indeed inevitable, especially with its role in debasements – so long as the public's psychological link between precious metals and 'money' could be broken. Once more we must call attention to the previous use of copper coins outside Europe: especially in the Islamic world (with *falus* coins), and before that, in ancient Rome. As demonstrated in Kenneth Harl's essay, third-century Roman emperors engaged in very extensive issues of largely copper ('silver clad') coins, known as *antoniniani* and *aurelianiani* – 'fiduciary coins', in his terminology – which proved most successful in financing the military and imperial recovery.

Within early-modern Europe, the government of the Habsburg Netherlands, and not of Habsburg Spain, was the first to issue pure copper coins: in 1543. France followed suit in 1577, and laggard England only in 1672. As Nicholas Mayhew demonstrates, a primary reason for the English issue of copper coinages was a severe dearth of silver that at least partly reflects the crown's and Parliament's refusal to engage in further defensive coinage debasements after 1601, largely for ideological reasons – reasons underlying the Great Recoinage of 1696–8: one undertaken fully at crown expense, with no alteration of the coinage (and no seigniorage). As the inevitable consequence, good silver coin was undervalued and exported, while barely any new silver came to the Tower Mint. The dearth of silver was gradually remedied by not only by the use of copper coins (chiefly now from Swedish mines) but also gold coins, whose supplies from Brazil grew strongly from the 1690s; but gold coins were obviously unsuitable for low-value transactions.

The Paradox of Coin Scarcities in a World Awash with Spanish American Silver: Bullion Exports to the East

Paradoxically, as several authors in this volume stress, both New Spain (Mexico) and western Europe experienced regional scarcities of silver during the very height of the Price Revolution era, when such seemingly vast quantities of Spanish American silver were entering Europe, especially from the 1550s to the 1620s, and were even then held responsible for that inflation.[14] In New Spain, as both Renate Pieper and Arturo Giraldez demonstrate, we find strong evidence for such a dearth of silver, even from the early seventeenth century. In their well documented view, despite evidence for the riches of the Zacatecas and other Mexican mines, the dearth of silver was largely due to the vast scale of silver exports: especially to Spain (via Seville) and elsewhere in Europe, but also, across the Pacific, to the Philippines, to finance the very important trade in Chinese silks. Evidently the remaining domestic supplies of freshly minted Mexican silver could not keep pace with the growth of the colonial economy and its population. Space limitations do not permit any discussion of Pieper's valuable

Money in the Pre-Industrial World

conclusions on how, when, where and why Spanish American silver imports, and re-exports to Asia, affected prices in Castile and more especially on the Amsterdam's exchanges (related to the role of the Wisselbank).

Thus, while the failure to engage in defensive debasements may explain some regional European scarcities of coined silver, the strongly growing West European exports of silver to southern and eastern Asia, the Baltic and the Levant, and as also discussed by Van der Wee and Nicolas, provide a more powerful explanation, though most especially from the 1660s. For by that decade, the English, Dutch and other European exports of silver to the Baltic, Levant and elsewhere in Asia were evidently surpassing the Spanish American silver imports (though Mexican if not Bolivian-Peruvian imports did revive in the early eighteenth century, as indicated in Pieper's chapter).[15] As tables I.2 and I.3 indicate, Europe's balance of payments deficit, with the consequent need to ship bullion to remedy those deficits, was far greater in trading with southern Asia than with the Ottoman Empire and the Levant, for two reasons: the latter offered a far more favourable market for western merchandise, especially textiles;[16] and trade with the latter involved far lower transportation and transaction costs, thus keeping prices of western goods in a reasonable range for consumers in Ottoman and other Levantine markets. On average, for the periods indicated in the tables, the composition of the East India Company's export trade with India and South Asia was 79 per cent in bullion and only 21 per cent in merchandise, while West European trade with the Ottoman Empire was almost the reverse: 33 per cent in bullion and 67 per cent in merchandise.

Table I.2: Exports of the English East India Company to Asia in 'Treasure' (Bullion and Specie) and in Merchandise with values expressed in pounds sterling in decennial means, 1660–9 to 1710–19.

Decade	Total Treasure in £ sterling	Merchandise in £ sterling	Total Value in £ sterling	Treasure %	Merchandise %
1660–9	74,022.400	41,085.200	115,107.600	64.31	35.69
1670–9	234,091.400	89,990.800	324,082.200	72.23	27.77
1680–9	383,707.700	56,170.200	439,877.900	87.23	12.77
1690–9	166,561.400	72,065.200	238,626.600	69.80	30.20
1700–9	337,008.900	60,876.500	397,885.400	84.70	15.30
1710-19	371,418.100	97,771.300	469,189.400	79.16	20.84
TOTAL	1,566,809.900	417,959.200	1,984,769.100	78.94	21.06

Source: K. N. Chaudhuri, 'Treasure and Trade Balances: the East India Company's Export Trade, 1660–1720', *Economic History Review*, 2nd ser., 21 (Dec. 1968), Table 1, pp. 497–8.

**Table I.3: European Exports to the Ottoman Empire (Levant) in 1686–7
in Merchandise and Bullion, with values expressed in Turkish Piastres.**

Exporter Nation	TOTAL PORTS Merchandise	%	Bullion	%	Total
France	660,636	52.16	605,900	47.84	1,266,536
England	1,415,138	80.76	337,075	19.24	1,752,213
Holland	926,780	62.88	547,000	37.12	1,473,780
Venice	569,200	78.92	152,000	21.08	721,200
Livorno	167,100	45.03	204,000	54.97	371,100
Genoa	115,250	100.00	0	0.00	115,250
Ragusa	0	0.00	8,000	100.00	8,000
Messina	0	0.00	20,000	100.00	20,000
Malta	0	0.00	7,000	100.00	7,000
TOTALS	3,854,104	67.20	1,880,975	32.80	5,735,079

Source: Michel Fontenay, 'Le commerce des Occidentaux dans les échelles du Levant en
1686–1687', in Bartolomé Bennassar and Robert Sauzet (eds.), Chrétiens et musulmans
à la Renaissance: Actes du 37e Colloque International du Centre d'Études Supérieures
de la Renaissance (1994) (Paris: H. Champion, 1988), Table 1, p. 351.

Finding such scarcities of silver in India may seem equally paradoxical, since we
are led to believe that so much of that silver ended up in India. As John Deyell
has demonstrated, however, many late-medieval Indian states (Delhi, Jaunpur,
if not so much Bengal) recorded periodic scarcities of silver; and India in general had not received all that much silver from Europe before the 1570s. Only
thereafter do European supplies make a major impact – an impact diminished,
however, by the vast scale of the Indian and other Asian economies. As indicated
earlier, a prolonged series of silver coinage debasements in the Delhi sultanate provide further possible evidence of an Indian 'silver problem' before 1575
(when Deyell's essay terminates).

Substitutes for Coined Silver, as 'Small Change': Indian Cowries and Mexican Cacao Beans.

One solution to that silver dearth, adopted in both late medieval India and
early-modern New Spain, was yet another silver-coin substitute: in both places,
non-metallic. In India, as elsewhere in the Indian Ocean basin, the most common alternative form of money was a seashell, known as cowries, produced and
distributed in the millions. Their exchange value was determined not by fiat
but by market operations through standard operations of 'supply and demand'
– with obvious problems in establishing stable money of account values in relation to traditional gold and silver coinages. Copper coinages were not unknown
in India; but the growing Portuguese copper imports (along with some silver,
though chiefly to the East Indies) – the product of the Central European min-

ing boom in *argentiferous cupric* ores – do not seem to have made any impact in India before Deyell's study ends in 1575.[17]

Our current concern thus directs us to the importance of Arturo Giraldez's research on the cacao bean, as an effective coin substitute, but with the same problems in establishing stable exchange rates with silver and gold coinages as seen with cowries in south Asia. Its value as medium of exchange, with a large geographic distribution, was based on its earlier and continuing role as an important commercial commodity: first, for as a major item in domestic food consumption and then as an export to Europe and Asia, where it created a new craze for chocolate (food and drink).

The Role of Bank Money and Paper Credit from the 1660s

The importance of cowries and cacao beans as coin substitutes lies more in reflecting relative monetary scarcities than in providing effective long-term solutions. In the Dutch Republic, from *c.*1610, and in England, from the 1660s (but more the 1690s), such a solution was found in expanding the role of 'bank money'. In Restoration England, the various new goldsmith banks soon came to excel the Dutch in issuing a wide variety of fully negotiable (and discountable) forms of paper credit – including bank notes – as effective money substitutes. Of even greater importance, was the Financial Revolution from the 1690s, including the vital role of the Bank of England, both in becoming a lender of last resort, to replenish cash reserves of financial institutions (a function that the Wisselbank as a *giro* bank could not fulfil), and in managing a permanent, funded national debt in the form of fully negotiable annuities traded on the Amsterdam and London exchanges. But those events take us from the monetary to the financial sphere, even if closely related, and thus lie beyond the scope of this volume.

Some Conclusions on the Role of Coinage Debasements in the Pre-Industrial World

Given the overriding importance of coinage debasements in this volume, we must attempt an answer to the inevitable question: were they, overall, harmful or beneficial? That depends on whether they were aggressive or defensive and on their extent. Without much doubt, aggressive fiscally motivated debasements often did have dire consequences: in transferring incomes from the wage-earning poor (including many proletarian peasants) to the profit- and rent-seeking merchants, but also from the church and landed aristocracy dependent on fixed incomes, as defined in nominal moneys of account. Yet many small farmers and those in natural resource industries, as well as merchants, benefited from rising prices of their products (often rising in fact in *real* terms). Furthermore, the findings of Harl (for ancient Rome), Spufford and Munro (for the fifteenth-century Netherlands and sixteenth-century England) refute the contention that debasements produced inflations that were in any way proportional to the extent of precious-metal reductions. Spufford indeed, as his major contribution to this debate, contends that percentage increases in mint prices for bullion rather than percentage reductions in precious-metal contents was the far more decisive method by which debasements affected both exchange rates and prices; and he demonstrates how debasements, though the exchange rates, promoted exports (and curbed imports).

Whatever the actual consequences of debasements, the still politically powerful aristocracies resolutely maintained their hostility to debasements in any form, in medieval and early modern Europe. That resolute consistent opposition (except in times of war) did not necessarily promote the public good in peacetime, when defensive debasements were so often clearly required.

Certainly, the historical record demonstrates that debasements, in either form, failed to provide any long-term solution to the two major 'bullion famines' of the later fourteenth and fifteenth centuries, when European debasements were the most prominent. At the same time, we must also admit the possibility that aggressive debasements aggravated monetary scarcities during this era, in two respects: first, by causing a Gresham's Law chain reaction that encouraged both hoarding and specie exports; and, second, by seriously curtailing the use of credit, since creditors were generally reluctant to accept repayments, those stipulated in moneys of account, in depreciated currency (i.e. to accept an anticipated *real* loss).

Another, very different view is presented in the recent, highly praised monograph, *The Big Problem of Small Change* (2002), by Thomas Sargent and his co-author François Velde.[18] They contend that the primary role of coinage debasements had long been to remedy chronic shortages of 'small change'. The historic record, for both medieval and early-modern Europe, does not support this view (in either motivation or results), as indicated in this volume and many other studies. Debasements certainly did not provide effective solutions for remedying shortages of small change. For if debasements had been confined just to the petty billon coinages, leaving the higher-denomination coins unchanged, the result would have been those examined in seventeenth-century Spain, with an aggravated monetary scarcity. The two authors fully admit, however, that the effective 'small change' solution lay in steam-powered technological innovations of the Industrial Revolution era, in coining money (to prevent counterfeiting, clipping, 'sweating', etc.), along with the subsequent establishment of a proper Gold Standard. Again, these monetary solutions lie beyond the temporal boundaries of this volume of essays.

1 THE TECHNOLOGY AND ECONOMICS OF COINAGE DEBASEMENTS IN MEDIEVAL AND EARLY MODERN EUROPE: WITH SPECIAL REFERENCE TO THE LOW COUNTRIES AND ENGLAND

John H. Munro

Coinage debasements in pre-industrial Europe, despite their frequency and especially their severity during the late medieval *guerres monétaires*, and despite their often important economic consequences, remain a subject that is often mentioned but remains ill understood in the economic history literature. Indeed, one often-cited article, aptly titled 'The Debasement Puzzle' (1996), by three highly respected economists, sought to demonstrate that coinage debasements were both impractical and economically futile.[1] Yet debasements continued to 'plague' Europe until the eighteenth century. The objective of this study is to demonstrate that they were both practical and often quite effective in their often very different goals, and were not always so deleterious in their effects as is traditionally portrayed.

Medieval Coinages and their Relation to Moneys of Account

The nature, techniques and economic consequences of European coinage debasements must be understood first in relation to the local money of account system for that coinage. In medieval and early-modern western Europe (except for the Iberian peninsula and parts of Germany), most local moneys of account were based upon the system that was established under Charlemagne, *c*.795. It was directly linked to the new Carolingian pound weight of fine silver (489.51 g) in that the pound money of account was given the precise value of this weight of fine silver.[2] Obviously no silver coins weighing a pound were struck; and for centuries, the only silver coins struck were the various regional pennies (and their subdivisions). Solely for accounting purposes, in reckoning prices, wages, values, etc., the pound money of account (*libra, livre, lira*) was subdivided into 20 shillings (based on the Roman gold *solidus*), which in turn were subdivided into 12 pence (based on the Roman silver *denarius*), so that this pound of account always consisted of 240 currently circulating silver pennies.[3] Not until the thirteenth century did some Italian city-states and then France introduce heavier weight silver coins, known as *grossi* or *gros*.[4] The primary reason for issuing such larger, 'full-bodied' coins was the deterioration in the silver contents of the original penny through the ensuing centuries of almost universal, if periodic coin debasements, and the consequent rise in prices in each region's silver-based money of account. At the accession of King Philip II Augustus in 1179, the French silver *denier parisis* contained only 0.509 g of commercially fine silver (*argent-le-roy*): only about half as much as the 1.020 g of fine silver contained in the original Carolingian *denier* of c. 795.[5]

The Forms and Nature of Medieval Coinage Debasements

Medieval coinage debasements normally took two different forms. The first, and by far the most common, was a physical decrease in the quantity of silver or gold contained in current coins of the same face value; and that meant, therefore, a corresponding reduction in the quantity of such precious metals represented in the related money of account: the penny, the shilling and the pound. The mint undertook such physical debasements by two different means, but often in combination: by reducing the weight of the coin itself and/or by diminishing the coin's precious-metal fineness. The latter method simply meant adding more and more base metal, copper, to the alloy. As a consequence of either or both physical methods a pound or *marc* weight of fine metal was struck into a greater number of coins, of each denomination, with a consequent increased money of account value of that pound or *marc* of fine metal so struck into the newly debased coins. At the same time, the face value of the currently circulating penny, whatever its fine silver content, always retained the value of 1d in the local money of account.

The alternative but mathematically related form of debasement was, paradoxically, the seeming opposite: an increase in the money of account value of the coin concerned, a method chiefly applied only to the gold coinages. Almost invariably, a physical debasement of the silver coinages necessarily required a compensatory debasement of the gold coinage, if only by raising that coin's money of account value, in order to maintain an equilibrium or balance between the market values of the two precious metals and the corresponding mint ratio. In this era, the normal bimetallic ratio – the ratio of the market values of gold to silver – varied between 11:1 and 12:1. If, for example, the prince debased just the silver coinage, thereby raising the relative money of account value of a *marc* or pound of silver, he would automatically have altered the mint's bimetallic ratio to 'favour' silver, and thus to 'disfavour' gold. He may have done so deliberately in order to attract an increased supply of silver into his mints. But the 'opportunity cost' of doing so was some corresponding loss of gold coins or bullion, which merchants would export to seek higher exchange values abroad, either on the market or at foreign mints. If the corresponding changes in these mint ratios exceeded the value of the mint charges (equivalent to the 'gold shipping' points under the modern gold standard), the prince would have suffered an unwanted loss of gold. Therefore, to protect his mints from such unwanted losses of gold, the prince would have debased his gold coinages as well, to some corresponding degree. While, as just indicated, many princes chose to do so simply by raising the money of account or exchange value for their gold coins, some did so either by physically debasing the existing gold coins, or by issuing entirely new coins with a lesser amount of gold, and with corresponding exchange rates calibrated to match the market ratios. Note that in most of medieval and early-modern Europe, the values of gold coins were always expressed in terms of the silver-based money of account.

When this technique was applied to silver coins, only the higher-denomination coins were subjected to such an increase in their money of account or exchange values, while the penny and other lower-denomination coins underwent physical debasements. The most famous example took place during the first debasements of France's Philip IV the Fair (r. 1285–1314), the monarch responsible for launching the disastrous late medieval *guerres monétaires*. Initially, from 1295 to 1303, he debased only the silver *denier* coins, while maintaining the fineness and weight of the prized *gros tournois*, the *sou* or shilling coin that Louis IX had introduced in August 1266. But he was forced to raise its money of account value from 12d to 15d *tournois*, and then (after 1303) to 26.25 d.t., while also reducing its fineness by 25 per cent.[6] Whatever the method employed, the consequence of any debasement, of both silver and gold, was a reduction in the precious-metal content of the money of account units: the penny, shilling and pound.

The Legal and Commercial Advantages in Using Legal-Tender Coin Instead of Bullion

Finally, the economic and legal distinctions between coined money and bullion are necessary to understand fully the nature and economics of medieval, early-modern debasements. In most European realms during this long era (except for the Italian city-states and early-modern Holland), especially from the commencement of the *guerres monétaires*, in the late thirteenth, early fourteenth century, trading in or exporting 'bullion' was illegal, with severe penalties in the form of both confiscation of the metals and fines (or even prison or exile). In most such realms, the legal definition of 'bullion' excluded all legal-tender coins and those metals allotted, by licence only, to goldsmiths and jewellers to be fashioned into plate, jewellery or other industrial goods. Some bullion exports were permissible: for government agents on official business abroad and for some merchants engaged in international trade, but only on the purchase of costly licences. Otherwise, all other forms of precious metals not covered by these exemptions had to be surrendered to the ruler's mints for conversion into domestic legal tender coins.

Similarly, these principalities also prohibited the importation and circulation of foreign silver coins and most foreign gold coins, with the exception of some favoured international 'dollars' of the day: e.g. Florentine florins, Venetian ducats, English nobles, French *écus*. Apart from those exceptions, they were also declared to be 'bullion', with the obvious requirement that they too be delivered to the ruler's mints for recoinage.[7] England's Parliament went even further, with legislation in force from January 1364 to May 1663 that prohibited the export of all forms of precious metal (except under licence) – all gold, all silver, in both bullion and legal tender coin – and also the domestic circulation of any foreign coins (except briefly, in the 1520s, under Henry VIII).[8] The aim of such bullionist proto-Mercantilist legislation was to protect the domestic realm from debased or otherwise fraudulent foreign and to promote an increase in the ruler's own mint outputs.

For most merchants and the general public, using coin rather than bullion provided two major savings in transaction costs. First and most obvious was in avoiding the risks and thus costs of confiscation and heavy fines, but also the costs of obtaining licences for legal exports of bullion. The second and far less obvious advantage lay in avoiding the costs of estimating the true market value of the precious metals: that is, the very error-prone costs of weighing the precious metals and assaying their true fineness, and of then ascertaining the proper money of account values. In contrast, legal-tender coins, stamped with identifying symbols on the obverse and reverse, as the sovereign's guarantee of their true precious-metal value, allowed them to circulate by 'tale' – i.e. by counting the coins, at their assigned 'face value'. The lower the denomination, the higher the transaction cost of assaying coins and not accepting them by tale.

One of the most contentious issues in monetary history is whether or not coins 'passed' or circulated by tale; and the denial that they did so constitutes a prime reason for doubting the efficacy of medieval debasements. All of the available commercial evidence does indicate that silver coins were accepted at official face value in domestic trade, with only rare exceptions. Consider the fact that by the later Middle Ages almost all European silver pennies had undergone some debasements, yet all were still treated as pennies in commerce. For example, the first Flemish silver penny groot, struck in May 1300, had an almost perfect fineness (95.667 per cent), containing 3.794 g pure silver; but, by the coinage ordinance of June 1418, that same Flemish silver penny groot had a fineness of only 41.667 per cent and contained only 0.850 g pure silver: just 22.40 per cent as much as in the original penny. Are we to assume that the 1418 single groot then circulated at a discounted value of just slightly more than one-fifth of a penny?[9] Thus, when did such discounting of silver pennies commence; and how was it calculated, in usable commercial values, over time? These questions reveal the very absurdity of denying the obvious: that penny coins always circulated by tale at this face value, irrespective of their intrinsic metal contents.[10] We might assume, however, that gold coins were more likely to circulate at 'market' values than by tale; but the evidence for England and the Low Countries indicates that, except for times of radical debasements, or sudden shifts in the market's bimetallic ratios, most gold coins did circulate at official values: but only so long as the public retained confidence in the ruler's coins, as stamped with his insignia.[11]

Considerable savings in these two sets of transaction costs correspondingly provided legal tender coins, including legal-tender foreign coins, with an *agio* or premium over their bullion values.[12] That premium value represented the sum of the mintage fees, which were deducted from the total value of the coins produced from the bullion: a value known as the *traite* in medieval Flanders, and the *pied de la monnaie* in France.[13] So long as this *agio* was at least equal to the sum of the mintage fees, so that coins remained more valuable than bullion, merchants would continue to deliver bullion to the mints. Conversely, whenever domestic coins lost that *agio*, bullion would cease to be delivered to the prince's mint, and would most likely be either hoarded or exported to some foreign mint, where it commanded a higher exchange value.

The Mint Price and the Mintage Fees: Brassage and Seigniorage Fees

The mint price for bullion was the total coined value (known as the *traite*) less the sum of the minting fees, which consisted of two distinct elements: brassage, for the mint-master, and seigniorage, for the prince (or republican government). Both fees were specified in nominal money account, in terms of the currently debased (or reformed coinage), though really as a percentage of the bullion brought to be coined.

Brassage was an economically necessary fee for the simple reason that it literally 'costs money to make money'. That fee thus compensated the mint-master for his own production costs: above all, the cost of the copper alloy; the capital costs of maintaining the mint, in the form of his dye tools (hammers), the furnaces, forges, melting pots, shears; the administrative costs of managing the mint – including light, heat, and rent; the labour costs of producing the actual coins and running the mint; and finally the cost of licence fees paid to the prince and other fees paid to official coin assayers and mint inspectors. Such costs were normally relatively modest, except for the low-valued petty coinage, whose production entailed a relatively higher cost in copper alloys and in labour (i.e. more coins cut per alloyed marc or pound). The capital cost of building the mint itself was usually borne by the prince or town government.

The other fee was the prince's seigniorage, arguably a less necessary fee from the vantage point of the economy, but not from the point of view of the prince. Most princes indeed claimed the right to exact a profit from the coinage, one based on their royal or princely prerogative in maintaining a monopoly on their realm's coinages. Depending on the circumstances that led to any debasement, the seigniorage fees might have been relatively modest or relatively high. In the latter case, whether the prince was driven to debase the coinage out of avarice or dire economic necessity, he was still restrained in setting his seigniorage fees by having to offer a mint price that was competitive with those from neighbouring mints. For obviously, the higher the seigniorage fee, the lower would be the mint price – and too low a price would thus discourage or even prevent an influx of bullion to his mints.

The objective of most debasements therefore was to set a new, higher mint price for one or both metals that would satisfy two objectives, which were not always compatible: first, to attract more bullion, foreign and domestic, to the prince's mint by offering a real gain to merchants; and second, to allow the prince to augment (or at least maintain) his mint seigniorage revenues. The domestic sources of bullion included both domestic precious-metal hoards, often in the form of household plate and jewellery, but especially the previous issues of the prince's coins, which were usually demonetized at the time of the debasement. Thus the new mint price had to be high enough to compensate merchants and the public for the total mintage fees that had been paid on the former coin issues. Obviously, the new mint price also had to be high enough to attract bullion away from foreign, competing mints, while also discouraging the export of precious metals. As indicated earlier, one danger inherent in all debasements was that 'favouring' one metal (by a more extensive debasement) might undervalue the other metal and thus promote its export abroad to mints and regions with a more favourable bimetallic ratio for that other metal.

Motives for Late Medieval Coinage Debasements, I:
Aggressive Fiscal Motives (Profit-Seeking)

Most monetary historians have focused on the aggressive debasements: as profit-seeking, fiscally motivated enterprises, chiefly to finance both warfare and defence. Indeed, the French philosopher and monetary observer, Nicholas Oresme bluntly and succinctly stated as much, in his famous treatise *De Moneta, c.*1355:[14]

> I am of the opinion that the main and final cause why the prince pretends to the power of altering the coinage is the profit or gain that he can get from it; [for] it would otherwise be vain to make so many and so great changes.

How a prince's mint profits could be so increased can be seen Table 1.1, for the debasement of the Flemish silver double groot coin (worth 2d) that Duke Philip the Good of Burgundy undertook in November 1428.

Table 1.1: Flemish Coinage Debasements, June 1418 and November 1428. Debasements of the Flemish double groot.

Part A: Changes in weight & fineness	June 1418		November 1428		% Change
Money of account value in d groot Fl.	2		2		0.00
Fineness in *argent-le-roy* in					
deniers and grains: 24 grains per denier	6	0	5	8	
% fineness AR*	50.00		44.44		-11.12
Percentage pure silver	47.92		42.59		-11.11
Weight: taille per *marc* (244.7529 g)	68.00		68.50		-11.11
Weight in grams	3.599		3.573		0.74
Fine silver (AR) content in grams	1.800		1.588		-0.73
Pure silver contents in grams	1.725		1.522		-11.76
Argent-le-roy = 23/24 pure silver = 95.833% pure					-11.76

Part B: Mint price, mintage fees, and *traite* per marc AR	shillings	pence	decimal £	%	no. coins	shillings	pence	decimal £	%	no. coins	% increase
Traite per *marc*: coined value of silver*	22	8.00	1.133	100.00	136.000	25	8.25	1.284	100.00	154.125	13.33
Brassage in shillings and pence	1	2.00	0.058	5.15	7.000	1	2.25	0.059	4.62	7.125	1.79
Seigniorage in shillings and pence	0	4.00	0.017	1.47	2.000	0	6.00	0.025	1.95	3.000	50.00
Total mint charges	1	6.00	0.075	6.62	9.000	1	8.25	0.084	6.57	10.125	12.50
Mint price for bullion: shillings, pence	21	2.00	1.058	93.38	127.000	24	0.00	1.200	93.43	144.000	13.39
Traite per *marc*	22	8.00	1.133	100.00	136.000	25	8.25	1.284	100.00	154.125	13.33

* *Traite* per *marc*: T = (taille per marc * value of coin) divided by the percentage fineness in *argent-le-roy*.

Sources: Louis Deschamps de Pas, 'Essai sur l'histoire monétaire des comtes de Flandre de la Maison de Bourgogne et description de leurs monnaies d'or et d'argent: Philippe le Bon (1419–1467): première partie', *Revue numismatique*, nouvelle série, 6 (1861), pp. 458–78.
J. H. Munro, *Wool, Cloth and Gold: The Struggle for Bullion in Anglo-Burgundian Trade, 1340–1478*. Centre d'Histoire Économique et Sociale (Brussels: Éditions de l'Université de Bruxelles; and Toronto: University of Toronto Press, 1973), Appendix I: Table G, p. 204

In comparison with the previous silver double groot issued in 1418, this debasement reduced the coin's fine silver content by 0.203 g, or 11.77 per cent. The fineness itself was diminished from 47.92 per cent purity to 42.59 per cent; and the weight fell from 1.800 g (68 to the *marc*) to 1.588 g (68.5 to the *marc*). As a consequence the number of double groot coins struck from a fine *marc* of silver increased from 136 to 154.125 such coins, thus increasing the *traite* or coined value of the *marc* from 22s 8d (136 * 2d) to 25s 8d 6 mites (8.25d) groot Flemish.[15]

By this debasement, the total mintage fees rose from 1s 6d to 1s 8d 6 mites per fine *marc* of silver. Of the two fees, the seigniorage was increased, in nominal terms, by 50 per cent: from 4d to 6d (in real terms, from 1.47 per cent to 1.95 per cent of the fine *marc* coined). The mint-master's brassage, on the other hand, was increased from only 1s 2d to 1s 2d 6 (2.25d) mites, and in real terms it fell: from 5.15 per cent to 4.62 per cent of the fine *marc* so coined. Obviously this debasement was instigated by the duke's own fiscal needs (during his wars in Holland and France), and can hardly be blamed on profit-seeking from the mint-master, whose minuscule increase of 6 mites per fine *marc* could hardly have compensated him for the increased costs in copper alloy and labour.

Indeed, the total mintage fees, as a percentage of bullion coined, fell from 6.62 per cent to 6.57 per cent of the bullion coined; and that decline necessarily meant an increase, in both nominal and real terms, in the merchants' price for bullion (the mint price). That rose, per *marc* of fine silver, from 22s 8d to 24s 0d groot Flemish: and thus from 93.38 per cent to 93.43 per cent of the bullion coined.

No medieval prince or ruler could have succeeded in undertaking an aggressive, profit-oriented debasement without having secured the cooperation of both domestic and foreign merchants, i.e. to entice them to bring more bullion to the mint by offering them an increased *real* gain in doing so. As Table 1.1 indicates, the 1428 debasement offered merchants a significantly higher mint-price for silver bullion, in terms of a *marc* of fine silver, *argent-le-roy*: 144 double groot coins, an amount 13.4 per cent higher than the previous mint price of 127 double groot coins.

Obviously, merchants converting their bullion into the newly debased coin could gain only if the public accepted them by tale. The previous explanations on the substantial savings in transaction costs in doing so – as opposed to treating such coins as bullion – may seem less convincing in these times of debasement. The ancillary argument to explain why the public would continue accepting debased coins by face value lies in the crudity of medieval minting technology.

The Technology of Pre-Modern Hammered Coinages and Coinage Circulation by Tale

The outputs of mints using that technology is known as *hammered* coinage. The first step in minting was to produce coin blanks: silver disks cut from thin sheets of silver, alloyed to the proper degree with copper. Each blank was placed on a lower dye, serving as the anvil, to allow the mint-master to use the other dye as a hammer, to strike the blank. Each dye, obverse (top) and reverse (bottom), was configured with the emblems or stamps that the ruler had designed for his coins. Once struck, the now flattened, elongated coin had to be trimmed with shears to approximate the desired circular shape of the coin.

As a consequence of all these procedures, no coins struck in one session of minting had exactly the same size, shape, and weight of the other coins in that lot. Indeed, mint regulations did not stipulate specific weights for each coin but specified rather a *taille*: the *number* of such coins to be cut from the pound or *marc*. These regulations necessarily permitted some reasonable variance – a tolerance known as the *remède* – per *marc* of fine silver. Thus, very few if any persons handling individual coins issued from a debasement by weight would have been able to tell the difference between current coins and past coins, and good coins from bad, provided that the changes were modest. Even if those who possessed accurate scales – a heavy cost for most tradesmen and retail merchants – would have had to weigh a very large number of such coins of the same denomination to be confident of detecting any debasement or any other fraudulent tampering.

Changes in the coin's fineness – especially when as minor as that indicated for the Flemish debasement of 1428 (a change of 4.16 per cent) – would have been even more difficult to detect, even with a touchstone, which most tradesmen also did not possess. According to some numismatic historians, medieval touchstones were at best accurate only for changes in fineness of from 5 to 10 per cent.[16] Even visual inspections that detected changes in the prince's stamps on the obverse and reverse sides of the coins would not have been conclusive since such changes often took place with changes in mint officials, without any debasements. Thus moderately debased coins – especially those from such a combination of hard-to-detect reductions in weight and fineness – would have continued to circulate locally by tale.

The Relationship between Debasement and Inflation

The second and even more important requirement for a successful debasement was that any consequent inflation – threatening to reduce or even eliminate the merchants' *real* gain – should have taken place only after the merchants had sufficient time to spend their newly acquired coins. Surely only those subscribing to a very crude quantity theory of money would believe that inflation was an immediate consequence of debasement. The historical record of prices almost always indicates some considerable time lag: the time required for the extra quantity of coins to enter full circulation and for the general public to become more fully aware of the consequences.[17] Medieval merchants converting bullion into coin generally enjoyed the benefits of asymmetric information: they were privy to knowledge about the particulars of the debasement that remained unknown for some time to the general public.[18]

The more important consideration, however, is that coinage debasements rarely, if ever, produced inflations in proportion to the percentage reduction in the particular coin's precious metal contents, even several years after the coinage changes. The obverse nature of that relationship must first, however, be clearly understood; for it is fallacy to believe that, for example, a 10 per cent debasement should have led to a 10 per cent inflation, even in accordance with the crude quantity theory of money. The relationship is instead one of reciprocals: an *increase* in prices as a consequence of a *decrease* in fine metal content, as indicated by the following formula:

$$\Delta T \ (\textit{traite}) = \left[\frac{1}{(1-x)} \right] - 1$$

In this formula, **ΔT** represents the percentage change in the money of account value of the *traite* – here, the coined value of the *marc* weight of fine silver (*argent-le-roy*); and the symbol **x** represents the percentage reduction in the precious metal of the coin (silver). Thus, by this formula, a 10 per cent reduction in the fine silver contents of the penny (groot) would automatically have increased the nominal coined value of the *marc* of silver (*argent-le-roy*), not by 10 per cent but by 11.11 per cent. It is the latter percentage increase (or the percentage increase in the mint price) that must be compared to the increase in the Consumer Price Index.[19]

Whether any increase in the money supply (probably less than indicated by the extent of the debasement) led to any comparable inflation is not supported by the historical record. For Flanders during the entire Burgundian era (1384–1482), for example, the fine silver content of the Flemish penny groot diminished from 1.173 g in September 1384 to 0.466 g in July 1482, a loss of 0.707 grams = 60.27 per cent of its 1384 contents. The corresponding value of *traite* per *marc argent-le-roy* rose from 16.667 s groot (= £3.553 per kg of pure silver) in 1384 to 41.920 s groot (= £8.936 per kg of pure silver) in 1482: an increase of 151.51 per cent. Over the 98-year period from 1386 to 1484 (allowing a two-year time-lag), the Flemish Consumer Price Index (base: 1451–75 = 100) rose from 139.658 to 224.457: an increase of only 60.72 per cent.[20]

A better if far more complex test would be to calculate the recorded price changes after specific debasements, in Burgundian Flanders, for subsequent two-year periods. The calculations for such changes, with these relationships between debasements and the price level, can be found in Table 1.2: for Flanders and England.

Table 1.2: Relationships between coinage debasements and rises in the price level (Consumer Price Index) in Flanders (1409–84) and England (1346–1544).

Part A : Relationships between the debasements of the Flemish silver penny groot
and changes in the Consumer Price Index from 1409 to 1484
Consumer Price Index: base 1451–75 = 100

Years	Silver Content of the Flemish silver penny in grams	% change from previous coinage	Value of 1 kg fine silver in £ groot Flemish	% change from previous coinage	Year 1	Year 3	Price Index in Year 1	Price Index in Year 3	% Change over 2 years
1409	1.182		3.524						
1416	0.958	-18.95	4.349	23.39	1416	1418	118.916	92.239	-22.43
1418	0.850	-11.30	4.903	12.75	1418	1420	92.239	98.118	6.37
1428	0.749	-11.91	5.566	13.53	1428	1430	112.317	125.849	12.05
1433	0.814	8.80	5.116	-8.09	1433	1435	139.210	108.046	-22.39
1466	0.703	-13.67	5.926	15.83	1466	1468	95.930	96.153	0.23
1467	0.677	3.77	6.158	3.82	1467	1469	102.146	96.000	-6.02
1474	0.597	-11.79	6.981	13.37	1474	1476	108.208	92.370	-14.64
1477	0.522	-12.50	7.979	14.29	1477	1479	98.775	149.327	51.18
1482	0.466	-10.71	8.936	12.00	1482	1484	193.932	120.307	-37.96

Part B: Relationships between the debasements of the English sterling silver penny
and changes in the Consumer Price Index from 1346 to 1544
Consumer Price Index: base 1451–75 = 100

Years	Silver Content of the English silver penny in grams	% change from previous coinage	Value of 1 kg fine silver in £ sterling English	% change from previous coinage	Year 1	Year 3	Price Index in Year 1	Price Index in Year 3	% change over 2 years
1346	1.199		3.476						
1351	1.079	-10.00	3.862	11.11	1351	1353	128.695	132.567	3.01
1412	0.899	-16.67	4.634	20.00	1412	1414	103.557	107.673	3.97
1464	0.719	-19.99	5.793	25.00	1464	1466	88.062	105.511	19.81
1526	0.639	-11.11	6.517	12.50	1526	1528	137.120	184.364	34.45
1542	0.491	-23.14	8.479	30.11	1542	1544	174.939	180.847	3.38

Sources: J. H. Munro, *Wool, Cloth and Gold: The Struggle for Bullion in Anglo-Burgundian Trade, 1340–1478* (Brussels: Éditions de l'Université de Bruxelles; and Toronto: University of Toronto Press, 1973), Table G, p. 204; Table K, p. 209. J. H. Munro, 'Wage-Stickiness, Monetary Changes, and Real Incomes in Late-Medieval England and the Low Countries, 1300–1500: Did Money Matter?' *Research in Economic History*, 21 (2003), pp. 185–297. J. H. Munro, 'Builders' Wages in Southern England and the Southern Low Countries, 1346–1500: A Comparative Study of Trends in and Levels of Real Incomes', in Simonetta Cavaciocchi, ed., *L'Edilizia prima della rivoluzione industriale*, *secc. XIII-XVIII, Atti delle "Settimana di Studi" e altri convegni*, no. 36, Istituto Internazionale di Storia Economica "Francesco Datini" (Florence: Le Monnier, 2005), pp. 1013–76. C. E. Challis, Appendix 2: 'Mint Contracts, 1279–1817', in C. E. Challis (ed.), *A New History of the Royal Mint* (Cambridge and New York: Cambridge University Press, 1992), pp. 717–21. E. H. Phelps Brown, E.H., and S.V. Hopkins, 'Seven Centuries of the Prices of Consumables Compared with Builders' Wage-Rates', *Economica*, 23:92 (November 1956), pp. 296–314, reprinted in E.H. Phelps Brown and Sheila V. Hopkins, *A Perspective of Wages and Prices* (London, 1981), pp. 13–59. British Library of Economic and Political Science (LSE Archives), *Phelps Brown Papers*, Box 1a.324.

For the sake of proper comparisons, the aforesaid money of account value of the two *traites* (Flemish and English) is expressed here in a measure common to both countries: the coined money of account values of a kg of pure silver. The object of the investigation is to compare the increases in these *traite* values with the ensuing changes in the Consumer Price Index, for the two years following each debasement.

In Part A, for the Flemish coinage debasements in the fifteenth century, up to the end of the Burgundian era (1482), we find, with two exceptions, that the percentage increase in the CPI was less than the percentage increase in the coined value of the silver *traite*. The first exception, for the 1416 debasement (the first in the fifteenth century), is a most curious one. It was followed by a fall, not a rise, in the price level: a decline of 22.43 per cent, from 1416 to 1418. In the second exception, for the debasement of 1477, the very sharp rise in the CPI over the next two years (1477 to 1479) was followed by a 22.5 per cent fall in the CPI (from 149.327 to 115.679). The subsequent Flemish coinage debasements, during the rule of the Habsburg Archduke Maximilian of Austria, from 1484 to 1489, are too complex to summarize in this table.[21] The accompanying bouts of inflation were also the product of warfare – wars with France and civil wars, with Flemish revolts against the Habsburg rulers. But, in summary, the rise in the mint's *traite* value of coined silver (as the direct reflection of those debasements) rose from £6.821 groot per kg of pure silver in 1484 to a final £15.804 per kg in 1489 (briefly at £17.480 in 1488): an overall rise of 131.70 per cent. Once more, the actual extent of inflation, as drastic as it may appear, was considerably less: from the Flemish CPI of 120.31 in 1484 to 231.87 in 1490, for an overall increase of 92.73 per cent.[22]

Part B of this table demonstrates that the monetary experience of England (for the far longer span of 1351 to 1542) did not differ from the Flemish. Again in the case of virtually all the debasements – in 1351, 1412, 1464, 1526 and 1542 – the increase in the Consumer Price Index over the subsequent two years was less than the increase in the coined value of the *traite*.[23] The debasements of 1351, 1412 and 1526 were all defensive debasements (see below); and the one exception, for these years, followed by a much more extensive rise in prices was Henry VIII's first debasement, of 1526; but that may have been due to silver influxes from the peak of the Central European mining booms.[24] Once again that rise in the English CPI (base 1451–75=100) – from 137.12 in 1526 to 184.36 in 1528 – was then followed by a sharp fall (of 15.50 per cent), to 155.80 in 1529. Even more remarkable is the statistically insignificant rise in prices – just 3.38 per cent – following the commencement of Henry VIII's Great Debasement, in 1542.[25] All these monetary and corresponding price data confirm the proposition that short-term inflation was less, often considerably much less, than would be expected by the quantity theory of money and less than the nominal gains that both the prince and bullion-supplying merchants would derive from participating in the debasements (at least in the later medieval Low Countries and England).

Debasement and Inflation through the Prism of the Modern Quantity Theories of Money

Furthermore, even the modern and properly formulated version of the Quantity Theory of Money should indicate why inflations were rarely if ever proportional to the extent of the coinage debasements (as interpreted by the previously cited formula). Consider the version based on the income velocity of money, a refinement of the classic Fisher Identity: $M.V = P.y$, in which M is the stock of coined money, V is the income velocity of money, P is the Consumer Price Index and 'y' is net national income (NNI = NNP). We may predict that increasing the stock of such money M – here, by a coinage debasement – would likely have led to an increase in output (for reasons noted below), in terms of net national product and net national income, but also to some decrease in the income velocity, and to some inflation. The extent of inflation (rise in P) would have been offset – to some unpredictable degree – by countervailing changes in V and 'y' (NNI).

Those consequences may be better understood in terms of the alternative Cambridge Cash Balances equation: $M = P.k.y$, in which the variable 'k' represents that proportion of net national income that the public chooses to hold in the form of cash balances, thereby deliberately forgoing investment income from using such cash. The Keynesian assumption, given an increase in the effective circulating money supply, and with no changes in Liquidity Preference, is that the rate of interest should decline (as it did in the sixteenth century), with two likely consequences: (1) an increase in real outputs ('y') and capital investments; and (2) an increase in 'k', with the reduction in the opportunity cost of holding cash balances, as expressed in the interest rate.[26] Since 'k' and V are mathematical reciprocals, that would mean a reduction in the income velocity of money – and that reduction also reflected the decreased need to economize on the use of money.[27]

One possible exception might seem to be the Henrician Great Debasement of 1542–53, when the overall debasement of the silver coinage, by an astonishing 83.1 per cent, should have provoked a veritable 'flight from money' – to convert debased coin into goods as soon as possible. Presumably doing so ought to have increased the income velocity of money and thus fuelled the very inflation that merchants had sought to avoid. Nevertheless, while we find that the coined value of the English silver *traite* rose, overall, by 492.00 per cent (by April 1551) – in exact mathematical correspondence to the 83.1 per cent reduction in the penny's silver content – the English CPI rose by only 51.73 per cent over this period: from 174.94 in 1542 to just 265.26 in 1553–4.[28] This historical evidence, for both England and Flanders, should provide sufficient proof that merchants as well as princes could have expected often substantial real gains from participating in coinage debasements, though both the merchants and the prince's government would always have been well advised to spend their newly acquired coins quickly.

Table 1.3 demonstrates the gains that Duke Philip the Good earned from the debasements that he undertook from his accession in 1419 – not only in Flanders, but also in his other territories of Namur, Holland-Zeeland, Hainaut and Brabant – up to 1433–4, when he decided to terminate his debasement policy and impose a unification of monetary reform of the now united Burgundian Low Countries.

Table 1.3: Seigniorage Revenues from Minting Gold and Silver Coins in the Burgundian Low Countries under Philip the Good, 1419–33 in pounds groot Flemish.

Year Michaelmas ending in	GOLD £ groot	SILVER £ groot	TOTAL £ groot
1420	0	965	965
1421	5	923	928
1422	43	1,130	1,173
1423	2	848	850
1424	23	808	831
1425	103	353	456
1426	2,156	226	2,382
1427	3,761	48	3,809
1428	692	123	815
1429	1,547	2,035	3,582
1430	351	1,316	1,667
1431	1,656	283	1,939
1432	5,088	55	5,143
1433	5,459	14	5,473
Total	20,886	9,127	30,013
14 yr mean	1,491.857	651.929	2,143.786

Source: J. H. Munro, *Wool, Cloth, and Gold: The Struggle for Bullion in Anglo-Burgundian Trade, 1340–1478* (Brussels: Editions de l'Université de Bruxelles; and Toronto: University of Toronto Press, 1973), Table III, p. 83; Appendix I, Table H, p. 205; Table J, p. 207. See pp. 193–6 for the archival sources of the mint accounts used for this table.

With that reform, Philip the Good agreed not to debase his coinages again, for thirty years, not without the consent of his Estates; and in doing so, he accepted a very modest seigniorage.[29] His next debasement, in 1466–7, undertaken with the consent of his Estates, was for defensive reasons, as explained in the following section.[30]

Motives for Pre-Modern Coinage Debasements, II: a Monetary Defence Against Gresham's Law

Oresme's hostile view of the motives of so many medieval princes in 'manipulating' their coinages took no notice of the possible defensive motives of those princes in being occasionally forced to debase their coinages. Consider that if aggressive, profit-seeking coinage debasements depended for their complete success on luring bullion from foreign lands, then the rulers of those victimized neighbouring principalities would understandably have reacted with retaliatory debasements. A particular problem arose when one prince sought to counterfeit the coins of his neighbours: i.e. by closely imitating such coins with issues that contained a lesser quantity of precious metals. One of the most prominent and flagrant examples were those of the dukes of Burgundy in striking inferior imitations of the English gold nobles, with varying degrees of success, from 1388 to 1428.[31]

At the same time, the counts of Flanders and their successor dukes of Burgundy were often victims of similar counterfeiting from their own neighbours.[32] For example, Duke Philip the Good's debasement of the Flemish silver coinage, at the Ghent mint in November 1428, portrayed above as an aggressive, profit-seeking venture – as it most certainly was – was partly undertaken as a defensive reaction against the issues of counterfeits of the Flemish silver double groot that the French Dauphin Charles (later Charles VII) had implemented, from June 1428, in his mint of Tournai, a French enclave within Flanders. That debasement soon reduced Ghent's silver coinage output to virtually nothing. During the entire Michaelmas year of 1428–9, the Ghent mint struck only 4,598.7 *marcs argent-le-roy* (1,126.54 kg fine silver); in the following year, after the November 1428 debasement, the Ghent mint output soared to 72,460.7 *marcs argent-le-roy* (= 17,734.97 kg fine silver), with the consequent seigniorage revenues listed in Table 1.3.[33]

Not surprisingly most late medieval coinage ordinances that implemented debasements justified them on purely defensive grounds, and many were indeed undertaken for such a combination of defensive and aggressive (profit-seeking) motives. The particular defensive problem that such foreign and domestic debasements produced is known today as Gresham's Law: commonly stated as 'bad money drives out good money'. The essence of this so-called law is based on the principle that, so long as coins circulated only by tale (face value), no rational, informed person would spend higher-silver content coins of the same face value. Instead, most merchants would melt down and hoard the better coins as bullion, or sell them for export to foreign mints, especially those engaged in debasements. Indeed that principle was well known long before the actual Thomas Gresham (1519–79), and can be found in many French and Flemish mint documents from the mid-fourteenth century.[34]

Gresham's Law pertained, however, not just to the circulation of fraudulent foreign coins (and thus especially counterfeits) but also to defective domestic coins, whose circulation provided an even more powerful defensive reason to undertake periodic coinage debasements. Many domestic coins had become defective through deliberate fraud, even apart from domestic counterfeiting: in particular from clipping and 'sweating' coins. The former was the common practice of using shears to clip off portions of the edges of coins; and the latter was the practice of shaking together a group of coins inside a leather bag, so that the resulting friction would remove some precious metal from the coins, which would then adhere to the sides of the bag, later to be scraped and removed as bullion. The previously discussed imperfect techniques of hammered coinages readily explain why such tampering could take place without being readily observed. Indeed, the only solution to this problem was the later introduction of steam-powered machinery to stamp coins with perfectly rounded and milled edges.[35] Finally, most coins lost their precious metals over time, without any such fraud, through perfectly normal circulation – from both physical and chemical erosion – even though the coins had always been alloyed with copper as a hardening agent. Low-denomination silver coins generally suffered a greater precious-metal loss than did higher denomination silver and gold coins, because they had a far higher circulation velocity.[36]

The inevitable consequence of such wear and tear and other physical losses, from clipping and sweating, was of course to eliminate the aforementioned *agio* or premium that coin normally commanded over bullion, so that the prince's mint ceased to receive bullion.[37] Faced with that prospect, most princes, legitimately concerned about protecting the operation of their mints, and maintaining the integrity of their circulating coinage and money supplies, would have been forced to undertake a defensive debasement: to reduce the silver contents of their newly issued coins to at least the level found in currently circulating coin and thus to restore the *agio* on their coinages, in order to reactivate their mints.[38]

The Test for Motives in Medieval Coinage Debasements: the Relative Seigniorage Rates

Even when the observable economic circumstances and mint ordinances for implementing coinage debasement reflect both defensive and aggressive motives for debasement, the predominant motive was readily observable in the seigniorage rates: high, for aggressive profit-seeking; and low for purely defensive protection of the mints. The latter was based on the obvious principle that the lower the mintage fee, the higher would be the mint price for bullion offered to merchants.

As already noted, for example, in Duke Philip the Good's debasement of the Flemish silver coinage in November 1428, the seigniorage was increased by 50 per cent, from 4d to 6d per *marc argent-le-roy*. But subsequently, when the coinages of Flanders and neighbouring Burgundian territories were unified and reformed in 1433–4, the seigniorage was reduced by two-thirds: to just 2d per *marc* (0.69 per cent of the *traite*). In his next coinage change of May 1466, a purely defensive coinage debasement, Philip reduced the seigniorage even further: to 1.5d per *marc* (= 0.45 per cent of the *traite*). Over this period, from 1433 to 1466, the total mintage fees were reduced from 6.60 per cent to 4.24 per cent of the *traite* per *marc*, so that the mint price for merchants' bullion rose from 93.40 per cent to 95.86 percent of that *traite* value. But when his successor Charles the Bold – killed at the Battle of Nancy in January 1477 – undertook a drastic and aggressive debasement of the silver coinage in October 1474, he tripled the seigniorage to 6d per *marc argent-le-roy* and necessarily reduced the mint price to 94.08 per cent of that *traite* value.[39]

As is indicated by Philip the Good's monetary reform of 1433–4, not all medieval coinage alterations were debasements. The opposite is known as a 'strengthening' of the coinage, for which the French term is even better: *renforcement*. In this monetary reform, Duke Philip augmented the fine silver content of the double groot coin from 1.522 g to 1.629 g fine silver (an increase of 7.04 per cent), thereby reducing the *traite* value of the *marc argent-le-roy* from £1.284 to £1.200 groot Flemish (from £5.474 to £5.116 per kg pure silver: a reduction of 6.54 per cent). Despite the drastic reduction in the seigniorage, as noted above, the Flemish mint price for bullion was still necessarily also reduced: from £1.200 to £1.138 groot Flemish per *marc argent-le-roy*, but with the prospect of deflation and thus of a higher-valued coinage.[40]

For obvious reasons, coinage *renforcements* were much more difficult to implement than were debasements and were undertaken only when the prince had decided that a restoration of his prestige demanded such a corresponding coinage restoration – since, as stressed earlier, coinage provided such an important symbol of sovereignty. In Flanders, the previous *renforcement* was undertaken by Philip the Good's grandfather, Philip the Bold (Philippe le Hardi), in 1389–90 (with a reduction in the *traite* from £5.337 to £4.050 per kg of pure silver).[41]

Especially because defensive debasements took place more often than did aggressive debasements, and certainly far, far more often than *renforcements*, for the variety of reasons earlier examined, most European silver coinages experienced a more or less continuous diminution in their precious metal contents until modern times. The best documented example is England, which practised chiefly defensive debasements (except for the aforesaid 'Great Debasement' during the reigns of Henry VIII and Edward VI). From the first fully documented coinage, in 1257 (Henry III), to Elizabeth I's recoinage of 1601, the pure silver content of the penny was reduced from 1.337g to just 0.464 g (only 34.70 per cent as much). By February 1817, when the final change in issues of silver penny took place, that precious metal content had diminished by another 6.06 per cent, to 0.471 g.[42]

Were Medieval Debasements Undertaken to
Counteract Monetary Scarcities?

The final question to be posed is closely related: did medieval rulers ever undertake defensive debasements as deliberately formulated monetary policies to 'reflate' and expand the supply of circulating coins in time of perceived monetary scarcities, especially during the so-called 'bullion famines' of the later Middle Ages?[43] That is a complex question that requires a separate study, but the short and simple answer is no: there is no evidence that any medieval rulers undertook any such deliberate monetary policies, other than the defensive debasements just discussed, and for the reason discussed here.

Nevertheless, one cannot ignore the conclusions of the recently published monograph, *The Big Problem of Small Change*, which the Nobel Prize-winning economist Thomas Sargent co-authored with François Velde. They contend that 'the motive for most debasements was to maintain adequate supplies of coins, not to raise government revenues', and more specifically such debasements were generally designed to remedy the chronic, pervasive shortages of 'small change'.[44] These petty coins, commonly known as billon or *vellón* coins, were normally those with a nominal or face value of less than penny, though by the sixteenth century the combination of debasements and the inflation of the Price Revolution era (from *c.*1520) meant, in some countries (e.g., France and Italy) that coins in denominations higher than a penny were then considered to be billon coins. Before the 1540s, such coins had always contained at least some silver, even if largely copper.[45] Whether or not such shortages of billon were truly chronic and pervasive is subject to considerable debate, even if the proportions of medieval coinages struck in denominations under one penny were indeed always small.[46] Nevertheless Sargent and Velde never prove their case with any concrete evidence of specific debasements. In particular, they cannot demonstrate that such debasements were ever undertaken to increase the supply of just such petty billon coins. For the evidence of all available mint accounts in medieval Europe demonstrate that debasements of the silver coinages almost always affected all denominations alike, and not just those below the penny in value – thus including the still silver-based billon coins.[47] Indeed, had such rulers debased only the petty coins, while leaving higher denomination silver coins intact, market forces would have either increased the latter's value, by adding a premium, or would have promoted the export of 'full-bodied' coins, had they remained undervalued.[48] With rare exceptions, therefore, late-medieval and early-modern European debasements were undertaken for either the aggressive or defensive motives that have been explored in this study. They were rarely, if ever, undertaken to replenish stocks of the coined money supply – i.e. independent of the reasons explored here.

2 FROM AURELIAN TO DIOCLETIAN: FINANCING IMPERIAL RECOVERY BY COINAGE DEBASEMENTS AND FIDUCIARY CURRENCIES

Kenneth W. Harl

Given the extent to which so many of the world's economies have suffered from excessive issues of fiat paper money and consequent inflations, often drastic, since the First World War and the end of the traditional gold standard, the coinage debasements in the Roman world during the third century AD should appear to be quite relevant to modern society. Yet, the great debasement of imperial Roman silver coins, along with the accompanying price increases during this era, has attracted little attention among current scholars of Antiquity. Debased silver or billon coins, especially the *antoniniani* of 238–74 AD, and the silver-coated coins struck between 274 and 371 – for almost a century – produced serious inflations that ruined traditional classes, while enriching much of the Roman autocracy and its servants.[1] A destructive expedient at best, these debasements led to a breakdown not only of the currency but of fiscal institutions and monetary policy.[2] Hence this inflation was once seen as a step backwards: a destruction of a well-developed, monetized market economy and a consequent shift to a 'natural' or barter economy (*Naturwirtschaft*) that marked the transition from the traditional Classical world to that of Late Antiquity. More recently, however, scholars have devoted far less attention to such questions of debasement and inflation, and have instead directed their primary efforts to quantifying the Roman economy. But the results are far from conclusive. There are insufficient data for, and even less agreement on, estimates of the GDP of the Roman Empire or even the scale of annual production of silver currency in the late first and second centuries.[3] The economy of the Rome under the Principate has also been compared, with varying degrees of success, to those of the traditional agrarian empires of Han China, Mughal India and the Ottoman Middle East.[4] Furthermore, social historians, writing in the tradition of M. I. Finley, have regarded coins as fiscal instruments issued to meet imperial expenditures rather than to promote markets and trade in what has sometimes has been dubbed an underdeveloped economy. Coins, which were also deemed to have been in limited supply, are thus minimized in their importance, along with the impact of debasement after 235 AD.[5] This view has led some scholars to contend that a change of social *mentalité* rather than political, military and economic crisis prevailed in the years from 235 to 284.[6] But such an argument confuses cause and effect; for the new *mentalité* resulted from other wider changes in state and society: especially those that were propelled by the impact of debasement and inflation.

Yet the fact remains that emperors, facing rising military expenditures after 235, did debase the imperial silver currency at unprecedented rates. The prime source for analysing Roman debasements are the coins themselves. Recently they have been subject to metrological analysis, in particular the imperial *denarius* and its double the antoninianus, revealing the decline in their intrinsic fine metal contents.[7] The overall analysis that Walker has offered in his seminal study on the metrology of Roman silver coins is still fundamentally sound, even though new analyses have revealed the practice of surface enrichment (known as 'silver-clad') of debased silver or billon currencies, and thus have led to some corrections of details.[8] These improved analyses have also demonstrated how carefully standards were regulated, and thus reveal a deliberate imperial monetary policy. Based on these metrological studies, we now know that successive emperors between 238 and 270 reduced the fineness of the antoninianus, tariffed at 2 *denarii*, from perhaps 55 per cent to 2.5 per cent; and at the same time, the third-century emperors minted these debased coins in ever greater numbers.[9]

The debasement in 235–70 can be readily documented, but the consequent surge in prices and thus the economic consequences of this imperial monetary policy are virtually undocumented for over a generation, until Diocletian (r. 284–305) restored order under his new regime known as the Tetrarchy. Various documentary sources – papyri from Roman Egypt, the Edict of Maximum Prices in 301 and imperial laws in the Theodosian Code – furnish potentially invaluable information on monetary policy, and prices and wages. From the era of the Tetrarchy, documentary papyri survive in greater numbers, but they quote prices in various units of account long in use in Egypt rather than real coins.[10] The Price Edict too cites the maximum price for many commodities in the unit of account *denarius communis (d.c.)*.[11] The rate of inflation in Egypt during the third century has been estimated by constructing tables of prices for wheat or the wages of unskilled laborers (reckoned in the base silver or billon provincial *tetradrachma* of Alexandria down to 296).[12] In Egypt during the Principate, the best estimates (or guesses) suggest a stability of wheat prices during the later first and second century AD, with due allowance for seasonal fluctuation until 170–90 when prices rose strongly, at least doubling at a time when the mint at Alexandria ceased to mint the *tetradrachmae*.[13] This price surge has also been attributed to the demographic impact of the plague in the reign of Marcus Aurelius (161–80).[14] Thereafter prices levelled off until the mid-third century, when it is presumed that prices for all goods and services rose sharply in the wake of imperial debasement of the silver currency.[15]

Gunnar Mickwitz, writing in shadow of the Great Depression and of Max Weber, believed that the rising prices quoted in Tetrarchic and later documentary sources indicate a ruinous inflation across the Roman world in the later third and early fourth centuries. Making use of both imperial coins and documentary sources, he concluded that such an inflation had an impact comparable to that of the 'Roaring' 1920s, before the ensuing Crash and then deflationary Great Depression of his own day.[16] The imperial Roman government, after having so seriously debased the currency, thereby triggering a run-away inflation, then decided, sometime in the late third or early fourth century, that debased coins would no longer be accepted in tax obligations.[17] Henceforth, taxes were to be collected in gold, commodities or even labour services. In short, in this still common historical view, imperial Rome returned to a barter economy or *Naturwirtschaft*, at least in its fiscal demands, if not in its economic institutions. Many scholars, especially those who subscribe to the Marxist dialectic, have viewed these monetary developments as a fundamental transition or turning point in the history of the later Roman Empire. Indeed, they have portrayed Diocletian as an emperor who imposed a form of state socialism, especially in continuing to demand that tax obligations be met in gold or like commodities, while mandating the use of debased coinage in domestic markets, with his Edict on Maximum Prices in 301.[18]

In the generation following the Second World War, the numismatists who produced the later volumes of the *Roman Imperial Coinage* accepted the thesis that debasement and inflation had led to an abandonment of payments of fiscal obligations in debased coins. In a seminal article, J. P. C. Kent contended that gold solidi circulated as privileged bullion rather than as true coins, during the fourth century, and that the imperial government met its rising military, ceremonial and bureaucratic costs in solidi, the majority of which were derived from tax collections.[19] Gold coins were thus continually being collected, melted down, and restruck as new solidi, almost entirely for tax payments and imperial obligations.[20] From Kent's work arose the assumption that two different currencies circulated in the late third and early fourth century, each of which had little connection to the other.[21] According to this view, the majority of gold coins thus functioned solely as fiscal instruments so that they played little role in Roman markets, even though some gold coins were indeed exported beyond the frontiers. As for the second currency consisting chiefly of base metal coins, Kent and the other editors of *RIC* never explained why the later imperial government struck such a large number of these coins or how these coins were intended to be used. Furthermore, numismatists did not then realize that the silver coating of these coins turned them into proxy silver coins that could be exchanged against gold coins at rates dictated by imperial fiat. These numismatists have influenced two generations of historians who, without the expertise to use the formidable *RIC*, have accepted the conclusions of these numismatists. Hence, leading historians of the period have based their understanding of late Roman coinage, monetary policy and inflation on a historiography written ultimately in response to the economic events of the 1920s and 1930s (inflation followed by sharp deflation).[22]

In my view, the extant documentary sources and coins do not sustain the underlying premise that the late Roman debasements had led to run-away or hyper-inflation and a retreat from the use coined money. First, prices quoted in documentary papyri or the Price Edict are in units of account, notably *d.c.* or drachmae during the Tetrarchy, and later in talents and myriads of *denarii*. Scholars have sought to create price indices by converting these sums, in sundry units, into the equivalent of gold or silver bullion; but these sums are misleading, because prices were in fact paid in real, silver-coated fiduciary coins.[23] Hence, these price indices tell us little about what vendors and customers paid out or what labourers received in real coins for their wages. Price tables presented in the units of account are deceptive, because especially after 313 little is known about actual exchange rates until both the imperial government and markets shifted to reckoning in terms of the gold *solidus* and its fractions (carats) in the fifth century.[24]

Second, the widespread hoarding of coins during this period indicates that the coins, even debased ones, still had some value. Finally, the emperors Aurelian (270–5) and Diocletian (284–305) paid for military recovery by means of a fiduciary coinage that had resulted from repeated debasements during the previous generation. In the absence of evidence of a marked increase in stocks of gold specie by mining or trade, the supply of gold coins alone was never sufficient to sustain the increased imperial spending of the Dominate.[25] Instead, silver-clad fiduciary coins made it possible for both Diocletian and Constantine to pay for the vast expansion of imperial government under the Dominate. In so doing, the imperial government applied two crucial lessons learned about the use of fiduciary coins, namely that prices responded directly to the numbers of coins in circulation, and that the coins must be acceptable in both fiscal and commercial market transactions.

The composition of hoards of *aurelianiani* or *nummi* from this period, documentary papyri and notices in imperial laws preserved in the Theodosian Code support the contention that the imperial government had understood the first lesson, namely that too many coins in circulation would drive up prices. Soldier emperors between Aurelian and Diocletian had experienced directly the impact of price surges resulting from debasements in 238–71, and the diminished buying power of their silver-clad coins during the darkest days of military crisis. Hence, Aurelian ended the policy of debasement and initiated a modest reform in 271; and many of these improved coins continued to circulate even after the second reform.[26] At his accession the antoninianus was a miserable base metal coin with a surface coating of silver that was only 2.5 per cent fine. Aurelian and Diocletian each instituted a reform of the currency, in 274 and 293, respectively.[27] Each emperor based imperial money on an improved silver-clad denomination, the *aurelianianus* or *nummus*, tariffed at 5 *denarii communes (d.c.)*, that is, the imperial money of account based on the traditional silver *denarius*. These silver-clad coins were struck in such large quantities that they were surely intended to meet imperial expenditures, and in this manner they entered commercial markets. Each reform required a massive recoinage to replace older coins in circulation, but thereafter production of the new fiduciary coins was regulated.

The relative scale of production of the new money required by the reform of Aurelian can be inferred from the total number of coins from each emperor's minting that has survived in the Venerà hoard. It was concealed in Italy in *c.*287 or five years before Diocletian's currency reform of 293.[28] This hoard contained nearly 46,000 *antoniniani* (41 per cent) and *aurelianiani* (59 per cent).[29] Of the nearly 19,000 older *antoniniani* coins, 45 per cent were struck by Aurelian before the 274 reform, and the other 55 per cent date from the decade before Aurelian's accession.[30]

Table 2.1: *Aurelianiani* by reign in the Venerà Hoard (287).

Reign	*N* of Specimens	% of *aurelianiani*
Aurelian (274–5)	3,042	11
Tacitus (275–6)	2,435	9
Florianus (276)	529	2
Probus (276–82)	13,206	49
Carus-Carinus (282–5)	4,491	17
Diocletian (284–305)	3,379	12
Total	26,992	100

Sources: The total no. of coins for Probus has been taken from Miliani, *Ripostiglio della Venerà*, p.266. All other totals are from the new catalogue. The 6 coins of the usurper Julian of Pannonia were included with those of Carus and Carinus (Venerà 4396–4404). Excluded from the table are 618 coins of *divus* Claudius II (struck by Aurelian in 270–1), 240 pre-reform coins of Aurelian (270–1), and 7,561 coins of Aurelian struck after the first reform (271–4). Also excluded were the coins struck before the reign of Aurelian: 10,459 specimens. These are 1 of Gordian III (238–44), 1 of Trajan Decius (249–51), 2 of Trebonianus Gallus, 131 of the joint reign of Valerian and Gallienus (253-260), 5,641 of the sole reign of Gallienus (260–8), 4,206 of Claudius II, 356 of Quntillus (270), and 121 of the Gallo-Roman emperors (260–73).

The composition of this hoard suggests that Aurelian, his short-lived successors Tacitus and Florianus, and then Probus struck a vast amount of coinage in less than eight years (274–82), because their coins comprise 71 per cent of the *aurelianiani* in the hoard. Furthermore, Aurelian very likely issued considerable numbers of the new denomination coinage in the last fourteen to sixteen months of his reign. Yet Probus (276–82), whose complicated and vast coinage will be elucidated in the forthcoming study of Estiot on the emperor's coins in the Venerà hoard, ordered an even more massive recoinage of the older debased imperial coins than had Aurelian. Together, Aurelian and Probus struck sufficient numbers of the new fiduciary coin, the *aurelianianus*, to meet most fiscal and market needs, so that their successors, at least the family of Carus, reduced production.

There was, however, at least one major region where sufficient numbers of new fiduciary coins failed to reach markets: Britain and the north-western frontier provinces. Here the demand for coins was met by numerous imitative coins, 'barbarous radiates', and older *antoniniani* of Gallienus, Claudius II and the Gallo-Roman emperors down to the reform of Diocletian in 293.[31] But in Egypt, Aurelian and Probus successfully provided the Nile valley with a new fiduciary coinage. In Aurelian's regnal years six and seven (274–5 and 275–6, respectively), the mint of Alexandria struck a distinctively new billon *tetradrachma* in fabric and and fineness that was almost certainly tariffed at par with the new imperial *aurelianianus*.[32] The new *tetradrachmae* were also minted in considerable numbers, as indicated by the surviving hoards, to replace the older currency in circulation.[33] At the same time, Aurelian's currency reform prepared Egypt for its monetary integration into the empire. In 295–6, Diocletian took the next logical step. He ended the province's distinct fiduciary currency, introduced the imperial or 'Italic' *nummus*, and ordered a revision of the province's taxation.[34] The outbreak of the short-lived revolt of Domitius Domitianus (295–6) delayed his reforms.[35] This obscure usurper, who had controlled Alexandria, struck a provincial multiple to the *tetradrachma* bearing Greek legends as well as imperial-style *nummi* bearing Latin legends.[36]

The impact of each reform on the rate of inflation is difficult to estimate, but the imperial government did take measures to check price surges. Although there are few documentary sources for prices in the period of 274–93, countermarks applied on civic bronze coins of Asia Minor indicate that the 274 currency reform had led cities to revalue downwards their fiduciary bronze coins, struck in 238–68, in response to what was likely a rolling back of prices. In the late 250s and 260s, cities in Asia Minor had doubled the value of bronze coins, which were denominated in *assaria* (the Greek equivalent of *asses*), by means of numerical countermarks. Hence, the common denominations of *assaria* were doubled in value: the 1 at 2 *assaria*; those of 3 or 4 *assaria* at 6; the 5 *assaria* at 10; the 6 *assaria* at 12; and 12 *assaria* at 24. After Aurelian's reform in 274, the bronze coins were halved in value to their original tariffing of fifteen years earlier.[37] In eastern cities, these civic coins were then exchanged against the new imperial silver clad *aurelianianus* down to the reform of Diocletian in 293.

There is one other indication from the coins themselves that Aurelian and his successors achieved some success with currency reform. The emperor Tacitus (275–6) might have revalued the principle fiduciary coin from 5 to 2.5 *d.c.*, because the mints of Antioch and Tripolis briefly struck improved *aurelianiani* in the names of Tacitus and Probus with the value mark of IA (1 = 10 *asses*). Probus soon discontinued this denomination in favour of the *aurelianianus* of 5 *d.c.*[38]

This analysis suggests that, once sufficient numbers of the new fiduciary coins were in circulation, production was regulated lest too many coins drive up prices. This can be surmised as imperial monetary policy even if it was not always implemented successfully. Supporting this conclusion is the fact that henceforth all silver-clad fiduciary coins bore mint marks and *officina* (or workshop) marks. Such control marks were devised so that officials could regulate production. In addition, the coins carried value marks: either XXI or the Greek equivalent KA; each designates 20 *sestertii* = one, or a coin of 5 *denarii communes*. The value marks not only informed users of the official tariffing, but also affirmed that the coins were fully negotiable in all debts public and private.

In 293, Diocletian replaced the aurelianianus, a successful fiduciary denomination, with an improved *nummus*, also valued at 5 *d.c.* and with a 5 per cent fine silver coating. The *nummus*, however, contained far more silver, perhaps as much as 50 per cent. The *aurelianianus* was first revalued downwards to perhaps 2 *d.c.*, and then might have been withdrawn from circulation, although many were still circulating as fractions of the *nummus* twenty years later.[39] The *nummus* could also be exchanged against full-body gold or silver denominations, but the initial exchange rates among the coins were perceived as unrealistic for reasons that remain unclear.[40] The market values of the *nummus* subsequently sank; and twice, in 300 and 301, Diocletian and his associates, the Tetrarchs, raised the coin's exchange value from 5 *d.c.* to 12.5 *d.c.*, and then to 25 *d.c.* This second revaluation is now known from a Monetary Edict issued on 1 September 301, preserved on an inscription found in the excavations at Aphrodisias.[41] The tariffing of 25 *d.c.* was officially maintained for the next twenty years, even during a period of imperial debasement that took place in a new round of civil wars, in 307–13.[42]

The rate of inflation under the Tetrarchy is difficult to estimate, because the only meaningful exchange rates and prices are cited in documentary papyri of Egypt. These figures, which are expressed in local units of account – the Attic drachma and talent – rather than in contemporary coins, pose problems of interpretation. Yet the very practice of reckoning by such units of account is significant. For it allowed a convenient means of calculating prices or tax obligations in terms of real coins during a period of fluctuating exchange rates.

In the prologue of the Edict of Maximum Prices issued in November or early December 301, the Tetrarchs speak only of increases of fourfold and even eightfold, attributing the blame to the avarice of vendors and money changes.[43] But these increases were in notational units. Most likely the same number of actual coins were exchanged in many transactions in this period. For example, the price of a commodity marked at 50 *d.c.* would have cost 10 *nummi* at the initial valuation of the *nummus* at 5 *d.c.* If the *nummus* had been revalued at 25 *d.c.*, the price would have been simply raised by the vendor to 250 *d.c.*, so that vendor still received the same ten actual coins. Hence, price indices denominated in such notational units of account (or even converted to equivalents of gold or silver bullion) convey little sense of how fiduciary coins actually circulated.

Thus, the Edict of Maximum Prices was issued in response to such practices, but it remained in force for only an indeterminate brief period, perhaps only a matter of months (if we are to believe Lactantius).[44] The Price Edict was not, as often suggested, a move towards state socialism. Nor may it be compared to the wage and price controls of modern nation states. The tone of the edict's prologue does convey the frustration of soldier emperors bred in the army camp and impatient, just like a requisitions officer, with markets and vendors.[45] Yet, the Tetrarchs' Price Edict was far more than just an expansion of traditional imperial market regulations to ensure the provision of essential commodities to the citizenry at fair prices.[46] It was, in effect, a means of communication between Tetrarchs and their subjects, for the edict set down maximum prices and wages that were to be used in settling disputes that arose in the markets. Vendors, however, refused to accept what they clearly regarded as artificially low benchmarks for prices and wages. Under the Price Edict, the daily wage of a skilled labourer was fixed at 25 *d.c.* or a single *nummus*, so that this fiduciary coin was intended to serve as a proxy for the silver *denarius* of the Principate.[47] Hence, vendors soon withdrew goods from markets, and operated with black-market dictated prices and exchange rates until the Price Edict was rescinded, thus permitting the free market once again to establish prices and wages.[48] The tariffing of the *nummus* at 25 *d.c.*, was acceptable only so long as markets determined the price of goods and services.

The next round of price surges appears in the documentary papyri during the debasements undertaken during the civil wars between Constantine and Licinius in 316–24. Revaluations of the fiduciary coinage and adjustments of exchange rates proved to be far more effective measures than did price and wage controls. Hence, the fraternal emperors Valentinian I and Valens issued new exchange rates between the gold *solidus* and fiduciary coins, possibly in 371, stating that: 'On account of the reduction that is being brought about in the exchange rate of the *solidus*, the price of all commodities ought also to decrease.'[49]

By their reforms, Aurelian and Diocletian established the imperial monetary policy that endured to 371, when the emperors Valentinian I and Valens issued an edict that ended the production of silver-clad fiduciary coins (*aes dichroneta*) in favour of gold and silver coins, along with base metal token fractions.[50] The imperial government clearly understood the relationship between prices and the number of fiduciary coins in circulation. In 362, Emperor Julian the Apostate reformed the fiduciary coinage, which had undergone debasements with consequent price surges during the previous decade. The new coin, which numismatists have called a double *maiorina*, approximated Diocletian's *nummus*. Although its exchange rate is unknown, the production of the new coins was apparently regulated, because the number of *officinae* among the thirteen imperial mints was reduced by over one-half in what was apparently a move intended to prevent price rises resulting from the issue of too many new coins.[51]

How well the imperial government effected currency reform in 274 and 293 is quite remarkable, for they struck fiduciary coins in the hundreds of millions without the information available to a modern state undertaking such monetary policies.[52] The imperial government also took measures to check inflation. By conducting so many debasements in the third century, the imperial government had learned from hard experience the danger of price rises resulting from the overproduction of coinage. Furthermore, the Roman imperial government had already gained some experience in using fiduciary coins in Egypt, from the time that Tiberius (AD 14–37) introduced the billon *tetradrachma* as the primary coin of the province.[53]

The imperial government had also learned the second important lesson about fiduciary coinage, namely that such coins must be acceptable for both fiscal obligations and commercial transactions in all domestic markets. There is no evidence that the late imperial government ever insisted on having tax obligations met in gold instead of its fiduciary coins in the later third century and thus no evidence that gold coins were treated as special specie that saw little circulation.[54] Indeed, on the contrary, the composition of gold coin hoards reveals that many solidi suffered wear, with other indications that many had circulated far beyond their mint of origin, thus proving that these gold coins were used for commercial purposes – well beyond tax payments. Instead, gold and fiduciary coins were part of a single currency that the Roman imperial government continued to accept in tax obligations. This salient fact can also be demonstrated from numerous tax registers recorded on the Egyptian papyri.

The surviving tax registers from Egypt in the Tetrarchic period record obligations in the notional unit of the Attic drachma, which was reckoned at par with the Roman silver *denarius*. In a series of tax registers from 303–5, these sums can be converted into *nummi* in convenient whole numbers when the established tariffing of 25 *d.c.* is applied. The results are too consistent and too numerous to be merely accidental. Evidently the Tetrarchic officials fully intended these tax payments to be collected in *nummi*. The famous monetary historian Sture Bolin commented on this same purpose for the sums cited in notational *d.c.* in the Price Edict of 301.[55] Bolin noted that the prices were based on two coin denominations: one valued at 2 *d.c.* and the other at 5 *d.c.* – the two units of reckoning for all Roman currency since 141 BC, when the *denarius* was revalued at 16 *asses*.

Furthermore, the silver-clad fiduciary coins were not only accepted in tax obligations, but were often preferred to commodities or labour services. Documentary papyri report the practice of *adaeratio:* the conversion of a fiscal obligation from coin into kind or the reverse. The papyri record many more instances of fiscal obligations in kind that were converted into coin payments rather than the reverse. Save for grain and olive oil – vital for provisioning the army and bureaucracy – the imperial government preferred coins by far, either gold solidi or the much more numerous silver-clad fiduciary coins.

Although all attempts to estimate the size of any late imperial coinage, either gold or fiduciary coins, still remain impossible, nevertheless we may conclude that gold coins alone were insufficient in numbers to ensure the entire collection of varied taxes, often calculated in fractions of the *solidus*. The majority of coins collected in taxes must have been fiduciary silver-clad coins.

One such example can be found in a register of land taxes that the scribe Victor drew up for the village of Skar in Egypt, around 435. The unit of account was then was the gold *solidus* (which had replaced the Attic drachma and talent by the early fifth century). The scribe notes that nearly 70 per cent of the taxes, while reckoned in notational solidi, were actually collected in 'small change' (*ta kermata*), the slang for the tiny AE4 bronze *nummi* measuring 18 mm and weighing 1.50 g.[56] Such a practice was to be expected. Registers of Roman Egypt in the second century AD, such as those from Karanis in the Fayyum, reveal that taxes were collected in the provincial fiduciary coins, the silver-clad *tetradrachma* (10 per cent fine) and copper fractions, rather than in gold or silver imperial coins.[57] In turn, most residents of the Nile valley had been successful in using a fiduciary money of copper coins in most daily transactions and to meet fiscal obligations under the Ptolemaic kings.[58]

Therefore, the soldier-emperors Aurelian and Diocletian were compelled to create a fiduciary coinage, exchanged against pure gold coins, to pay their soldiers and officials, thereby allowing them to finance a remarkable political and military recovery. Furthermore, as noted earlier, their monetary policy remained in force until 371. To be sure, subsequently, in the fourth century, civil wars and invasions led to further debasements of the fiduciary coins; but once each crisis had passed, the emperors immediately reformed the fiduciary money. The subsequent monetary changes of 371, however, still remain unclear: why, after a century of a successful fiduciary coinage based on silver-coated base metal coins, did the imperial government then abandon this currency, returning to gold and silver coins accompanied by base metal fractions? Part of the explanation may lie in the evident disdain with which the imperial army's barbarian soldiers held this fiduciary coinage; and from the later fourth century on emperors recruited more and more tribal regiments of barbarian *federates* who clearly expected payment in gold and genuine silver coins.

In conclusion, I suggest that a good modern analogy, for a comparison of Aurelian's and Diocletian's monetary reforms, would be the replacement, in 1965, of United States silver coins with cupro-nickel fiduciary coins and the issue of Federal Reserve bills that are not backed by silver, in contrast to the early gold or silver certificates in American history. As a result of a series of silver-coinage debasements, the Roman imperial currency experienced the same shift to a fiduciary money that the currencies of contemporary leading powers experienced in the early twentieth century.

More particular details, for comparison, may be cited from recent American monetary history. In March 1900, the American paper dollar, in order for it to adhere to the international gold standard, was officially backed by gold fixed at the rate of $20.67 to the Troy ounce (25.8 grains and 90 per cent fine).[59] High coin denominations were still in silver: the dollar coin, the half-dollar, quarter and dime (10 cents). The nickel 5 cent piece and the copper 1 cent piece (penny) alone were the true token coins. But subsequently, in 1933, four years after the onset of the Great Depression, and just after the inauguration of President Franklin Delano Roosevelt, the new Democratic government suspended the gold standard for domestic transactions; and by the Gold Reserve Act of 1934, it devalued the gold dollar by 69.3 per cent, in fixing the dollar's value now at $35.00 per ounce of gold Troy (a link of convertibility later broken in 1971, under President Nixon). Silver was demonetized in 1964.

Since 1965, therefore, the currency of the United States has had no backing other than its fiduciary value: that is, the value of the money itself, in paper bills and coins, is established by the fiat of the federal government. This is a money of trust that can be negotiated for public and private debts. If faith in this money collapses, then all paper money and assets denominated in dollars become worthless. Imperial Rome had similarly learned that, for any fiduciary currency to work, it must be acceptable for negotiation of taxes and all debts, public and private.

3 THE MAKING OF A GOLD STANDARD: THE DUCAT AND ITS OFFSPRING, 1284–2001

Alan Stahl

In the late fourteenth century, a French royal adviser cited the ducat of Venice as a worthy example for his young king to emulate: 'the fine gold ducat of 24 carats that has not changed its standards for nine centuries'.[1] In fact, the ducat at that point was barely a century old, but it had already impressed itself on the minds of contemporaries as an unchanging standard of immemorial presence. By the time it saw its last issue on the eve of the birth of the euro in 2001, it had indeed survived as the main gold denomination of Europe for the better part of nine centuries.

When authorized in 1284, the ducat standard was not an original invention of Venice; it was a conscious appropriation of the gold coins of identical standard introduced by Florence and Genoa, apparently simultaneously, in 1252.[2] While the genovino had a restricted circulation and would not be copied by other issuers, the florin had great success throughout Europe, partly as a result of the influence of Florentine bankers in collecting papal revenues. Its image of St John (standing) on the obverse and the heraldic lily on the reverse served as the visual model for gold coins for centuries. However, its standard was not universally adopted along with the imagery, and even in Florence its weight was lowered before the end of the thirteenth century.[3]

The Venetian ducat was introduced with an authorization that specifically recalled the standard of the Florentine florin.[4] Like the florin, the ducat was intended to have a fineness as pure as medieval refining technology allowed, generally within a quarter of a carat or about two per cent of absolute purity. The florin was cut at the rate of eight coins to the Florentine ounce, resulting in a coin weight equivalent to about 3.53 grams Venice set the ducat at 67 coins to its *marc*, which resulted in a slightly heavier standard, about 3.545 g. The types of the ducat were derived from Venice's silver *grosso* (in turn derived from Byzantine prototypes): on the obverse the doge, kneeling before St Mark, both holding a central flagstaff, and on the reverse an image of Christ delivering a benediction in an almond-shaped field of stars. The ducat took more than a half century to be fully established; for even in the Mediterranean the florin was the dominant coin in the early fourteenth century. Only with the glut of gold that followed a shift in the bimetallic ratio in the 1330s did Venice begin minting the ducat in such quantities that it became the predominant gold coinage of the eastern Mediterranean.[5]

Like most medieval minting authorities, Venice had a money of account based on the penny (*denaro*) introduced by Charlemagne in the late eighth century, counted in terms of a shilling (*soldo*) of 12 pennies and a pound (*lira*) of 240 pennies. And, like most of continental Europe, the penny on which the Venetian pound of account was based underwent successive debasements in the course of the Middle Ages; by the time that the ducat was introduced, the fineness of the Venetian *denaro* had declined to under 20 per cent pure silver and its weight had been reduced to just over 0.30 g. In the course of silver-coinage debasements over the next century and a half, the link to the Venetian lira had been shifted to higher denomination silver coins. But these coins were also were debased, so that the pound of account lost more than 50 per cent of its silver between 1282 and 1421. As elsewhere in medieval Europe, some of the debasement can be attributed to changes in the bullion market and the competition of other issuers, but it was also the result of an increased reliance of the Venetian state on mint profits, in the form of the seigniorage derived from producing silver coins.[6]

From its very beginnings in 1284, the gold ducat was produced under a minting regime that was very different from that for the silver coinages. Indeed, the ducat was coined in separate facilities, under its own administration. Rather than being tied into the local money of account, and being viewed as a source of fiscal revenue, the ducat was established as a coin of fixed content but variable market value, whose benefit to Venice was more as a trusted means of exchange for its merchants than as a source of mint income. While silver was coined for individuals from the bullion they brought to the mint, with a significant delay in turnaround, the gold mint was supplied by the state with significant capital so that bullion could be exchanged on the spot for coins. Repeated regulations were enacted to make sure that the mint was producing ducats of unimpeachable reputation. The gold was repeatedly assayed to ensure that it was as close to pure as possible, and the weight tolerance was held to about 0.2 per cent. Most importantly, the surplus value of the ducat (the difference between its value as metal and as coin) was kept to as low a level as possible; it was maintained at about 1 per cent or even lower, compared to the silver coinages that were overvalued by as much as 20 per cent and a colonial coinage that carried an added value of 100 per cent.[7]

The imagery adopted for the Venetian ducat in 1284 would remain almost unchanged for the next five centuries, but its weight would undergo slight modifications, and the name of the coin itself would change. In the course of the late fifteenth century and early sixteenth century, the weight of the ducat was continually adjusted; finally in the middle of the sixteenth century it was fixed at 3.494 g, a standard it would retain for the next two and a half centuries.[8] During the early sixteenth century as well, a change in the bimetallic ratio produced a change in the value of the gold ducat from 124 soldi or 6.2 lire, the one that had prevailed for the previous half century.[9] The term 'ducat' (whose original significance was related to the status of Venice as a duchy and to the last word in the reverse legend of the coin) remained associated with the unit of account for 124 soldi, while the actual minted gold coin, whose value continued to float against the silver-based lira of account, was now called the *ducato di zecca* (mint ducat). But then, in 1562, a new Venetian silver coin with the size of the *thaler* (the Habsburg *Joachimsthaler*) was introduced at a value of 124 soldi, and it was called a 'ducat'. Henceforth the Venetian gold coin that formerly bore that name would be called the *zecchino*, popularized in English as 'sequin'.[10] In the beginning of the seventeenth century, a new lighter Venetian gold ducat was introduced with the same obverse imagery as the *zecchino* of the doge kneeling before St Mark, but with a winged lion as its reverse type. This additional gold denomination would last for a couple of decades.[11] The *zecchino* continued to be minted with the types and standard of the original ducat until the end of the republic in 1797.[12]

Outside of Venice, the imagery of the ducat was only rarely copied, with short-lived issues, but the weight, fineness and name of the Venetian original would carry on as the basic gold standard of modern Europe. The only major medieval European issue to adopt the actual imagery of the ducat was produced in Rome, where an apparently large issue of ducats was minted by the commune during the fourteenth-century 'Babylonian Captivity of the Papacy', when the papal curia was transferred to French-dominated Avignon (1309–1417). This type was taken up again by the papacy in the late fifteenth century under Paul II (1464–71).[13]

The ducat type had its greatest success in the eastern Mediterranean. It remained the prototype for the issues of the Knights of St John on Rhodes and then Malta from the early fifteenth century until the middle of the eighteenth century.[14] There were briefer issues from medieval rulers of Genoese origin on Chios and Mytilene.[15] A series of anonymous imitations of Venetian ducats, produced in many mints stretching from the Aegean to India, appears to have continued as a significant trade coinage well into the modern era.[16] The imagery of the Venetian ducat resurfaced rarely in western Europe, appearing only in Savoy in the early fifteenth century, in Bavaria in the sixteenth and seventeenth century and in the French seigniorial coinage of Dombes in the late sixteenth. But none of these issues was significant or long-lived.[17]

Although the name 'ducat' would have the longest monetary tenure as a denomination for European gold coinage, the use of that name did not always correspond to the original Venetian standard: that is, of a pure gold coin weighing something over 3.50 g. The term 'ducat' came to be applied to coins of various southern European mints in the course of the fifteenth century. When the anti-pope John XXIII enjoyed his brief reign, from 1410 to 1415, he took control of the communal mint of Bologna, replacing the gold bolognino with a papal ducat. Despite John's deposition, his gold coin remained characteristic of that mint for the following century.[18] In mid-century, Ferrara and Mantua began minting gold coins called ducats, with portrait types appropriate to their identities as seigniorial issuers; the rulers of Milan and Naples soon followed.[19]

The ducat denomination was brought from Naples to Spain by Juan II, who minted his ducat in Valencia while continuing to mint the well-established, but very debased, florin in his realm of Aragon. In the last decades of the fifteenth century, Ferdinand II of Aragon (r. 1479–1516) introduced the ducat denomination to his territories of Aragon and Mallorca.[20] In 1497, after his marriage to Isabella of Castile, he introduced a new gold denomination to replace both his ducat and her dobla (derived from an Islamic denomination); although the new coin was called the *excelente*, it was minted on standards specifically stated to be those of the ducat.[21] The *excelente* and its multiples bearing the facing busts of Ferdinand and Isabella were minted into the early seventeenth century. An index of the currency of the ducat at the beginning of the modern period may be found in the hoard of Saint Pere de Rodes buried around 1520 in Catalonia; its 348 gold coins included ducats of Salzburg, Bohemia, Hungary, Rhodes, and fifteen Italian mints, as well as Spanish *excelentes*.[22]

North of the Alps, the florin, of the traditional type of a standing figure on the obverse and a heraldic reverse, dominated that region's gold coinages: first as an exact copy of the Florentine prototypes and then with images adapted to the identity of the issuer. Centred in the Rhineland mints, these *Rhinegulden* began to be issued in the mid-fourteenth century, on the same standard as the Florentine florin (and the Venetian ducat), but gradually their fineness declined to 19 carats (79 per cent), retaining that fineness through the fifteenth century.[23] The gold coins of Austria followed those of the Rhineland in reduced fineness and Florentine prototypes, but changed to pure gold and took on the name of ducats late in the late fifteenth century.[24] In Hungary, as well, gold coinage started in the fourteenth century with gold gulden on the florin model; but these were always of fine gold. Only in the last decades of the fifteenth century did these coins take on the name of ducats.[25] With the imperial coinage decree of 1510, Archduke Maximilian I (king of the Germans from 1486; emperor 1493–1516) sought to standardize the gold coinage of the Holy Roman Empire on the Venetian standard and with the name ducat. But the transition in the name was irregular through the next century, and nowhere was there an attempt to adapt Venetian imagery.[26] The Austrian ducat survived until the First World War, to be outlived only by the Netherlandish ducat, which saw its last issue in 2001, still bearing the image and the accounting abbreviation derived from the florin.

These gold ducats stood apart from the local coinages, usually based on alloys of silver and copper, in the regions of their minting and often circulated into neighboring monetary zones. The various European coins called ducats, those that were minted over the course of the later Middle Ages and the modern era, were not always of a consistent weight or fineness, nor did they all resemble the original Venetian prototype. Nevertheless, they represented the closest thing the Western world has had to a unified coinage standard since the age of Charlemagne, and indeed provided Europe with a gold standard that long predated the now more famous British gold standard (from the 1720s). The gold ducat and its family provided the later medieval and early-modern European economy with a truly international, indeed almost universal medium of exchange, that was vastly different from and much superior to the wide varieties of often debased and thus unstable silver coinages, even including the much touted English sterling silver coinage which saw a loss of 59.6 per cent of its fine silver content from 1351 (1.079 g) to its final issue in 1816 (0.436 g).[27]

Introduction to the Ducat Table

Table 3.1 represents the issues of European mints between 1250 and 2001 of coins that were either of the same standard as the ducat or were called a ducat. The florin of Florence, the genovino of Genoa, and the ducat of Venice are represented in different shadings. Those coins which copied the appearance of one these models are charted in the same shading as their prototype. All coins called ducats (whether they were of the same appearance, standard or metal) bear a lighter shading.

Table 3.1: The making of a gold standard: the ducat and its offspring from 1285 to 2001.

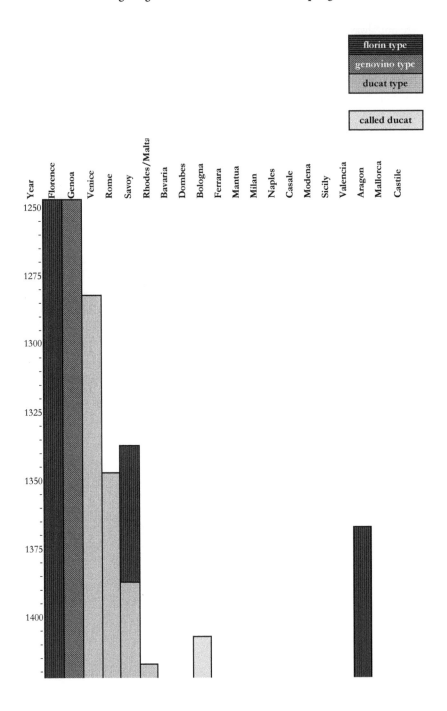

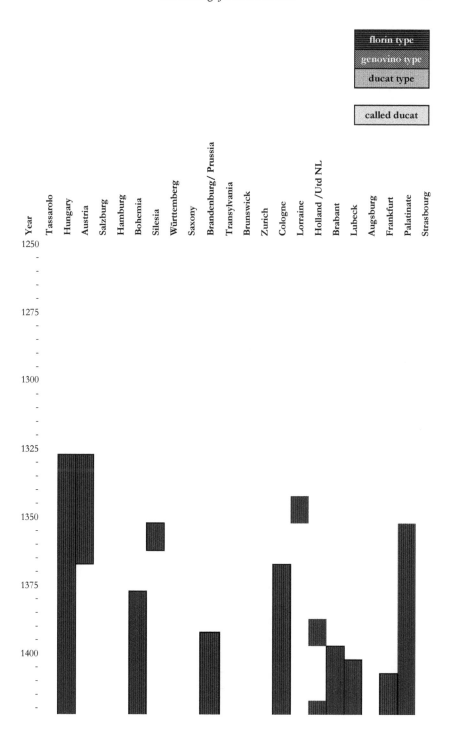

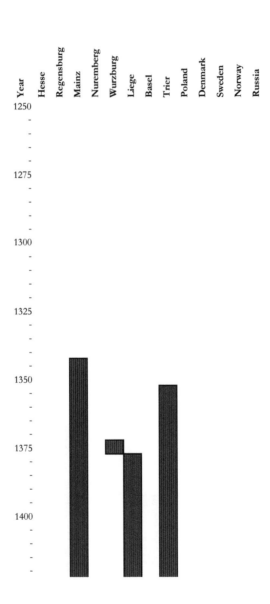

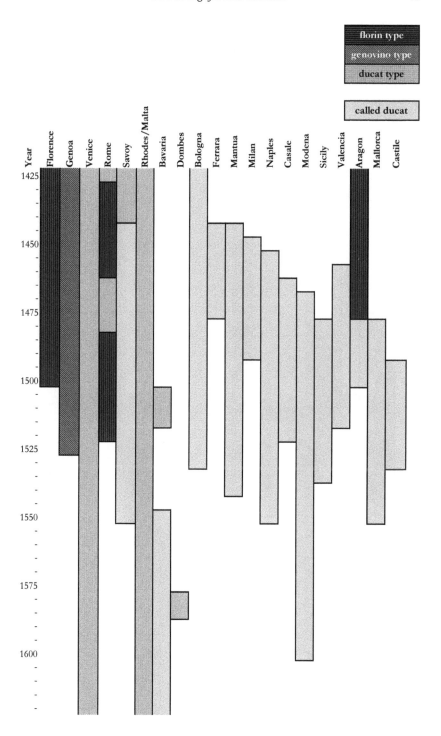

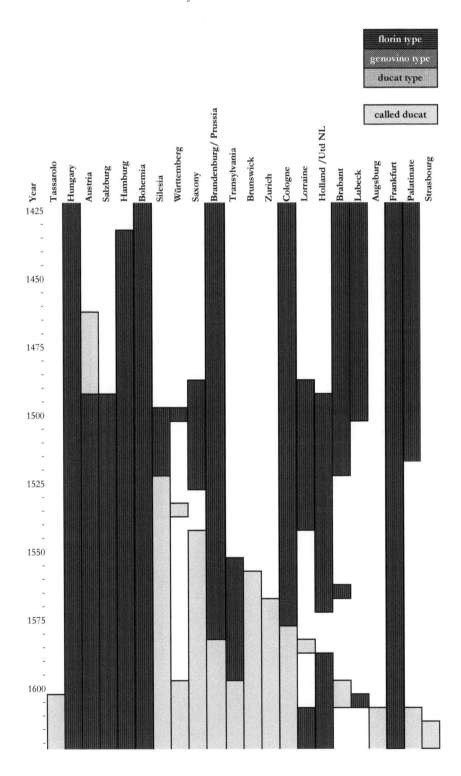

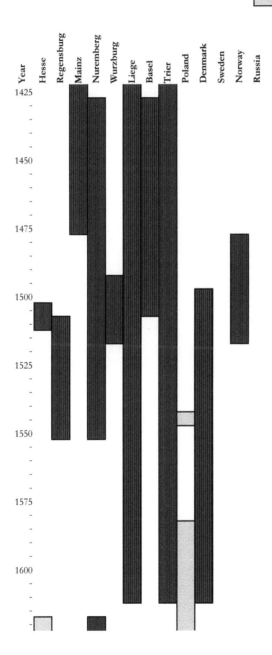

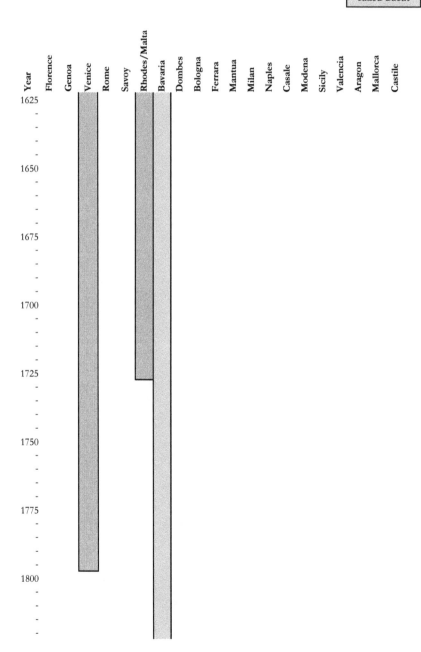

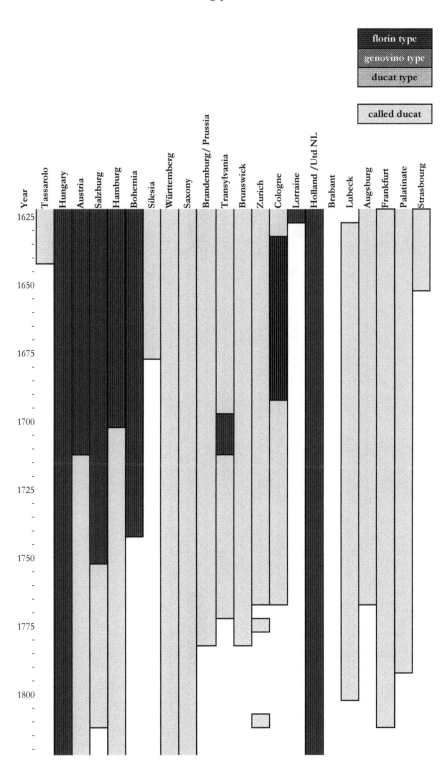

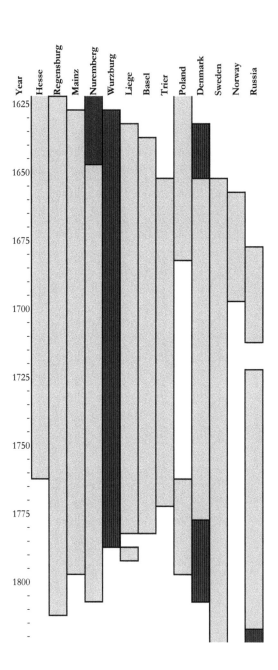

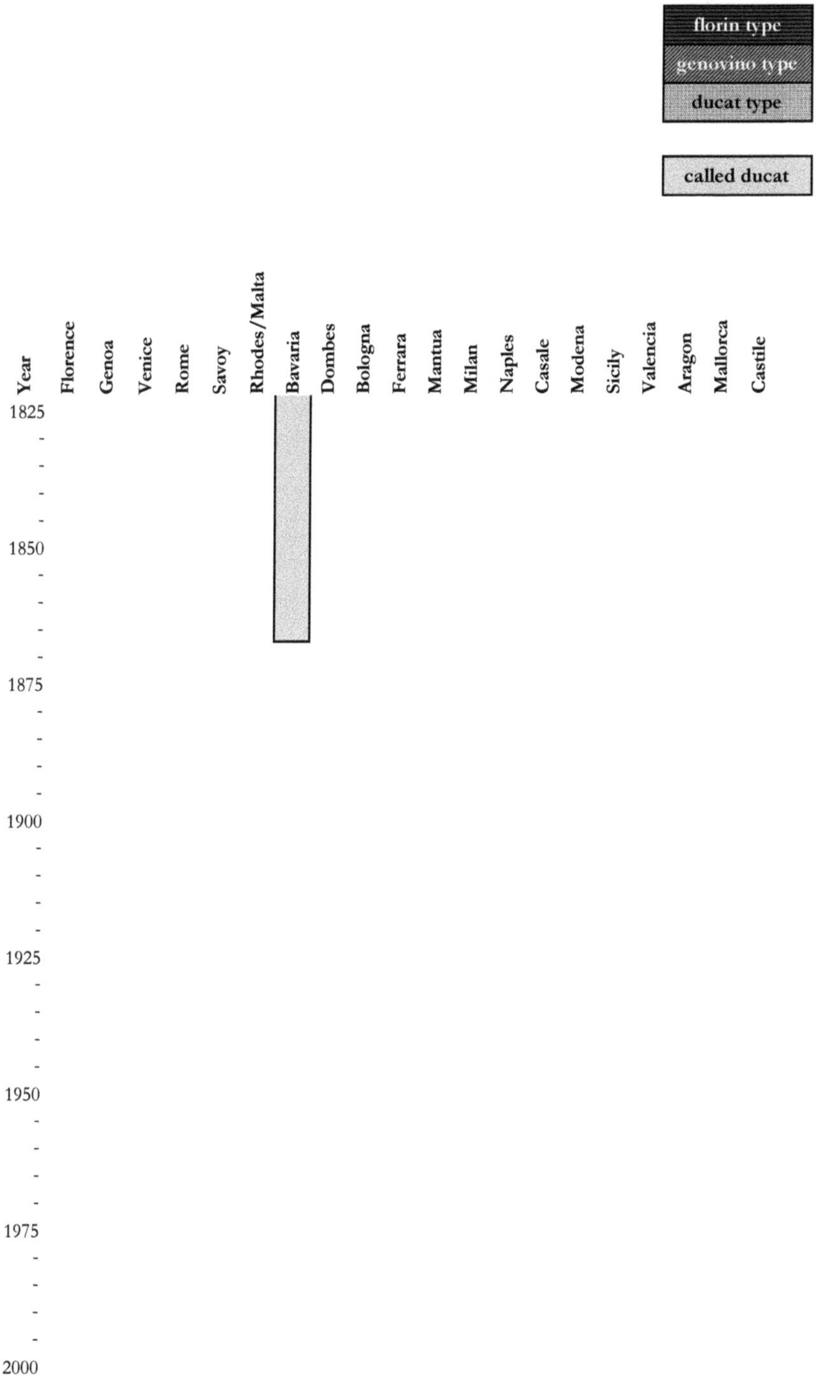
florin type
genovino type
ducat type
called ducat
Year
Florence
Genoa
Venice
Rome
Savoy
Rhodes/Malta
Bavaria
Dombes
Bologna
Ferrara
Mantua
Milan
Naples
Casale
Modena
Sicily
Valencia
Aragon
Mallorca
Castile
1825
1850
1875
1900
1925
1950
1975
2000

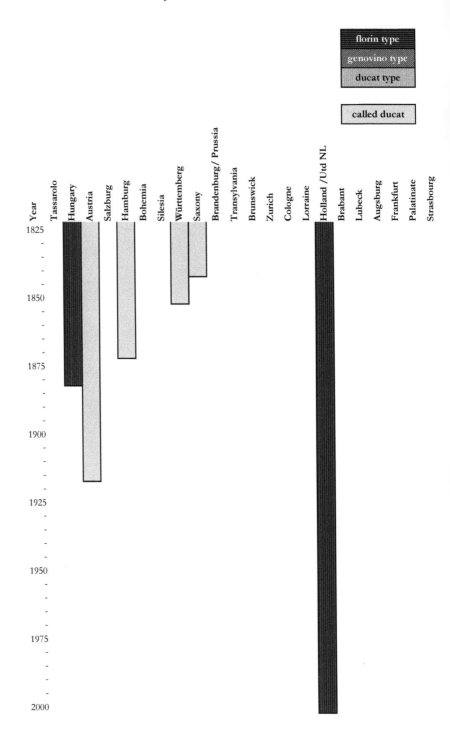

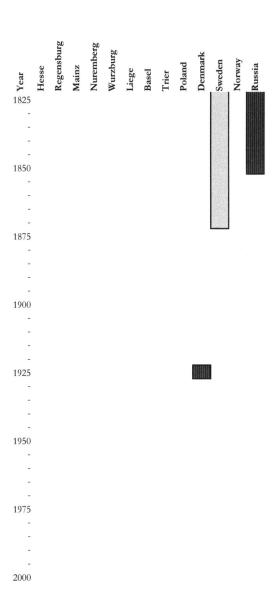

4 DEBASEMENT OF THE COINAGE AND ITS EFFECTS ON EXCHANGE RATES AND THE ECONOMY: IN ENGLAND IN THE 1540s, AND IN THE BURGUNDIAN-HABSBURG NETHERLANDS IN THE 1480s

Peter Spufford

I: England in the 1540s

In the introduction to my *Handbook of Medieval Exchange,* I presented the hypothesis that exchange rates by and large oscillated about the intrinsic metal contents of the coins underlying the moneys of account concerned.[1] I still believe this to be true *in normal times,* when the intrinsic metal content of a coinage was basically equal to the price of the metal in it, minus the costs of coining, and with negligible profit or loss to the ruler. However, my hypothesis does not work when currencies were debased, for example in France at the end of Charles VII's reign, between 1417 and 1422. Numismatists, concerned with the coins themselves, have naturally concentrated on their weight and fineness. For normal times this is also what economic historians need to know. However, it is now apparent that in abnormal times, in debasement conditions, economic historians should be more interested in the prices offered by the mints for silver than with what the mints did with it afterwards. In periods of debasement there was quite frequently a deliberate official policy of secrecy to prevent the public from know-ing the extent of debasement. If the public did not know how far the coin was being debased, they did know how much the mint was prepared to pay for silver, and adjusted their expectations to this, on the false assumption, that, as in normal times, debasement was in proportion to the rise in the price offered for silver.

In the Dauphin's parts of France a sequence of debasements meant that 46 times the value of coin was actually made from the marc of silver in 1422 than had been made in 1416. The public did not know this. What they did know was that at the same time the sum paid for the marc of silver had increased twelve-fold. If they thought that debasement was of this order they were hopelessly wrong. The rival governments of the Plantagenets and of Burgundy in their parts of France were doing approximately the same. The profits of these competitive debasements were used to keep rival armies in the field. Much of the money was sent or taken by military leaders, and to a lesser extent the generality of the soldiery, back to England or the Netherlands, and by mercenary captains and their companies to Switzerland and the Italian states. Even so we can believe that there was an increase in the money supply in France itself in all three parts of the country. The inflationary effects were not however forty-six-fold. There are, as yet, no proper price series for France, but David Sorenson and Nathan Sussman, working independently, both concluded that prices for grain and wine in Dauphiné followed the mint price for the marc of silver, not the value of coin minted from it.[2] Even such a twelve-fold increase was far greater than the largest increases in agricultural prices brought about by bad harvests. The consequences distorted all sorts of relationships. In particular peasant producers, unless their land was devastated by the wars, gained from high prices, while their rents, their principal outgoings, generally remained fixed. By contrast landlords lost out, since so many rents in France were by then fixed, while they were the principal consumers of imported goods which increased in price to reflect the perceived loss in the value of French currencies.

In comparison, the English 'Great Debasement' of the 1540s was a relatively minor debasement.[3] However, by contrast with France before 1422, there is an abundance of price material. Twenty years ago I was able to show that, with a one or two month time-lag, exchange rates, and hence the prices in sterling of imported goods, fairly accurately reflected the mint price offered for silver in England between April 1545 and August 1553, not the extent of debasement. Some domestic prices then adjusted themselves upwards on the same basis.[4] Since then Oliver Volckart has accumulated a much greater number of exchange rates between England and the Netherlands than I had access to in the 1980s. Table 4.1, derived from his material, shows even more clearly what happened.

The first set of columns give the sums minted from the Troy pound of silver between 1526 and the 1560s, showing a six-fold increase between 1542 and 1551. This was unknown to the public. The second set of columns gives the prices paid by the mint for the Troy pound of silver during the same period, showing only a two-and-a-half-fold increase. This was deliberately made public to attract silver bullion to the mint. The third set of columns gives the ranges of exchange rates for the pound sterling in Flemish money groot, primarily in Antwerp. It will be noticeable that the exchange rates reacted to changes in the prices offered by the mint, rather than to the sums minted from the Troy pound, and that, even then, they did not fully keep up with them. In the final column I suggest how soon after a change in the price paid for silver bullion the exchange rates made both the cost of goods purchased abroad dearer and English goods sold abroad cheaper. It is particularly noticeable that nothing happened to the exchange when 30 per cent more coin was minted from the Troy pound in May 1542 because it was not public knowledge. It is also noticeable that on four occasions between April 1547 and August 1550 the exchange reacted to the increased price for silver offered by the mint, although there was no change in the amount being minted from the Troy pound.

Table 4.1: Sum Minted from a Troy Pound of Silver at the Tower Mint and the Price Paid for it, with rates on the London-Antwerp Exchange 1542–60.

Date	Sum Minted	Index	Price Paid	Index	Exchange information	range of rates	median rate	Index	= cost in sterling if goods purchased in Antwerp paid in Flemish money groot.
Nov.1526-May 1542	£2-8-8	100	£2-7-6	100	1537until July1542	26s6d-28s	26s10d	100	
May 1542-June 1544	£3-3-3	130	£2-8-0	101	Aug 1542-Aug1543	no rates			
June 1544-April 1545	£3-4-0	132	£2-12-0	109	Sept 1543-April 1545	25s8d -27s2d	26s8d	101	
April 1545-April1546	£4-16-0	197	£2-16-0	118	May 1545-May 1546	25s-26s8d	26s	103	reaction next month
April 1546-April 1547	£7-4-0	296	£2-16-0	118	May - Sept1546	23s-25s2d	24s4d	111	reaction next month
					Nov1546-March1548	21s11d-23s6d	22s6d	119	
April 1547-Oct 1548	£7-4-0	296	£3-4-0	135	March - Nov 1548	21s5d-23s1d	22s3d	121	
Oct 1548-Oct 1549	£7-4-0	296	£3-8-0	143	Dec 1548 - Feb1549	20s6d-21s8d	21s6d	125	reaction 2 months later
					Mar-Sept1549	19s11d-20s9d	20s4d	132	
Oct 1549-Aug 1550	£7.-4-0	296	£3-12-0	152	Sept 1549- May 1550	18s11d-20s5d	20s	134	
					May - Aug1550	18s6d-19s11d	19s3d	139	
Aug 1550-	£7-4-0	296	£4-0-0	168	Aug-Nov1550	17s7d-18s6d	18s	149	reaction same month
					Jan-Feb1551	16s7d-16s10d	16s8d	161	
April 1551 - July 1551	£14-8-0	591	£6-0-0	253	April-May 1551	15s3d-16s3d	15s6d	173	reaction same month
					May-June1551	13s1d-14s3d	13s8d	196	
					June-Aug 1551	12s1d-13s4d	12s6d	215	
Oct 1551- Aug 1553	£3-5-2	134	£3-4-1	135	Sept 1551-Feb1553	15s9d-19s11d	18s4d	144	reaction when announced
Aug 1553-Nov 1560	£3-5-5	135	£3-3-10	134	Aug 1553-Aug1559	20s3d-22s6d	21s10d	123	reaction same month
					Sept 1559-July 1560	22s-23s4d	22s6d	119	
Nov 1560-	£3-4-10	133	£3-3-3	133					

Cost of minting represented 2 2 % difference between silver price and sum minted before 1542 and after 1560. rates for £1 sterling in Flemish money groot collected by Oliver Volckart

Sources: C. E. Challis, 'Appendix: Mint Output', in C. E. Challis (ed.), *A New History of the Royal Mint* (Cambridge and New York: Cambridge University Press, 1992), pp. 685–7, 717–34. Data supplied by Professor Oliver Volckart, Department of Economics, London School of Economics.

At the beginning of the sixteenth century, England was primarily exporting cloth and, to a lesser extent tin, lead and wool. J. D. Gould recognized the importance of the London–Antwerp exchange rates and how they related to the specie points, which derived from the mint prices offered in the mints of England and the Netherlands. He wrote extensively on how cloth exports increased as a consequence. As the value of the English pound gradually halved abroad between 1545 and 1551, in reaction to the rise in the price the English mints paid for silver, the prices at which English mercers and Hanseatic merchants could sell English cloth dropped in other currencies. Broadcloth exports consequently increased enormously, reaching the equivalent of very nearly 150,000 standard cloths by 1549–50.[5] Such exports had not even surpassed 100,000 pieces until the mid-1530s. Debasement brought down the overseas prices of very expensive cloths, to a point where they became more easily sellable, so that not only the numbers, but also the overall qualities of cloths exported were raised, increasing the revenue stream still further.[6]

J. D. Gould did not concern himself either with other exports, or, more importantly, with the effect of England's debasement on her imports. England's imports were much more varied than were her exports. At the beginning of the sixteenth century, linen, iron and wine were the most important, but England also imported brass and copper, salt, silks, spices (including sugar), cottons, fustians, furs, glass, tapestries and other works of art.[7] As early as 1549 Sir Thomas Smith, the newly deprived Secretary of State under the Protectorate of the fallen duke of Somerset, in his *Discourse of the Common Weal of this Realm of England* has the 'Merchant' in his dialogue point out how:

> all other merchandise that we bye beyond the seas, as silkes, wynes, oyles, woode, madder, Iron, steyll, wax, flax, lynnen clothe, fustians, worstedes, coverlettes, Carpettes and all arrasies and tapesterie, spices of all sortes and all haberdsashe wares as paper, bothe whyte and browne, glasses as well drinkiinge lookynge, as for glasinge of windowes, pinnes, nedles, kniues, daggers, hattes, cappes, broches, buttons and lases; I wote well all theise doe coste me more nowe by the third parte well, then theyn did but seauen yeares agoe.[8]

This fits very neatly with an exchange rate that had increased by 34 per cent from 1542 ('7 yeares agoe') by the autumn of 1549. As we know, worse was to come. Thomas Smith has well-to-do English consumers, in the person of his 'Knight', point out that merchants can accommodate such price increases for imported goods, but the eventual consumers cannot do so, squeezed between customarily fixed rents and rising prices for such goods as were primarily consumed by the aristocracy and gentry. What Thomas Smith himself, in the person of his 'Doctor', suggests, is import substitution. Joan Thirsk has pointed out that import substitution did indeed begin to be attempted at this very time. The most successful import substitution was the working up of English iron ore in place of importing Spanish or Swedish iron, particularly from 1543. Not quite so successful were the manufacture of sailcloth from 1547, and the growing of woad from 1548. Consideration was also given at this time to the manufacture of fustian, the making of worsteds and the creation of a linen and canvas industry. All these were to come about later in the century, but the germ of the idea was born in the 1540s. What did happen then was an increase in the growing of flax and hemp which provided the material for later developments.[9] Only a little later an unsuccessful attempt was made to introduce silk manufacture into England.[10]

The import of iron did shrink, but so did that of wine, for which the only native substitution was a further shift to drinking beer, since wine could no longer be made in England in this colder period. By 1551 wine imports were well below the level of 1503–9. The English aristocracy and gentry found that they had to do without their wine, or pay a great deal more for it, as they had to do for fine linens for themselves and coarser fustian for their servants. Spices, too, for which there could also be no substitute, similarly increased in price, as did carpets and tapestries and all the other luxuries listed by Sir Thomas Smith. The price of velvets increased by 50 per cent between October 1546 and September 1550.[11] Squeezed between static rents and increased expenditure, it is no wonder that pressure built up among landowners for a return to sound money.

When the return to sound money was announced in September 1551, the exchange rate reacted immediately, and the price of English cloth in Antwerp climbed accordingly. John Oldland suggests that the London mercers who were selling English cloth in Antwerp at the time could do so only at a loss, by contrast with the gross profit margin of 25 per cent or more that they had been making.[12] However by November 1551, they had still managed to sell enough to be buying linens and other goods in quantity, at prices that customers in England would afford, even though the £1 sterling was not yet accepted there at a value appropriate to the level of the new coinage.[13]

With a lower exchange rate English wine imports recovered. By the end of the 1550s they had doubled, from around 30,000 to around 60,000 tuns per annum.[14] In 1559 the value of wine imported was £68,000 sterling. Imports of linens, linen thread, fustians and canvas were still enormously more important than wine with a value of £139,000, besides £20,000 worth of flax and hemp which suggests that the import substitution was beginning to take off by then. In the new normality of 1559 materials for the English cloth trade took second place among our imports. Some £95,000 of them were imported, including £33,000 of woad, and £6,000 of Spanish wool, presumably to mix with English wool in cloth manufacturing. £36,000 of spices and £26,000 worth of silks came ahead of the imports of iron and steel, which because of the successful growth in English iron-founding had shrunk, from a value comparable with that of linen imports to an insignificant £20,000, barely ahead of hops, of which £17,000 were imported.[15]

'Sound money' and cheaper imports restored the lifestyle of landowners. However, what did affect a much larger part of the population very adversely was not the debasement, but the sudden calling down of money. All the coin in everyman's purse was halved in value by proclamation on 17 August 1551. It took ten years for the coinage to be properly re-established. Unlike the situation in France 130 years earlier, debasement did not have a greater effect on domestic prices than did harvest fluctuations. For example in the 1550s when both the sum minted from the Troy pound of silver and the price paid for it were virtually unchanged, the domestic prices for grains fluctuated quite wildly. In the harvest year 1556–7, categorized as one of 'dearth', wheat prices were three times as high as in the 'good' harvest years of 1553–4 and 1558–9.[16] The English debasement was too small to produce that sort of change in domestic prices. Agricultural price changes could be much greater, and affected almost the entire population, while the smaller price changes to imports only affected the vocal minority who had a say in running the country.

II: The Burgundian-Habsburg Netherlands in the 1480s and Early 1490s

Although the scale of the debasements in the Netherlands in the 1480s was comparable with those in England by Henry VIII and Somerset in the 1540s, the conditions were in many ways quite different. First, the Burgundian-Habsburg debasements were in the context of a civil war, while the English debasements were in the context of an overseas war. Second, the Netherlands' debasements were much briefer and prosecuted much less vigorously. Third, England was self-sufficient in food, while the Netherlands had to import both grain and livestock. Fourth, the evidence for what happened is much flimsier than for England in the 1540s. Both the English experience in the 1540s, and the Netherlands experience in the 1480s, were very mild compared with that in fifteenth-century Castile or France at the end of Charles VI's reign. A further comparison might be made with Brittany in the 1480s or with Prussia in the time of Copernicus, who wrote against coinage debasement on behalf of landed interests.

Even after the Battle of Nancy (1477), when the expense of defending the Netherlands was even greater than the costs of Charles the Bold's expansive policies, Mary, surrounded by the survivors from her father's group of noble counsellors, resisted the temptation to debase the coinage. However, in the spring of 1482 Mary died unexpectedly young from a hunting accident. Her infant son, Philip 'the Handsome', was universally recognized as heir of the united Burgundian-Habsburg Netherlands. The problem was one of who should rule during his minority. Should it be Mary's widower, Maximilian of Austria, theoretically excluded by the terms of his marriage contract? At a joint meeting of the assemblies of estates of all the provinces, Maximilian was reluctantly recognised as regent, except by the estates of Flanders, where a council was formed by a group of the infant Philip's major subjects to rule on his behalf.[17] Civil war resulted. The war affected much of the counties of Flanders and Artois, the southern parts of the county of Hainaut and of the duchy of Brabant, the bishopric of Liège, the northern parts of the county of Holland, and much of the bishopric of Utrecht and the duchy of Guelderland, in other words a very great deal of the Netherlands. It was exacerbated by French intervention on the side of those in Flanders. Only the northern parts of Brabant, including Antwerp, the lordship of Malines (Mechelen), Zeeland, and the southern parts of Holland, which remained in Maximilian's hands throughout, were exempt from war.

During the preceding half century of 'monnoye ferme et durable', since 1433, the dukes had taken 2, 3, 4 and occasionally, 5 d. groten as seigniorage on each *marc* of silver minted. Maximilian, coming from an Austrian tradition of frequent debasements,[18] and unable to raise money to pay his troops from the assemblies of Estates, broke with that traditional Low Countries' policy of strong money (i.e. from the monetary reforms of 1433–4). In 1485, and again in 1488–9, he engaged seriously in debasement, and took seigniorage at a much greater rate. In the first, brief, relatively mild, debasement in 1485 he was able to take 24 d. groten from each marc de Troyes of silver minted. In the second, more serious debasement of 1488–9, Maximilian took 62 d. groten per marc in 1488, and, from December 1488, 120 d groten per marc (= 10 s. groot Flemish).

From the Burgundian monetary reform of 1433–5, Philip the Good's total revenue from his mints had only been in the region of 240 Flemish pounds groot per year,[19] while Duke Charles (1467–77), whose reign covered the end of the European silver famine, had received around 500 pounds groot per year from a much greater volume of coinage. These were negligible sums, of no use for military adventures. The entire profit from all Charles's mints for his whole reign was less than his expenditure on clothing for his entourage when he went to Trier to meet the Emperor Frederick III! In the single year 1488, by contrast, Maximilian received nearly 19,000 pounds groot (113,000 livres of 40 gros) from the mints in only the area under his control, at Malines,[20] at Zaltbommel for Guelderland and at Dordrecht for Holland. The revenues from the debasement of the coinage in Maximilian's three mints were providing nearly a quarter of all the revenues passing through the hands of his receiver-general.[21] Maximilian used the profits of debasement to pay the wages of the German and Swiss troops that were employed to fight the Council of Regency, which was administering much of Flanders and Brabant in his son's name.[22] Since much of the additional money created by debasement passed into the hands of these foreign troops, who would have taken at least part of it away from the Netherlands, it is not clear whether in this case the debasement increased the money supply locally at all.

In the summer of 1489 the market price of bullion evidently rose above the price offered to merchants, so that the mints were closed. The regulations for opening a mint at Veurne (Furnes), in Flanders, on the coast to the west of Ghent and Bruges, newly reconquered in November 1489 for Maximilian's government, oddly specified the same price to be offered to merchants as in February. Since the market price was by then much higher, no bullion was brought to the mint; it coined nothing so that no accounts were ever rendered. It seems to have been some sort of propaganda exercise, to show that there was at least nominally a mint in Flanders on Maximilian's side ahead of the reform of the coinage that was about to take place.

Even from the limited information that we have, it is already quite clear that, as in England in the 1540s, exchange rates to and from Maximilian's Netherlands in the 1480s reacted very directly to the market price of bullion, which, in a period of debasement, was generally the mint price for bullion.

Table 4.2: Mint Prices and Exchange Rates in the Burgundian-Habsburg Netherlands 1485–9. All rates are in Flemish money groot.

Date	Value of coin minted from *marc* fine silver		Price paid by mint *marc* silver		against Venetian ducat		against Hungarian ducat
3 Nov. 1485	£2	100					
Dec 1489					6s 4d	95	6s 8d
31 Jan 1486			£1 18s 4d.	100			
31 Aug 1486					6s 8d	100	6s 10d
Sept 1486					7s	105	
20 Apr 1487	£2 8 s.	120					
28 Apr. 1487			£2 6s. 8d.	111			
May/June 1487					7s	105	7s 2d
July 1487					7s 10d	118	
20 Dec 1487					9s	135	
20 May 1488					9s	135	9s 2d
8 Dec 1488	£4 3 s	208	£3 10 s. 6d.	184			
Dec.1488					10s 8d	160	
Winter 1488-9					11s	165	
2 Feb. 1489					10s 10d	163	11s
12 Feb. 1489			£3 12 s.	188			
in or before			further				
June 1489	£6 11d ?	302	increase?				
July 1489					13s 6d	200	
26 July 1489					14s	210	
14 Dec 1489	reform		£1. 5s. 6d	67			
Dec 1489					4s 2d	63	4s 4d

Source: Exchange rate data supplied by Professor Oliver Volckart, Department of Economics, London School of Economics.

Between 1486 and 1489 the Venetian ducat, along with the Hungarian ducat and the gulden of the Rhineland monetary union, dominated international exchanges with the Low Countries. The exchange rate against the Venetian ducat slightly less than doubled. The rates show a rise from 84d. groten (7s gr. Fl.) in September 1486, before the debasement of April 1487, to 162d groten (13s 6d gr. Fl.) in July 1489, the last available before the return to strong currency in December 1489.[23]

Surprisingly few exchange rates between the Rhine gulden and Maximilian's Burgundian Flemish money groot are now available, although the gulden of the Rhineland monetary union were clearly circulating in the Habsburg-controlled Netherlands in the 1480s.[24] In the ecclesiastical principalities of Utrecht and Liège, however, the bishops' mints were producing silver coins that were debased more or less in parallel with those produced for Maximilian in the parts of the Netherlands that he controlled.[25] We may therefore use the rates known for Utrecht as a proxy for the Habsburg-Burgundian rates. The building accounts of the cathedral provide an evaluation of the Rhine gulden in money of Utrecht from 1484 to 1490.[26]

Table 4.3: Rhinegulden values in money of Utrecht.

Year	rate	index	index of Venetian ducat in s.d.gr. Flem.
1484	31 stuivers	103	
1485	31 ½ stuivers	105	
1485	30 stuivers	100	
1486	30 stuivers	100	100
1486	322 stuivers	108	105
1486	33 stuivers	110	
1487	33 stuivers	110	105
1487	33½ stuivers	112	
1487	34 stuivers	113	
1487	35 stuivers	117	118
1487	36 stuivers	120	
1487	37 stuivers	123	135
1488	40 stuivers	133	135
1488	42 stuivers	140	160
1489	45 stuivers	150	163
1489			200
1490	19stuivers	63	63
	moneta gravis		

Source: W. Jappe Alberts (ed.), *Bronnen tot de bouwgeschiedenis van den Dom te Utrecht*, part 2, vol. 2: *Accounts, 1480/81 – 1506–07*, Rijks geschiedekundige publication. Large Series, 129 (Utrecht, 1946).

A halving of the value of money groot against Venetian gold ducats would lead us to expect a doubling of the cost of eastern spices imported through Venice in money groot. This is effectively what we do see. The Venetian galleys were now bringing their goods to Antwerp, in the heart of the lands controlled by Maximilian, rather than to Bruges. South Indian short pepper imported into Antwerp from Venice virtually doubled in price, between October 1485 and October 1489. Prices for other spices, such as cloves, nutmeg, cinnamon, ginger, mace all did much the same. Some more than doubled in price, and so did Mediterranean products like saffron, cumin, almonds and fine olive-oil based soap, probably from Spain or possibly Italy. Vinegar rose in price even more. It may also have come from the Mediterranean, or alternatively, like so much wine, from the Rhineland. We have no prices for Italian and other silks, but we can assume that the rising exchange rate would have approximately doubled these prices as well.

Table 4.4: Prices at Antwerp for imports from or through the Mediterranean 1485–90.

Commodity	October 1485	October 1489	Change	October 1490
pepper per lb	2s 10 2 gr. Brab	5s 7 2 gr. Brab	× 1.96.	2s 1½ gr. Brab
cloves per lb	5s gr. Brab	8s gr. Brab	× 1.6	2s 9gr. Brab
nutmeg per lb	4s gr. Brab	9s 8gr. Brab	× 2.42	4s gr. Brab
cinnamon per lb	4s 9 gr. Brab	6s 9 gr Brab	× 1.42	3s gr. Brab
ginger per lb	1s 10½gr. Brab	7s 6 gr. Brab	× 2.65	2s 6gr. Brab
mace per lb	8s gr. Brab	18s gr. Brab	× 2.25	8s gr. Brab
saffron per lb	1li. gr. Brab	2li 8s gr. Brab	× 2.4	£1 2s 8 gr. Brab
almonds per lb	3s 9d gr. Brab	7s 6gr. Brab	× 2	3s 9gr. Brab
soap per half vat	17s 3 gr. Brab	1li 16s gr. Brab	× 2.1	12s 9gr. Brab
vinegar per aime	12s gr. Brab	2li. 5s gr. Brab	× 3.75	£1 2s 6gr. Brab

Source: Annual purchases in October for St Elisabeth Hospital Antwerp, extracted by E. Scholliers in Charles Verlinden (ed.), *Dokumenten voor de geschiedenis van prijzen en lonen in Vlaanderen en Brabant*, vol. 1 (Bruges: de Temple, 1959), pp. 332, 334, 336–8, 340–1, 359.

Wine growing had virtually ceased in the Low Countries by this period, and it was beer, brewed by now in Holland and Brabant, that was largely drunk. Wine therefore had become a drink for the rich. Wine from Burgundy and Gascony had become much less available. Imports were mostly Loire wines and above all Rhine wines. Rhine wine, bought in Lier (Lierre), nearly doubled in price by the autumn of 1489, rising in price from 1s gr. Brab per gelte in 1485 to 1s 10½ gr. Brab in 1489. Its price fell back to 1s gr. Brab in 1490.[27]

Commodities of such great variety do not permit the construction of a price series. Just as we can have no price series for Italian silks, so we can have no price series for the furs from the Baltic that reached the Netherlands. Bruges had for long been the most important market for furs in Europe. What we do have are prices for north European and Baltic beeswax, imported into Antwerp in the summers, and used for high-quality candles, as burnt by the wealthy and in grand churches. Its price also nearly doubled, rising in Antwerp from £5 14s 9d gr. Brab per 100 lb in 1485 to £9 6s gr. Brab in 1489, before falling back to £3 16s 6d gr. Brab in 1490.[28]

The rich were particularly conscious of the rise of the cost of imports, for it was they who mainly consumed spices, wine, beeswax, silks, furs and other goods imported from abroad. The eventual consumers were those most seriously afflicted by such rises in price, since merchant intermediaries were sufficiently flexible to be able to cope with changes in prices themselves, although they were affected by changes in the volumes of imports and exports. The volume of cloth imported from England diminished remarkably. The amount of cloth sent from London by denizens, i.e. the Merchants Adventurers, mainly London mercers, primarily to the Low Countries, had been in the order of 18,000 standard broad-cloth equivalents a year in the decade before debasement.[29] The amount dropped suddenly from 21,500 cloth equivalents sent between September 1485 and December 1486, to only 7,400 cloths between December 1486 and July 1487, and remained low at 7,900 cloths between July 1487 and Michaelmas 1488.[30] At first sight this seems to be a violent scaling back of demand in the Low Countries in the 1487–9 debasement period, because English cloth had become too expensive. However, it does not correlate neatly, for the recovery in shipments in 1489 preceded the end of debasement. Thus 15,400 cloths were sent between Michaelmas 1488 and Michaelmas 1489. Evidently, the civil war itself was more important than the related debasement. In 1487 and 1488, French ships, based at Sluis in support of those opposing Maximilian, attempted to blockade the entry to the Scheldt. This situation was worsened by the poor relations between Henry VII and Maximilian, since the latter supported Yorkist claimants to Henry VII's throne. In 1488 Henry VII ordered an English boycott of the Brabant Fairs (Antwerp and Bergen op Zoom). Thus this decline in imports does not seem to be a consequence of debasement. Much of this cloth was unfinished and after finishing it was re-exported, along with woollens from the Low Countries cloth, so that the Low Countries were not the final destination.

Some imports however did affect everybody. The amount of salt produced in Zeeland was utterly inadequate for the needs of the Netherlands. Earlier, much salt had been imported from Lüneburg (near Lübeck), but by the 1480s the prime source of salt had become the Bay of Bourgneuf on the west coast of southern France (Bay of Biscay). With the fall in exchange rates, the cost of Bay salt at Antwerp rose correspondingly: from 2s 7.2 Brabant groten per bushel in 1487 to 6s 7¾ Brabant groten in 1489, nearly 2.2 times the price of two years earlier.[31]

Grain too was in the category of imports that affected everybody, since not enough grain could be grown within the country. From 1477 to 1483, when Louis XI closed the French frontier, the regular supplies of wheat from Picardy were cut off, so that the Netherlands had to rely on other sources for grain to supplement what could be produced at home. Much grain came to Dordrecht and Delft down the Meuse and the Rhine and to Amsterdam from the rivers of northern Germany, the Ems, the Weser and the Elbe. It was at this point that imports of rye from the Baltic began to be noticeable. Unfortunately, we have no figures for the 1480s, but it was a time of change. Around 2,000 lasts of rye were sent out of Danzig (Gdansk) in the 1470s, while about 10,000 lasts were sent in the 1490s. It was a significant beginning, although negligible compared with the quantities that would be sent from the second half of the sixteenth century. This rupture in supplies of Picard wheat gave a great boost to the grain importers of Holland, particularly those of Amsterdam. Even when Picard wheat again became available after 1493, the alternative sources of grain continued to be exploited.[32] The sources of grain were a consequence of war, but the price changes were a product (in part) of coinage debasements.

Although the Netherlands formed one of the most heavily urbanized areas in Europe, nevertheless two-thirds of the inhabitants still lived in the countryside. Even in the county of Holland, now more heavily urbanized than the county of Flanders, over half the population still lived in the countryside, while in the duchy of Limburg, a normal European proportion of over nine-tenths did so, as in England or France or Germany. So 'what happened in the countryside' mattered enormously.

The possibility that domestic producers could increase their own prices in correspondence with debasements came about because of the increase in the price of imported grain that resulted from changes in exchange rates. There is some evidence to suggest that in this way internal grain prices did approximately reflect what debasement was thought to be. At Lier (Lierre), in the duchy of Brabant, 17 kilometres south east of Antwerp, and well away from the war, we have figures for monthly sales of wheat on the local market by Lier's 'Table du Saint Esprit'.[33] We have to keep in mind that such prices were far more affected by harvest quality than by this scale of debasement. The price of wheat therefore generally showed major changes in the autumn, when the size of the new harvest became clear, but normally only minor changes during the harvest year, often rising slightly in the summer before the new harvest was available. In some years it is just possible to distinguish effects of debasement on the change of prices *within* the harvest year, rather than *between* harvest years. In the spring of 1486, when there was no change in the coinage, the price of a viertel of wheat at Lier crept up by a normal 3 per cent between the spring (February–April) and the summer (May–July). In the following year, 1487, it rose by an exceptional 11.2 per cent at the same time of year. The first stage of the currency debasement had taken place in April. The year after, 1488, it rose even more, by very nearly 30 per cent, which coincided with the debasement in June that followed Maximilian's release. Normally, there was not much change in prices between winter and spring quarters, but in spring 1489 the price of wheat rose by 20 per cent, coinciding with the known alterations in the mint price for silver in December 1488 and February 1489. Prices went up again between the spring and summer quarter that year, by 11 per cent, an increase possibly confirming the supposition that some further change, presumably in the mint price as well as the silver content of coin, was made at some time before July. Overall, wheat prices at Lier rose from 6s 6 gr. Brab per viertel, before April 1487, to 11s gr. Brab per viertel, by early December 1489. This rise of 70 per cent partially reflects the sequence of debasements that had taken place in between, but also reflects the fact that the harvest of 1489 was better than that of 1486. Wheat at 11s in December 1489 was effectively *cheaper* than at 6s 6 gr. in March 1487. In other words the grain-producing farmers, or at least the middlemen, were partially able to adjust the price of grain to fit with the perceived debasement of the coinage. The mint price had gone up overall by at least 90 per cent, without taking account of the rise in the summer of 1489, although the silver money minted from a *marc* had increased by 202 per cent. We also have figures for the quantities of rye sold by the St Elisabeth hospital (*gasthuis*) in Antwerp and the prices that it fetched. Since the hospital did not sell rye at regular intervals round the year, but concentrated its sales in the autumn and the spring, the pattern is harder to discern, but still shows the same effects.

Table 4.5: Price of Rye at Antwerp by harvest years 1485–6 to 1489–90.

sold for St Elizabeth gasthuis
(Per viertel [quarter] of Antwerp in money of Brabant)
1 d. gr. Brab = 2/3d gr. Flem.; 1.5 d gr Brab = 1.0d gr. Flem

Harvest Years	year 1485–6	year 1486–7	year 1487–8	year 1488–9	year 1489-90
Autumn new harvest prices uncertain					
August		54d	54d	72d	
September	30d			72d	90d
October	36d				78d
Winter new harvest prices certain					
November				mint price increased	mint price reduced
December	41d	72d	60d	72d	
January					
Spring little change likely					
				Mint price increased	
February					36d zwaar = 108d licht

Harvest Years	year 1485–6	year 1486–7	year 1487–8	year 1488–9	year 1489-90
March			54d		
		Mint price increased			
April			60d		
Summer			Mint price increased		
slight rise likely					
May		54d			30d zwaar = 90d licht
June	45d				
July		57d			

Sources: Annual purchases in October for the St. Elisabeth Hospital, Antwerp: in E. Scholliers and C. Verlinden (eds), *Dokumenten voor de geschiedenis van prijzen en lonen in Vlaanderen en Brabant*, 4 vols (Bruges: De Tempel, 1959), vol. 1, pp. 332, 334, 336–8, 340–1, 359. H. Van der Wee, *The Growth of the Antwerp Market and the European Economy, Fourteenth-Sixteenth centuries*, 3 vols (The Hague: Martinus Nijhoff, 1963), vol. I: *Statistics*: Appendix 1, 'Rye in Antwerp', pp. 173–7.

In the harvest year 1487–8, rye was being sold at 4s 6d to 5s gr. Brab a viertel up to April 1488. A debasement took place in June, so that the next sales were at a markedly higher price: in August and September at 6s and 6s 7.2d gr. Brab. Although this was the next harvest, the wheat prices at Lier suggest that this in itself made little difference . The increases in the mint price in February 1489 and again later in the year are reflected by sales in the next harvest year, after a good harvest, at 7s 6d gr. Brab the viertel in September 1489 and at a price in February 1490 of 9s *licht* (i.e. in the coinage struck before the reforms of December 1489). Overall the price received for rye tripled between the autumn of 1485 and the reforms of December 1489.[34] However, even the principalities under Maximilian's control did not yet enjoy a unified market. In each individual city the market price of wheat was observed monthly to calculate the required weight of the loaves at which bakers were to make different types of bread.[35]

Not only could the Netherlands not grow enough grain to feed itself, despite having adopted intensive cultivation,[36] it could also not raise enough livestock to provide meat for its inhabitants. By the 1480s, the cattle trade from Denmark was firmly established, replacing that in horses. Again it was the increase in the price of imported cattle, resulting from the change in exchange rates, that made it possible for domestic livestock farmers to increase their prices. The prices of livestock also fluctuated from year to year, although they did not vary as dramatically as grain prices, except when herds or flocks were reduced by disease. The evidence that we do have shows that livestock prices did go up appreciably, although they did not double between 1487 and 1489. In Antwerp, not in a war zone, the prices paid for cattle by the St Elisabeth hospital rose only from £2–0–6d groot per head in 1487 to £2–18–0d groot in 1489, a rise of only 43 per cent. The price they paid for sheep rose from 37 groten a head to 60 groten, a rise of 62 per cent and for geese from 13 groten to 22 groten, a rise of 73 per cent. In other words livestock farmers, or at least the middlemen, were also able to adjust their prices, but not completely, to compensate for the perceived debasement of the coinage. Because of this need to import foodstuffs, the changed prices of imports affected everyone in the fifteenth-century Netherlands. While rural dwellers depended primarily on sales of produce, many townsmen depended on some form of money wages. The wages we know about moved remarkably little, in many cases not at all. It is, of course, in the nature of wages to change less easily than market prices, although more easily than rents. However, the sort of wages we know about are the wages of such people as gardeners or building workers, bricklayers and carpenters, very often those employed by the day by churches or charitable institutions.

Wages were expected to be static: i.e. not to rise or fall with agricultural prices from harvest year to harvest year. Long-term trends in wages do correspond with trends in agricultural prices although usually lagging behind; and the changes with debasements were no different. Typical urban day wages, for craftsmen and labourers, only rarely including food, and generally varying with the length of the working day between winter and summer (except in Bruges), were quite different from the piece-work payments in the various textile industries in both the great cities and the small towns of the Netherlands. Such artisans as weavers, fullers and dyers were paid by the job done, and were sub-contractors to drapers rather than employees, owning their own looms, fulling- or dyeing-vats. We know a little about payments to master fullers, for example. The fees paid to full cloths also covered the use of their equipment and the wages they paid to their workers, as well as remuneration for the masters themselves, who might have several fulling-vats in operation at once. There is little evidence that payments in the textile industries rose either. In other words ordinary urban incomes remained static, while food prices rose significantly, or rather, in the case of bread, the size of the loaf diminished in proportion to the rise in the price of grain. The ordinary townsman was substantially worse off. Professor Leo Noordegraaf has shown in poignant detail how, in the towns of the county of Holland, the purchasing power of static wages was heavily depressed at this time.[37] It was not merely ordinary 'wage-stickiness', but also major unemployment that suppressed wage increases in the face of inflation. Wages were not entirely static everywhere. In the town accounts of Malines (Mechelen), although the daily wages paid to masons' aides and journeymen remained unchanged, the summer wages of the master masons themselves did eventually go up slightly in the summer of 1489, from 12d to 13½d. groot, a rise of 12.5 per cent at a time when wheat and rye prices had risen by 60 per cent and 67 per cent since the harvest year 1486–8.[38]

If the rich in the fifteenth-century Netherlands were anything like their counterparts in England – and there is no reason to suppose they were not –

they distinguished themselves from the 'poor' by eating an extraordinarily high protein diet. By contrast the poor had a high carbohydrate diet. The contrast was still significant in the late fifteenth century, although not as marked as it had been a century and a half earlier, since ordinary fifteenth-century wage earners ate more meat and fish than did their ancestors. A possible reason why livestock prices did not rise as much as grain prices is that in the late 1480s ordinary wage earners had temporarily given up their newly acquired possibility of eating meat to concentrate more on buying bread. This enforced change in diet perhaps explains why the price of meat did not go up as much as the price of grain between 1487 and 1489, nor did the cost of fish.

One effect of static wages was that goods manufactured within the Netherlands, in which labour was a major component, did not increase in price. At Lier the nominal price cost of bricks actually went down from 30d Brabant groten per 1,000 in 1487 to 24d Brabant groten per 1,000 in 1489.[39] Demand was undoubtedly utterly depressed. Those normally likely to commission buildings were property owners, who were of course dependent on rents whose purchasing power was falling. In such a situation, there was very little chance that building wages or brick prices would rise. But even if the labour costs did not increase prices for manufactured goods at home, the exchange rate mechanism made manufactured goods much dearer abroad.

Town governments seem to have been among the few beneficiaries of the situation, apart from those farmers who survived the disturbances unscathed. This was because of the way their finances were organized. Irregular expenditures, for example large payments for walling or paving, or for meeting demands of the central government, were met by selling *renten* (annuities). The interest on these was paid out of local excise dues, bearing heavily on beer and wine, which rose with the price of beer and wine. The remainder of the income from excises was spent on ordinary regular expenditure, mostly wages. In these debasement years the income from excises rose, while the payment on wages hardly rose and annuities remained constant. For example in 1489 at Mechelen, outside the war zone, the city paid out £5,872 gr. Brab on its annuities, only slightly more than in previous years, but the return from excises had risen so much that the annuity payments only took up 54 per cent of the receipts. The previous year annuities had taken up 73 per cent of the excise and before that nearly 80 per cent. Some cities actually paid out less in these years. There was a lively market in *renten* so that they were held as investments by people living quite far away from the issuing town or city. As a consequence in the civil war situation the parties involved might be on opposite sides. In order to put additional pressure on his opponents, Maximilian wrote to the city of Dordrecht on 1 June 1488, instructing them not to pay out on any of their *renten* held by people from Bruges, Ghent or Ypres, against whom he was resuming military operations.[40]

The corollary of the cities' having gained from only paying out constant sums in money of account on annuities, was, of course, that the holders of *renten* received exactly the same nominal income in money of account as they had done before debasement, but, in 1489, they were actually receiving half the amount of silver or gold equivalent that they had been given two years earlier. The countryman basically depended not on wages, but on the prices he received for his produce and the quantity he was able to produce. If the Lier and Antwerp figures are in any way typical, the farmer was able to ride the debasement well, particularly since his principal expenditure was the rent that he paid for his farm. This was normally fixed for long terms of years and rarely changed, unlike the prices he received for his produce. Since their rents remained unchanged, both grain farmers and livestock farmers were effectively better off at the end of the period of debasement than they had been at the beginning, provided that their farms had not been devastated by the civil war.

The other side of this situation was that the landlords were effectively worse off, since property, particularly agricultural property, was generally let on very long leases. The income from it was therefore virtually unchangeable in the short run. This meant that in any inflationary situation the tenant gained and the landlord lost, until the lease ran out and could be renegotiated. In any period of time as short as two years, very few leases could be renegotiated, and this meant that virtually all landlords saw their real incomes drop dramatically. Furthermore many of those who owned property in areas directly afflicted by war received no rent at all for some properties. Those with land on the 'front line' in Flanders Brabant or Hainaut were particularly badly affected.

An example of how rents could respond in practice is provided by two adjacent houses in Antwerp, on the Kamerstraat, both rented from Our Lady's Church. The first house was let on a 25-year lease from 1471 to 1495 at £2 gr. Brab a year, and no change could be made in the debasement years. It was then leased again in 1496 at a higher rent, at £3 gr. Brab on a 39-year lease. The house next door was let on much shorter leases, thus indicating how hard it was for both parties to get it right in negotiations over the rent and the term. First there was a four-year lease in 1472 at £2 10s, then a five-year lease in 1476 for £3 2s, then a single year lease for £3 3s, then another single year for £3 2s again, then it disappears from the church accounts until 1486, when the church was able to demand appropriately higher rent for the time of £3 10s for seven years. This turned out to be too much, and in 1493, in the expectation of post-debasement stability, a 33-year lease was negotiated at a reduced rent of £3. At the end of this long lease the tenant was doing very nicely, for by 1526 Antwerp was booming and the new lease for this city centre property was at the new realistic figure of £12.[41]

All those who lived on fixed incomes were in the same situation – and this included all members of the nobility, and most churchmen, who primarily depended on income from property or city annuities. Furthermore it was these very people who were particularly badly affected by increasing expenditure, because they were the primary consumers of imported goods.

The tradition of not debasing the coinage without the consent of the estates went alongside the grant of *aides* by those same assemblies. It is noticeable that Maximilian's breach with tradition, in the debasement of 1485, had followed the refusal of the estates for his request for an *aide*. It is equally noticeable that after 1493 the grants of *aides* again became normal, alongside the return to the tradition of coinage stability. By the 1480s, there was already a long tradition of noble opposition to currency debasement, based on a very clear appreciation of the effects of debasement on landowners. They had no doubt that debasement increased the prices of what they consumed, particularly imports. Since their nominal incomes remained static, they were faced with a choice between a catastrophic drop in their standards of living, or plunging deeply into debt, unless they could suddenly find extraordinary additional sources of income.

Maximilian went back to Austria in December 1488, effectively defeated, having been captured in Bruges, earlier that year, in January. In return for his release in May, Maximilian had given up his claims to rule the Burgundian Netherlands instead of the noble Council of Regency during the rest of his son Philip's minority. However the Treaty of Frankfurt of 19 July restored his right to rule, so that the civil war continued. When Maximilian gave up the unequal struggle for personal dominance in the Low Countries, he left Albert III, duke of Saxony, as *Stadhouder Generaal* (general deputy), supported by Engelbert II count of Nassau, to rule his parts of the Netherlands. They were much more effective in the prosecution of their side of the civil war than Maximilian had been, as well as being better at negotiations. As a parting gesture, on 8 December 1488, Maximilian began to fund Saxony's campaigns against the Council of Regency, by further debasing the coinage, taking over 14 per cent seigniorage. After the first few months the supply of bullion began to dry up, when the market price caught up with the mint price for bullion. Saxony raised the mint price slightly in February, but does not seem to have debased the coinage any further at that time. Even with a higher mint price, he was still taking nearly 12 per cent seigniorage. The supply of bullion now markedly dried up, because the market price first caught up with, and then went higher than, the mint price. Minting shrank to a trickle, if it did not actually stop A final debasement in the summer, presumably accompanied by an increased mint price, did attract some more bullion for coining, so that it became possible to pay Saxony's mercenaries over 23,000 livres of 40 gros (= £3833 6s 8d groot Flemish) from the Malines mint in September 1489.

As well as using force, Saxony and Nassau realized how much negotiation was also necessary. They learned from Maximilian's experience that it was necessary to placate Philip's greater subjects, who were the ones principally suffering from the effects of debasement. To do this involved not only engaging in personal negotiations to win over powerful individuals, but also in making some settlement with the assemblies of estates, who had been alienated by Maximilian's autocratic imposition of taxation and debasement of coinage without their consent. At a prolonged meeting in the autumn of 1488 representatives of the estates of all Philip's principalities had made a treaty between the assemblies in which they had asserted against Maximilian their ancient privileges of securing consent. In it they stated that for the common coinage of all principalities, there should be no change without the consent of all.[42] One of Saxony and Nassau's first effective moves was to make a truce with France, and so to remove French support from the Council of Regency. The truce was followed up by the peace of Plessis-lès-Tours of 30 October 1489. This was followed up by a meeting of the estates of Artois and Picardy (an area still occupied by the French), which allowed Maximilian's debased coin to circulate there. By 20 November, Charles der Croy, prince of Chimay, had conquered Hainaut for Maximilian, and gone through southern and western Flanders to the coast, reducing the area controlled by the Council of Regency to the area around Ghent and Bruges. In the autumn of 1489 Saxony and Nassau engaged in lengthy negotiations with the estates. One of the key outcomes, in December 1489, was the promulgation by Saxony, under pressure from the estates, of an ordinance to return to the traditional Netherlands policy of ' monnoye ferme et durable'. By doing so they won over many of the nobility. The chronicler Molinet described the negotiations:

> A cause de l'entretenement et nourreture des guerres dures et austères ès pays de monseigneur l'archiduc, les monnoyes estoyent tellement montées en valeur que une pièche d'or valloit trois, samblement d'argent, qui estoit grant dhommage et desplaisir tant pour ceulx qui avoyent rentes comme pour gens d'eglises ... qui estoit chose exorbitant et hors de règle, dont pluseurs consaulx et assemblées se tindrent à Malines sur la reduction d'icelle. Jehan de Lannoy, abbé de Saint-Bertin, chancelier de la Thoison d'Or, principal directeur de ceste matière, fit convocquier de pluseurs quartiers gens experimentés en ceste faculté, affin d'y remedier ou mieulx que possible seroit.[43]

The reform of December 1489 was very successful from the point of view of those consuming foreign goods. The exchange rate against the Venetian ducat improved very rapidly (see Table 4.2) and the prices of imported spices and Mediterranean goods responded with the arrival of the next ships from the Mediterranean in 1490 (see Table 4.4) to levels last seen in 1485, and so did the prices for Rhine wines and beeswax. We may safely assume that prices for silks and furs returned to their earlier level as well.

In 1485, the coinage had been restored to the way it had been immediately before the recent debasements. The December 1489 reform did not, however, produce the expected return to the coinage that had been in force before April

1487. Instead there was an attempt to go back over twenty years to Philip the Good's final coinage, at the end of his reign, in 1466–7.[44]

The coin produced in the debasement years was allowed to circulate until enough new coin could be produced to replace it, but its exchange value had to be reduced to just one-third of the rates for which it had previously passed. The intention was that new coin should be produced in five provinces: Brabant, Flanders, Holland, Hainaut and Guelderland. However the mint in Hainault was never reopened, although the Luxemburg mint (closed since 1443) was reactivated. When enough new coin was produced, as much as possible of the debased coin was melted down and reminted, rather effectively, which means that although huge numbers of coins had been minted in 1488, they are now relatively rare. The difference between the mint price and the amount minted from it was reduced to a much more traditional rate in December 1489. Less than two per cent was allowed for seigniorage, together with the brassage costs of minting. Once again it was possible to reckon that what was being minted was closely related to the price offered for bullion by the mints.

The accompanying regulations dealt with the valuation of debts and obligations incurred at various dates during the debasement period since St John's day in 1487, but lumped together all obligations entered into before that date, even though the coinage had been changed a number of times between 1467 and June 1487. [45] The rates given were lopsidedly and decisively in favour of creditors, and of those who were in receipt of sums fixed in money of account, whether rents or *renten*, the very people who had lost out the most badly in the intervening two and a half years.[46] One effect of this was that an annuity of £10 gr. Fl, which could have been met by payments of 40 Andries gulden (florin) early in 1487 (when the gulden was actually passing for 5s), and by payments of only 20 gulden in the second half of 1489, was now reckoned to need payments of 60 gulden.

Despite the penalties built into the ordinance, it was not easily enforceable, and litigation continued for many years. The jurist, Nicolaas Everaerts (1462–1532), eventually the eminent President of the Great Council of Malines, the supreme court of the Netherlands, kept a note of much of the advice he had provided in tricky legal cases. These were published by his heirs as *Responsa sive Consilium* in 1554, long after his death. They included his advice on the value of money left as a bequest in 1488 which was disputed after the reforms of December 1489.[47]

Tariffing the money of account against gold at a pre-1466 level did not work. Monetary difficulties continued for the next seven years. It not only proved impossible to mint much, but the ordinance was disregarded. At the beginning of 1491 an instruction was published in Hainaut against defiance of the ordinance. At a meeting of Estates in May it was noted that the ordinance on coinage recently made was not being upheld, and a means was sought to uphold it, particularly because at Tournai, in France, and at Ghent and Sluis coinage had a higher value. A joint assembly of the estates of all the provinces, in May and June 1491 requested that the Andries gulden no longer to be tariffed at 20 patards (i.e. double *groten*), but at 24 patards (= 48d = 4s gr. Fl), as it had been from 1474. This request was repeated at the meeting in February and March 1492, and this new tariff was approved by order of Engelbert count of Nassau, by then Maximilian's deputy. It was still not right. On November 1493 the money of account was adjusted again, with the gold gulden of St Andrew retariffed at 27 patards (= 54d = 4s 6 gr. Fl). It was only in 1496, after Philip's majority, that the right level for coinage was finally achieved. A proper return was made at last to the Burgundian tradition of a stable strong coinage, which had been broken by Maximilian in 1485. The new stable coinage of 1496 lasted until 1521. The changes introduced in 1521 involved only a reduction in the weight of the silver by 4.4 per cent, the necessary generational adjustment to cope with wear and tear in circulation. In effect the stable coinage of 1496 lasted for the whole of the first half of the sixteenth century.

The monetary uncertainty of these seven years was accompanied in the early 1490s by some of the worst harvests of the fifteenth century. Furthermore the civil war continued until October 1492, but with those governing on behalf of Maximilian increasingly in the ascendant. The consequences in terms of food prices and the purchasing power of wages meant that the early 1490s were more dreadful for ordinary citizens and townsmen than the earlier years of debasement.

In the areas of the Netherlands outside Maximilian's control, the mint of Ghent was continuing to strike gold and silver coin in 1488, in the name of the young Philip, for the Council of Regency, backed by the authority to do so of Charles VIII, as nominal overlord of most of Flanders.[48] In Brabant the Estates reopened the old mint at Brussels. In the next year, 1489, the mint of Ghent went on minting gold and silver coin in Flanders in the name of the young Philip, for the Council of Regency, and in Brabant the mint at Leuven, previously operated in the 1460s and 1470s, was restored to coin production. Saxony and Nassau wore down their opponents, by force and negotiation, so that both Brussels and Leuven fell to them in August 1489, bringing to an end independent minting in Brabant. The Ghent mint continued to operate, however, through 1490 and 1491. It closed after the peace of Cadzand at the end of July 1492, which marked the end of the Flemish alternative government. Only Sluis (L'Écluse) held out, under the command of Philip of Cleves, lord of Ravenstein, and an alternative mint was set up there, until Ravenstein became reconciled to Maximilian's government in October 1492.

In contrast to Maximilian's mints, the Ghent mint went on minting a silver coinage on the same standard as that of 1482–5 and 1485–7. The Council of Regency refrained from using the coinage to pay for their troops fighting against Maximilian's. Noble and rentier elements on this side remained strongly opposed to debasement. They preferred direct taxation in the form of *aides*, or loans from the sale of interest-bearing *renten*. The coin produced at Sluis to pay for the defending troops came not from any profits of debasement, but from the personal plate of the commander, Philip of Cleves.

When I looked for prices and wages in the accounts of hospitals in Bruges, Ghent and Leuven/Louvain, I expected to be able to find much more stable prices than in Maximilian's areas of control. Unfortunately these accounts, which had been kept meticulously up to this point, either became very haphazard or skipped the war years entirely.[49] However even in these war years Adrian Verhulst found a series of wheat prices recorded, at three times each year in the accounts of the chapter of St Donatian in Bruges. As I had hoped, they show changes *between* harvest years, but not *within* harvest years until November 1490, when the price of wheat, which had been at 9s gr. Fl per heud in the harvest year 1489–90, shot up to 24s gr. Fl in mid-November.[50] This increase was not due to debasement but to the terrible siege of Bruges, which was then brutally sacked by Saxony's *landsknechts* on and after its fall on 29 November 1490.

Similarly G. Croisiau found prices for Rhine wine purchased for St Peter's Abbey at Ghent. They show that the prices paid did not rise in the same way as in the Maximilian-controlled provinces. The prices for Rhine wine varied between 9d and 13d gr. Fl per stoop in the accounts for 1485–6 and between 10d and 14d gr. Fl in 1489–90. After that, there are no further records until 1494–5. He also found that the price paid for sugar remained stable from 1485–6 to 1487–8 at 8d gr. Fl per steen.[51]

If these fragmentary pieces of evidence are representative of what has been lost, prices in those parts of the Low Countries where sound coinage was maintained were indeed much more stable, and provide a remarkable contrast to what happened in those provinces that suffered from Maximilian's debasements.

In France in the 1420s, the competitive debasements by the warring parties were so severe that they even overwhelmed the effects of changing harvest qualities. In England in the 1540s, and Maximilian's parts of the Netherlands in the late 1480s, the effects on agricultural prices are difficult to see and in any case were clearly less significant than was the quality of harvests. Furthermore in the Netherlands the effects of the civil war in themselves also generally outweighed the effects of debasement. In both England and the Netherlands exchange rates can be seen to relate to the market price of bullion, generally the price offered by the mints, not to the extent to which coin was debased. In England it is possible to see the effects of changing exchange rates on both exports and imports, and it is possible to pick out the consequent moves towards import substitution. In the Netherlands the effects on some imports can be seen, but the effects on exports cannot be determined, and no import substitution can be detected. However, in both England and the Netherlands the consequences of such relatively small debasements, included the doubling of the prices of selected imports, maddened those living on fixed incomes, in England on rents and in the Netherlands not only on rents from property, but also on municipal *renten*. These included the politically important nobility. Even such relatively small debasements upset the nobility. In both cases the pressure of the groups so affected built up to be able to force a violent return to strong money. In neither case did this work properly to begin with. In England it took ten years to sort out, and in the Netherlands seven.

I therefore believe that it is possible to disentangle some of the effects of debasements, even ones of this limited scale, from the direct effects of civil war and variations in the quality of harvests. I also believe that it was through exchange rates and imports that most such changes took place.

5 THE AMSTERDAM WISSELBANK'S INNOVATIONS IN THE MONETARY SPHERE: THE ROLE OF 'BANK MONEY'

Herman Van der Wee

Introduction

From its very foundation, the Amsterdam Wisselbank has been praised by bankers as well as by scholars for its pre-eminent role in early-modern national monetary policies and international finance.[1] In 1776 Adam Smith called it 'the great warehouse of Europe for bullion' and more recently Simon Schama described it as the 'watchdog of capitalism in Amsterdam', the 'church of Dutch capitalism'.[2] In 'European Banking in the Middle Ages and Early Modern Times', in *A History of European Banking*, I put forward the hypothesis that in the early-modern period the Low Countries produced an autonomous Financial Revolution, one that should be considered as a crucial link between the late-medieval Italian Financial Revolution and the eighteenth-century English Financial Revolution.[3] I also suggested that the real innovations, as far as financial techniques were concerned, occurred in Antwerp during the sixteenth century. In this hypothesis the Amsterdam Wisselbank was, from a technical point of view, a primarily conservative institution, simply following the Italian banking traditions of the fifteenth and sixteenth centuries. If innovations in financial techniques did occur in Amsterdam during its Golden Age, they originated mainly in the sectors of private banking.

The purpose of this chapter, therefore, is to explore to what extent this thesis is still valid or, on the contrary, has to be restated or revised on the basis of recent research. No spectacular new discoveries will be revealed, but this chapter attempts to combine the new insights of the many scholars who have studied these problems in recent years, and to connect their findings with my own hypothesis. While this chapter examines early modern banking institutions, and related innovations in credit instruments, it also provides a clear link with the previous studies on coinage debasements in this volume. For one of the most pressing, indeed urgent, concerns in both the private and the public spheres of the new

Dutch republic (created in 1579, as the United Provinces, to use its more formal title) was how the government, bankers, merchants and money dealers would deal with the problem of an increasing circulation of foreign coins generated by Dutch regional and foreign trade: a circulation that contained a large proportion of debased and counterfeit coins, to the extent that, by the early seventeenth century, public confidence in the coinage system was being seriously undermined. What is so remarkable is how the Wisselbank of Amsterdam, a seemingly traditional and very conservative exchange bank, dealt with this problem, essentially by creating a new form of 'bank money' – even if *moneta di banco* had been pioneered much earlier by late medieval Italian banks – and one that promoted both Dutch and European economic growth.

The Hypothesis of Conservatism

The hypothesis of conservatism, as far as the Amsterdam Wisselbank is concerned, refers primarily to its origins and first statutes. The formula of a municipal deposit and transfer bank originated in late medieval Spain and Italy and became, particularly in sixteenth-century Italy, very successful. The Amsterdam Wisselbank, founded by the Amsterdam municipality in 1609, was as a matter of fact a copy of the Venetian model of a municipal deposit and transfer bank, the Banco della Piazza di Rialto, founded in 1587. Another much praised structural aspect of the Wisselbank, i.e. its system of payments, exclusively to be made in a single and stable money of account, represented by a fixed weight of precious metal, was not new either: the principle had already been applied during the fifteenth and sixteenth centuries at Geneva, Lyons, Besançon and Piacenza. For example, at the end of each of the four fairs at Lyons, the final payments for all transactions had to be made in *écus de marc*, a money of account, representing a fixed weight of precious metal, rather than a traditional money of account tied to some currently circulating silver (or gold) coin.

The fact that the Wisselbank had to send to the Dutch mints all coins and bullion it received, except the full-weight great silver Dutch *rixdollars*, was an obligation, which for centuries all money-changers, in principle, had respected for illegal and worn coins. In this respect the obligation of the Wisselbank, once again, was not new – having been found, as noted, with earlier Italian banks – but it was still more restrictive.

The Wisselbank, moreover, was officially declared to be and was stipulated to serve as the only cashier and money-changer of the town, since other edicts had prohibited the profession and practice of private cashiers and money-changers. These measures implied that the bank, in fact, was continuing, in a centralized way, some functions of both of these professions: the activity of money-changing and the banking function of the cashiers. From the beginning of the sixteenth

century, Antwerp's merchants had been instructing cashiers to pay their creditors and to collect the payment of debts by their debtors. Later, in the course
of the century, cashiers had extended their activities to more modern banking
functions, such as the granting of credit in current accounts or by discounting
commercial paper, the latter one of Antwerp's great financial innovations of the
later sixteenth century. The cashier system had been taken over by the Amsterdam merchant community, chiefly under the aegis of Antwerp merchants who
had migrated to Amsterdam in the later sixteenth century. The Wisselbank, by
becoming the only cashier of the town, continued therefore an old practice,
albeit again in a much more limited way. Indeed, the statutes of the Wisselbank,
fundamentally based on the statutes of Venice's Banco della Piazza di Rialto
(1587), did not permit the granting of credit in any form to merchants: whether
in the form of loans or advances in current account, or by way of discounting.
Its involvement in negotiating current commercial paper remained limited to
settling bills of exchange at the bank, in nominal Dutch currency. We do know,
however, that three exceptions to the Wisselbank's ban on credit were permitted
in practice: loans or advances to the municipality, to the East India Company
(VOC) and to the local Lombard bank (Bank Van Leening). But these exceptions do not really undermine the basic financial principle of the Wisselbank:
that it should function primarily as a giro (exchange) bank.

The Wisselbank, in 1609, was not allowed to issue notes to bearer or to
order: it was permitted only to issue 'assignations', that is, requests by merchants
to transfer specified sums from their own credit balances (deposits) in the Bank's
ledgers to some designated assignee. The Bank, therefore, did not acquire the
character of a central, money-creating credit institution that, in times of need,
could act as lender of last resort, as did the later Bank of England (in the course
of the eighteenth century).

To summarize: from the point of view of financial techniques, the Amsterdam Wisselbank was conceived as a conservative institution and it remained so
in essence during its whole existence, notwithstanding some adjustments, particularly at the end of the seventeenth century, to the changing circumstances
of Amsterdam's money and capital markets. Does this statement thus imply that
the Wisselbank was not innovative from other points of view either? This question will be answered in the next section.

The Innovative Aspects of Amsterdam's Wisselbank

In discerning the banking and monetary innovations of the Wisselbank, we
must first make a distinction between the four major functions that the bank
assumed during the course of the seventeenth and eighteenth centuries: a monetary function, a banking function, a commercial function and finally, so to speak,

a necessary function in responding to challenges. In its monetary function, the Wisselbank no doubt played an innovative and most important role. For the system of concentrating all important commercial transactions in one public institution, with a single monetary denominator, representing a fixed weight of silver to record those deposits and transactions in the bank's ledger, certainly did inspire trust, thereby contributing substantially to the stabilization of the whole monetary system in the Dutch Republic.

How that monetary stabilization was achieved may now be briefly summarized. In the sixteenth century during the rule of Charles V (r. 1506–56; emperor from 1519), the guilder (or florin) of 20 stuivers (= 40d groot Flemish), as the newly established money of account, was used not only for daily transactions in the domestic economy of the Low Countries, but also in the international trade of north-western Europe. That latter role was due principally to the commercial and financial pre-eminence of Antwerp, until the outbreak of the Revolt of the Netherlands or the Eighty Years' War against Spain (1568–1648). For that reason, Charles V's new money of account became internationally known as the 'Brabant' guilder of 20 stuivers, since Antwerp was a major town in the duchy of Brabant. After the Dutch closure of the Scheldt in 1585, followed by the rapid rise of Amsterdam, this money of account remained in fashion, in both the northern and southern Low Countries; but it now became known internationally as the 'Dutch' guilder of 20 stuivers, since, of course Amsterdam was the primary town and port in the county of Holland (whose citizens were now commonly called 'Dutch').

Both the Brabant and the Dutch guilders, as moneys of account, were handicapped, however, by one major weakness: that their value was based upon a small current coin of unstable silver content, the stuiver (2d). In the sixteenth century, Charles V had been able to minimize that deficiency by maintaining a more or less stable metallic content of the stuiver. However, from 1559 onwards and particularly during the first half of the Eighty Years' War, that monetary stability no longer prevailed, especially with so many coinage debasements in the northern and southern Netherlands that reduced the fine silver contents of the Brabant and Dutch stuiver.[4] The result was the circulation of a great variety of stuivers and of other medium-size coins of unequal value, generating much uncertainty about the exact value of the money of account. The confusion was enhanced by the increasing introduction and circulation of heavy-weight, high-denomination silver coins from all over Europe. The popularity of these coins encouraged the minting of imitations with a slightly lower silver content, especially at the periphery of international trade centres. The widespread circulation of the various imitation silver coins soon affected the value of the Brabant and Dutch money of account, by increasing the premium on the value of coins with higher fine-silver contents.

By the beginning of the seventeenth century, according to many financial reports, more than 500 different coins, legal as well as illegal ones, were circulating on the Amsterdam money market. The Amsterdam money-changers and cashiers were in an optimal position to take advantage of the consequent general monetary confusion. The money-changers and cashiers indeed earned large profits by selecting the better coins and selling them at a substantial premium. Decrees by the Amsterdam municipality to maintain the official monetary tariffs (exchange rates) were to no avail. Finally, in 1609, as previously indicated, the municipal government of Amsterdam prohibited individuals from practising the functions of money-changer and cashier, and transferred those functions as the exclusive monopoly of the new Wisselbank van Amsterdam.

Those combined measures immediately stabilized the value of the Dutch guilder money of account for the settlement of large international commercial transactions. All bills of exchange with a value exceeding 600 guilders (later to be reduced to 300 guilders), payable at Amsterdam, now had to be settled at the Wisselbank in these bank guilders of 20 stuivers; and also, as indicated above, each stuiver in this Dutch money of account represented a fixed weight of silver: from 1619 to 1681, 0.4367 g fine silver; and from 1681 to 1791, 0.4725 g fine silver per stuiver. All deposits at the Wisselbank therefore were converted into Bank guilders, along with the intrinsic silver value of foreign coins or bullion deposited. When a merchant wanted to withdraw cash from his deposit account (credit balance at the Bank), he was paid in Dutch *rijksdaalders* or *rixdollars* (87.50 per cent fine) at a conversion rate of 2 Bank guilders 8 stuivers. Indeed, the *rixdollars* would soon be called *negotiepenningen*, because of their predominant use in international trade, especially in the Baltic, the Levant, South Asia and the East Indies. The merchant could also transfer, without cost, Bank guilders from his own account to the account of a third party.

The new system was thus a great success in stabilizing the Dutch money of account in the sphere of international trade and finance, and, at the same time, it also stabilized the current money of account in the domestic economy. Before this stabilization, a creditor was, as it were, embarking on a venture when he received in cash a sum worth 100 guilders current money of account. Indeed, he did not know, at the moment of payment, the exact silver content of the coins he was then receiving, since so many coins were seriously deficient in their quality: whether they were debased, counterfeit, 'clipped' or just seriously worn. On the contrary, if he received payment through a transfer at the Wisselbank, he was certain of being paid in coins of perfect quality, since he was always entitled to convert the sum so transferred into *rixdollars* of perfect quality. Later, some other large-denominated coins of perfect quality became official *negotiepenningen* as well, thus enlarging the choice of good coins paid by the Bank.

Not surprisingly, such bank payments were soon earning a premium over current coin. A dual monetary system thus came into being, in that the Bank's money of account (the Bank guilder) was receiving an *agio* of 5 to 10 per cent over the current money of account (the current guilder). Over time, however, because of the ease of switching from one system to the other, the quality of all high-denomination coins in the daily circulation improved so much that their quality tended to become close to the quality of the *negotiepenningen* that the Bank delivered to its customers. In this way Gresham's Law was effectively reversed: so that, in striking contrast to the monetary situation of the early seventeenth century, good money was now driving out bad money.

Other developments also had an impact. The favourable balance of payments that the Dutch generally enjoyed in the seventeenth century and the abundance of American silver at Amsterdam increased the supply and circulation of high-quality, large-denomination coins to such an extent that they were soon determining the value of the current Dutch money of account. At the same time the stuiver and its multiples were losing their traditional link with the value of the current guilder: they were being downgraded over time to small-change currency, or 'token money'.

Certainly from 1638 onwards, but probably earlier, the relation between the two moneys of account, therefore, stabilized at about 5 per cent, as the value of both now depended upon the silver content of all legal, high-denomination silver coins. Oscillations of the *agio* still occurred, but from the second third of the century onwards they were limited and depended exclusively upon demand and supply of the *negotiepenningen* at the Bank. In 1681 the dual monetary system was legally confirmed, and consolidated by the simultaneous issue of silver coins, which were worth respectively 1 and 3 guilders and denominated as such. The dual system remained operative in this fashion until the closure of the Wisselbank in 1816, but it had become a purely artificial construction. Nevertheless, in stabilizing the whole monetary system of the Dutch Republic in the course of the seventeenth century, the Wisselbank was clearly playing an innovative role.

The Wisselbank was also achieving innovations in its related banking activities. The spectacular expansion of Amsterdam's world trade during the seventeenth century promoted the international payments in Bank money. Along with 'Dutch' merchants from Holland and Zeeland, foreign merchants from all their major firms maintained accounts with the Bank; and a growing number of international commercial transactions, even those contracted or arranged abroad, were being settled by bills of exchange, now more commonly called acceptance bills, payable at the Bank. Furthermore, the Bank became instrumental in executing purely international financial transfers.

The growing concentration of international payments on such a large scale made Amsterdam the most important money market of the world; and because of its expanding trade in domestic and foreign government securities (*rentes* or *renten*), Amsterdam soon became as well the largest capital market in the world. The concentration of all these payments at the Wisselbank made it a dominant international clearing-house, through which debit and credit balances from all over the world were offset against each other, or offset multilaterally, through the medium of Bank guilders, which, to repeat, always had a fixed silver value and were always convertible into high-quality large-denominated coins. This system may be considered as the seventeenth-century 'silver' equivalent of the nineteenth-century gold standard

The innovative role of the Wisselbank in its function as a dealer in precious metals was, at first sight, less clear. Initially this function was a very limited one. The statutes indeed specified that all precious metals, coined or uncoined (i.e. bullion), except for the full-weight *rixdollars*, that were received in international trade and other payments had to be sent to one of the licensed mints in the Republic in order to be converted into official full-weight *negotiepenningen*, which the Bank could then use for paying those merchants who chose to withdraw cash from their accounts. And that was it. Very soon, however, the Bank, in view of extra profits earned, began to deviate from this rule, by purchasing (for example) large quantities of Spanish *reals* from the Dutch West Indies Company and selling them directly to the VOC (East India Company) for export to the Far East or to the Amsterdam gold and silver thread drawers (for the jewellery and other *objets d'art* trades).

Over time the Bank found another, and even more important, reason for deviating from the rule. In 1621, when the 1609 prohibition on private exchangers was repealed, the private cashiers were again able take up their business. The cashiers took advantage of the new legislation by starting *inter alia* a trade in Bank money, so that merchants were no longer required to maintain accounts at the Wisselbank. As a result the rate of increase in the number of account-holders began to diminish, and indeed, from the 1660s, the total number started to decline, forcing the Bank to take other measures to enlarge its profitable trade in precious metals. In 1683, the Amsterdam municipality authorized the Bank to accept precious metals and coins as security. Thus, merchants who deposited an amount of coins of a particular type with the Bank would receive credits in their accounts for such deposits in Bank money. Such merchants could use this money to effect transfers from one account to another, while at the same time receiving a receipt (*recepis*), specifying the quantity and type of coins provided as security. This document was negotiable and could be put on sale at the Amsterdam Beurs (Exchange).

The negotiability of the *recepis* became the cornerstone of a far-reaching innovation. When the exchange rate for a given foreign currency moved beyond the specie points on the Amsterdam Beurs, merchants soon found it more profitable to buy a *recepis* – instead of buying bills of exchange (acceptances) –, exchange it at the Wisselbank against the foreign currency needed, and send the coins to the foreign money market, where the debt had to be settled. The fact that buyers of foreign currencies always enjoyed such an alternative led sellers of bills of exchange to establish or fix the exchange rate as close as possible within the brackets of the specie points. The system of the *recepis* thus contributed substantially to reducing the volatility of exchange rates at Amsterdam; in other words, this arbitrage function increased the stability of the exchange market, thereby fulfilling one of the major tasks of a modern central bank.

The straitjacket of restrictive regulations, within a very expansive and dynamic commercial, financial and industrial context, that were imposed on the Bank in 1609 generated great tensions within the Dutch economy, providing merchants in the private sector with the opportunity to introduce important innovations in the field of financial techniques. The private cashiers and great merchant bankers indeed proved to be very inventive. Cashiers became important suppliers of commercial credit in current money and also became important brokers for Bank money. They developed deposit, transfer and discount banking, specializing in the negotiation and discounting of bills of exchange, issuing negotiable receipts, assignations and notes on order. Together with the great merchant-bankers they developed 'acceptance credit', a new form of short-term international trade credit, as a refinement of the old traditional bills of exchange. The merchant-bankers, finally, set up a successful international securities market for long-term government debt instruments (especially *renten*).

Conclusions

The hypothesis that the Amsterdam Wisselbank was a conservative public institution in its financial techniques remains, no doubt, valid. But its innovative role in other fields has to be emphasized as well. In its monetary function the Wisselbank played a decisive role in stabilizing the monetary system, not only in the sphere of international trade and finance, but also in the sphere of the domestic economy. In its banking function the Wisselbank managed to become the first multilateral clearing-house in the world for settling international balances. As a dealer in precious metals the Wisselbank was the first public institution to be instrumental in making exchange rates less volatile. And finally, the Bank, by respecting the restrictive regulations imposed upon its functioning, spurred the private sector to introduce new financial activities and new financial instruments.

Of particular importance for the international trade of Dutch merchants, during the later seventeenth and eighteenth centuries, important indeed then for the entire western European economy, was the Wisselbank's use of its Bank guilder, with the privilege of converting funds in merchants' bank account deposits into *negotiepenningen* or bullion. In an era of increasing European scarcities of silver – as exports abroad were, by the 1670s, exceeding influxes of Spanish American silver – this bank system allowed merchants to economize on such valuable silver and reserve its restricted supplies for silver's most profitable use: in settling trade balances with the Baltic (and Russia), the Levant, South Asia and the East Indies, from which eastern regions Europeans had always purchased goods of greater value than those that they exported and sold to these regions. It is often said that the most important role that Spanish American silver played in promoting such an augmented 'globalization' of the early-modern world economy was to provide western Europeans with the monetary instruments (in good coin and bullion) to engage in such trade with these eastern regions. At the same time, the monetary and banking operations of the Wisselbank greatly reduced the transaction costs and thus increased the ease of doing so, to the very great benefit of Dutch merchants, during the seventeenth and eighteenth centuries.

Table 5.1: Exports of silver to Asia by the Dutch East India Company, decennial means, 1602–1795.

Decade	Value in gulden (guilders)	Kg fine silver	Index: 1600–49 = 100
1600–09	647,375.0	6,959.7	71.9
1610–19	965,800.0	10,382.9	107.3
1620–29	1,247,900.0	12,610.8	130.3
1630–39	890,000.0	8,994.0	92.9
1640–49	880,000.0	8,892.9	91.9
1650–59	840,000.0	8,488.7	87.7
1660–69	1,190,000.0	11,563.1	119.5
1670–79	1,220,000.0	11,854.6	122.5
1680–89	1,972,000.0	18,847.0	194.8
1690–99	2,900,500.0	27,720.9	286.5
1700–09	3,912,500.0	37,392.9	386.4
1710–19	3,882,700.0	37,108.1	383.5
1720–29	6,602,700.0	63,104.0	652.1
1730–39	4,254,000.0	40,656.8	420.1
1740–49	3,994,000.0	38,171.9	394.5
1750–59	5,502,000.0	52,584.3	543.4
1760–69	5,458,800.0	52,171.4	539.1
1770–79	4,772,600.0	45,613.2	471.4
1780–89	4,804,200.0	45,915.2	474.5
1790–99	3,233,600.0	30,904.5	319.4

One current Dutch guilder: in 1606–20 = 10.751 g fine silver; in 1621–59 = 10.106 g fine silver; in 1659–81 = 9.717 g fine silver; in 1681–1795 = 9.557 g fine silver
Source: F. S. Gaastra, 'The Exports of Precious Metal from Europe to Asia by the Dutch East India Company, 1602–1795 A.D.', in J. F. Richards (ed.), *Precious Metals in the Medieval and Early Modern Worlds* (Durham, NC: Carolina Academic Press, 1983), pp. 447–76.

6 SILVER IN ENGLAND 1600–1800: COINAGE OUTPUTS AND BULLION EXPORTS FROM THE RECORDS OF THE LONDON TOWER MINT AND THE LONDON COMPANY OF GOLDSMITHS

Nicholas J. Mayhew

Debasement has always commanded a high degree of interest among historians, and rightly so. Strong currencies of high intrinsic worth are associated with successful trading nations, but also have connotations of probity and high moral worth. Reductions in the intrinsic content of the coinage seem in contrast to speak of spendthrift government policies, and dissolute behaviour born of lax personal and national standards of behaviour. Debasement is also often associated with deception and downright fraud, since the extent of the reduction in intrinsic content was often concealed from the public. Nevertheless, despite such attempted secrecy, debasements usually resulted in some (unpredictable) degree of price inflation, which was almost always widely unpopular.

Debasement undermines the functions and use of money in all its principal respects. Whether money was used as a measure or store of value, its alteration obviously reduced its ability to fulfil its core functions. Debasement also disrupted the operation of money as a medium of exchange, arguably its principal use in medieval and early modern societies. It introduced uncertainty, created winners and losers, and undermined confidence in established social and economic values, in both domestic and international trade and certainly also for all payments made for factors of production (labour, land, capital).

Nevertheless, despite the unpopularity of debasement, consideration of the needs of commerce leads to a more rounded view, which recognizes that reduction in the intrinsic content of the money was not in every case mistaken. Indeed, it is clear that in certain circumstances a currency might be too strong. Rather than simplistically declaring sound money to be good and weak money to be bad, a more sophisticated analysis is required which also considers how far the currency was capable of supplying the needs of the economy.

This chapter, rather than charting the sorry progress of debasement and its effects, looks instead at a period of English history in which too much stress may have been laid on the importance of retaining a high value silver coinage of unchanging worth, despite major shifts in the international values of precious metals. In marked contrast to English medieval practice, when periodic adjustment to align the mint and the market price for silver had been the norm, any such adjustments had come to be deemed unacceptable by the seventeenth and eighteenth centuries.[1] The entirely unintended consequences of this shift in monetary policy, which brought about the effective disappearance of silver coin in eighteenth-century England, are considered below.

But first it is necessary to explore the market for, and uses of, silver in the period 1600 to 1800. Global movements of bullion in the early modern period have been the subject of important and detailed work charting the role of precious metals in world trade. From the European perspective the activities of the Dutch and English East India Companies have been the focus of contemporary attention since the early seventeenth century, and studies in our own times have refined and sharpened our understanding of the nature and scale of this trade.[2] It is clear that these oceanic powers extended and increasingly supplanted the Venetians, who had earlier dominated the medieval eastern trade.[3] However, the European perspective has been enhanced by more truly global studies, identifying different phases of production, and charting the transmission of bullion all round the world by patterns of trade and the power of internationally varied bullion ratios.[4]

Within this international context, however, more limited national studies still have a role to play, supplying the local detail from which the world picture must be built up. For example, Stephen Quinn's study of the complementary roles of bills of exchange and the import and export of bullion in the late seventeenth century adds a new dimension, made possible only by the survival of documents concerning the operations of the goldsmith-banker, Stephen Evance.[5]

The second half of the seventeenth century saw the emergence of a group of English proto-bankers, whose financial operations developed alongside their existing activities as goldsmiths.[6] Many of these men – Backwell, Duncombe, Meynel, Vyner – also figure as suppliers of coin and bullion for export by the East India Company.[7] Combining banking with their expertise in precious metals placed the goldsmiths at the heart of the developing financial institutions. The purpose of this short note is, therefore, to draw attention to the surviving records of the Company of London Goldsmiths. Hitherto these have largely been explored by those interested in antiques and fine art, but they also provide important quantitative information about the weight of silver hallmarked each year in London. Graphs of this data have been published separately by Forbes and by Mitchell,[8] but the data are of sufficient interest to justify presenting the annual totals in the tables which follow below. The tables demonstrate that the scale of London's manufacture of silver plate often surpassed mint output, and sometimes even approached the volumes exported. To ensure the fineness of the metal used, goldsmiths were required to have all their work tested and certified fine by a hallmark.[9] The weight of silver thus hallmarked in London each year was often very considerable, and comparison with the known mint output of the period is instructive. Ever since medievalists began to examine the supply of coin, identifying periods of relative glut and scarcity, historians have wondered how far the use of bullion for the production of plate may have influenced mint output. In the same way contemporary commentators and modern historians have associated scarcity of coin in England with the export of bullion by merchants, especially by the East India Company from 1600. Clearly all three uses for silver – the production of coin, the manufacture of plate and the export of silver in the course of international trade – were closely linked. In turn, the relative prices for silver offered by the Mint, the goldsmith bankers, and the East India Company largely determined the choices that silver owners exercised in disposing of their metals.

This unsurprising conclusion nevertheless confounded contemporaries who hoped that the allocation of silver to one or other of these institutions might have been guided by moral or legal principles. The most obvious point about mint output and the goldsmiths' production is the very large proportion of the available bullion devoted to plate. For example, annually between 1609 and 1631, when the Mint struck only low thousands of Troy pounds weight in silver, the goldsmiths regularly hallmarked between 13,000 and 31,000 pounds weight.[10] In the 1630s the goldsmiths' figures are largely lacking; and hallmarking was at a low ebb throughout the Civil War years, though minting boomed at this time. From the 1650s both mint and hallmarking figures are strong; but in the 1690s mint output stagnated until the huge recoinage of 1696–8, while the weights hallmarked remained high throughout this decade. In the eighteenth century, the English mint price for silver was lower than those prevailing elsewhere, both in Europe and globally, so that English silver coinage almost disappeared. Silver continued to flow plentifully to Britain, however, and the goldsmiths' production boomed.

Although this problem of mint scarcity in the face of the goldsmiths' plenty became most acute in the eighteenth century, attempts were made much earlier to divert silver from the owners or makers of plate to the mints. The stories of how Charles I caused all the college plate in Oxford to be brought to his mint are well known, but the quantities of coin which this exercise created were insignificant compared with the output of the Tower Mint in London.[11] Parliament also put pressure on its supporters to bring their plate to the Tower Mint. We know that at least £100,000 was coined from this source, though at this time the Tower Mint was coining literally millions of pounds sterling, most of which came from Spanish America and other international trade flows.[12] Thus, even when plate was converted to coin during the Civil War, the quantities were relatively modest.

While it was always difficult to compel the owners of silverware to bring it to the Mint, silver continued to flow in the other direction, out of the currency, as a result of clipping. Thomas Violet, writing in 1643 understood the process well:[13]

> The silversmiths ... presently fell a-culling the silver moneys current; and the money being coined in the Mint at 5s2d, the Goldsmiths, Finers, and Wyre-drawers did raise it up to 5s3d an oz, and melted down all the weighty shillings and sixpences, and left none to pass betwixt man and man.

The problem was particularly acute after the Restoration. Coins were commonly clipped and the proceeds melted and sold for a better price than the Mint was able to offer. As John Garrill, Gent., wrote to the Goldsmiths' Company in 1669:[14]

> The Refiners and others give the Goldsmiths 2d the ounce or more above the rate of the Mint, which is the cause why the Goldsmiths and others doe melt down such vast sumes of Coyne and make them covett to bee Casheers – This advantage is the reason of their combination and them jointly to seek for the preservation of this cloke which has soo longe covered their cheats named Refined silver.

The introduction of milled coin by Charles II was designed to combat the problem of clipping. Machine-made coin with a properly defined edge was indeed less vulnerable to clipping since attacks of this sort on milled coin would have been much more obvious than on hand-struck 'hammered' pieces, and of course the profit in clipping depended on being able to pass the diminished coin at its full face value. A clipped milled coin would have been much more likely to have been rejected. Nevertheless, while worn and clipped hammered coin continued to pass at face value, full-weight milled coin seemed in contrast to contain too much silver. It was quickly picked out of the currency, and illegally melted for use as bullion in the goldsmiths' trade or for export. The key to the problem was that the price at which the Mint bought silver for coinage was lower than that prevailing on the open market. The abolition of mint charges in 1666 attempted to address this difficulty, but new coin continued to be issued with a face value below its intrinsic value. The new money was too good, compared either with the old coin, or with the international price of silver.

Spanish American silver production continued to boom throughout the seventeenth and eighteenth centuries, but the demands of international trade and domestic consumption of plate grew even more, so that the open market price for bullion rose above the unchanging English mint price. Gold coin, unlike the silver, was permitted to find its own value, and commanded a gradually rising price, so that the guinea, originally intended as coin of 20 shillings, always circulated for higher values.

The poor condition of the circulating silver currency eventually resulted in serious government action to melt and reissue the entire stock of silver coin in 1696. Simultaneously a further attempt was made to tackle the problem of competition for bullion from the goldsmiths. A Bill was proposed arguing for a duty of 6d per oz. to be laid upon

> all wrought silver that shall not before 4th November 1697 bee brought in to be coined due to the end [that] persons having such plate may be the more disposed to have the same converted into the lawfull coins of this realm, whereby it may become more useful to the benefit of trade which at present laboureth under great difficulties for want of sufficient specie.[15]

The plan was that plate not brought to be coined would be counter-stamped to show that the levy of 6d per lb had been paid. Yet the Bill was never passed. Although the Goldsmiths' Company was not without influence, those Parliamentarians possessing plate evidently had good reason to oppose the Bill. Whatever the economic needs of the country at large for coin, the scarcity was least felt by the well-to-do owners of plate, who consequently saw little reason to give it up. Clearly, a serious shortage of silver coin was allowed to coexist alongside great wealth in plate.

One serious attempt to separate coinage metal from that required for plate was actually enacted. In 1697 a new 95.8 per cent standard for silverware was introduced, known as the Britannia standard, explicitly to separate silver bullion for coinage – still on the Sterling standard of 92.5 per cent – from that used for plate. However, in 1720 the Sterling standard was reintroduced for silverware alongside the Britannia standard, which was less hard-wearing than the old standard.[16] There is little evidence to suggest that the experiment made much difference to the supply of silver to the Mint. The key factors influencing mint production remained the gold–silver ratios and mint prices offered for bullion in England and abroad, and the price for silver offered by the goldsmiths. Thus when in May and June 1711 the mints were permitted to offer an enhanced price for plate, the bullion flowed in.[17]

This was, however, quite exceptional. The government had given serious consideration to raising the mint offer price for silver before the 1697 recoinage, but sound economic arguments gave way to John Locke's insistence that the fineness of the coinage not be altered in any circumstances. The high-minded, though utterly unrealistic, principle that money should be constant thus won the day, and (mis)guided government policy for a century thereafter. The unintended consequence was that English silver coin became increasingly scarce throughout the eighteenth century. Its place in the currency had to be filled by gold coins, by newly introduced copper or tin small change, and by the increasing use of paper money, which could pass for very small sums as well as much larger ones.[18]

The paradox that, despite plentiful supplies of Spanish American silver in Europe, everywhere copper coinage became more plentiful, is noted elsewhere in this volume.[19] This trend was earliest manifest in Spain itself, which quickly discovered that the glut of silver lowered its value at home, causing it to flow abroad for the purchase of goods which could everywhere else be purchased more cheaply than at home. England continued to attract silver throughout the sixteenth, seventeenth and eighteenth centuries, but during the second half of the seventeenth century, as we have seen, the price offered by the English Mint fell below that offered elsewhere, whether in London or abroad. Faced with the increasing inadequacy of the silver coinage for the needs of small transactions, the crown introduced a copper and/or tin coinage of halfpennies and farthings from 1672. Additionally private issues of small change had been licensed by the government earlier in the century, and tradesmen's unofficial tokens were tolerated in the period 1650 to 1670. In the eighteenth century unofficial imitations of the royal coinage became extremely plentiful. Although it is difficult to quantify the extent of these private issues,[20] the output of royal halfpennies and farthings by the Mint is recorded. From their introduction in August 1672 until 1696 £131,674 was struck in official halfpennies and farthings. Issues were then suspended till 1718, but a further £30,289 were then struck between 1718 and 1725, and from 1729 to 1754 £175,762 was struck in halfpence and farthings.

Though the size of these issues of 'small change' may appear to have been small compared with the output of gold when expressed in terms of total face value, they amounted nevertheless to a significant number of individual coins. The seventeenth-century issue of £131,674, for example, could have amounted to some 31,601,760 halfpennies and 63,203,520 farthings.[21] The £175,762 struck in copper between 1729 and 1754 would have made over 84 million halfpennies, if entirely struck in halfpennies. Taken altogether the official English and Irish issues, plus tokens and counterfeits, amounted to a huge volume of small change, which for the most part appears to have been answering a genuine need. This level of demand for copper coin speaks powerfully both of the scarcity of silver coin and of the thorough monetization of eighteenth-century English society.

If copper supplied the deficiency of silver at the bottom of the system, gold increasingly came to replace the use of silver at the top. Throughout the eighteenth century the Sterling currency remained technically silver-based, in that the weight of silver deemed to be worth one pound was fixed by law, and silver coins were accepted at face value. Gold was allowed to find its own value in accordance with the current open market valuations, until Newton fixed the value of the guinea at 21s in 1717. By 1730, John Conduitt, who had succeeded Newton as Master of the Mint, believed that 'nine parts in ten, or more, of all payments in England, are now made in gold'.[22] By the 1770s, when the condition of the gold coinage was causing serious concern, the government spent some £750,000 recoining about £16.5 million pounds in gold, thought to be about 75 per cent of the total quantity of gold in circulation.[23] Yet in addition, of course, ever larger amounts of paper currency were in use. The full social and economic consequences of this eighteenth-century revolution in the nature of the payments system have not perhaps received the attention they deserve.[24]

However, the purpose of this short note is to draw attention to the quantitative data surviving in the records of the Goldsmiths' Company. The quantities indicated rank consideration alongside the more thoroughly researched figures for mint production and East India Company bullion exports. The fact that very large amounts of plate could exist side by side with a scarcity of silver coin, evident in this early-modern period, may also be relevant for the Middle Ages. Plentiful holdings of plate did not guarantee a plentiful silver coinage. The goldsmiths' records also have much to interest historians of the luxury trades, not so much for the great showpieces of a Bateman or a Lamerie, but as evidence of a growing trade in small silverware that may prove a sensitive indicator of economic trends and cycles. Forbes noted a marked increase in the manufacture of watch-cases from the mid-eighteenth century,[25] while small wares, which did not include watch-cases, grew across the century as a whole.[26] In short, both the scale and the detail of English silverware production in the seventeenth and eighteenth centuries are worthy of consideration.

Table 6.1: Silver hallmarked by the London Company of Goldsmiths.

Years	Pounds Troy	Years	Pounds Troy
–1600	No data	1633–34	n.d.
1600–01	n.d.	1634–35	n.d.
1601–02	n.d.	1635–36	n.d.
1602–03	n.d.	1636–37	n.d.
1603–04	n.d.	Nov 1637–June 1638	13,520
1604–05	n.d.	June 1638–June 1639	18,973
1605–06	36,420	Nov 1639–June 1640	24,561
Oct 1606–July 1607	15,744	1640–41	n.d.
Nov 1607–July 1608	17,064	1641–42	n.d.
1607–08	n.d.	1642–43	n.d.
1608–09	n.d.	Nov 1643–June 1644	341
1609–10	n.d.	June 1644–June 1645	823
1610–11	n.d.	1645–46	n.d.
1611–12	n.d.	1646–47	n.d.
1612–13	n.d.	July 1647–June 1648	4,946
Nov 1613–July 1614	17,040	Nov 1648–June 1649	4,790
Nov 1614–July 1615	14,760	Nov 1649–June 1650	8,881
Nov 1615–July 1616	16,716	July 1650–July 1651	14,851
Nov 1616–May 1617	15,972	July 1651–June 1652	18,229

Years	Pounds Troy	Years	Pounds Troy
Nov 1617-May 1618	15,996	July 1652-June 1653	23,085
Nov1618-July 1619	13,872	1653–54	40,792
1619–20	20,700	1654–55	31,580
1621–22	19,416	1655–56	32,062
Nov 1621-May 1622	17,172	1656–57	27,142
Nov 1622-June 1623	19,692	1657–58	28,275
Nov 1623-May 1624	21,192	1658–59	26,131
Nov 1624-June 1625	21,192	1659–60	28,507
June 1625-Nov 1626	23,119	1660–61	37,295
Nov 1626-May 1627	22,656	1661–62	33,827
1627–28	n.d.	1662–63	32,331
June 1628-June 1629	27,228	1663–64	n.d.
Nov 1629-June 1630	31,476	1664–65	n.d.
1630–31	n.d.	1665–66	n.d.
1631–32	n.d.	1666–67	25,825
1632–33	n.d.	1667–68	3,206
1668	n.d.	1704–05	49,435
1669	n.d.	1705–06	53,957
1670	n.d.	1706–07	45,891
1671–72	39,147	1707–08	52,924
1672–73	39,947	1708–09	51,046
1673–74	41,002	1709–10	48,021
1674–75	39,805	1710–11	43,676
1675–76	42,273	1711–12	43,736
1676		1712–13	44,425
1677–78	46,204	1713–14	50,197
1678–79	34,159	1714–15	51,357
1679–80	42,251	1715–16	51,649
1680–81	43,467	1716–17	50,898
1681–82	36,144	1717–18	52,845
1682–83	11,013	1718–19	52,371
1683–84	19,810	1719–20	64,538
1684–85	84,728	1720–21	35,981 OS
			10,797 NS
1685–86	61,796		
1686–87	n.d.	1721–22	15,632 OS
			23,789 NS
1687			
1688–89	46,613	1722–23	21,519 OS
			17,697 NS
1689–89	44,940		
1690–91	44,057	1723–24	25,776 OS
			11,580 NS
1691–92	52,866		

Years	Pounds Troy	Years	Pounds Troy
1692–93	43,859	1724–25	32,159 OS
			9,278 NS
1693–94	45,412	1725–26	30,972 OS
			7,623 NS
1694–95	46,422	1726–27	32,719 OS
			4,604 NS
1695–96	29,743	1727–28	36,244 OS
			3,638 NS
1696–97	18,743 OS	1728–29	32,394 OS
	2,038 NS		2,328 NS
1697–68	38,393	1729–30	30,642 OS
			1,503 NS
1698–99	46,931	1730–31	40,313 OS
			1,591 NS
'99 –1700	44,623	1731–32	36,016 OS
			1,505 NS
1700–01	46,130	1732–33	35,815
1701–02	48,899	1733–34	35,112
1702–03	51,033	1734–35	35,280
1703–04	52,551	1735–36	36,856
1736–37	34,240	1773–74	93,936
1737–8	33,396	1774–75	107,952
1738–39	33,264	1775–76	109,560
1739–40	n.d.	1776–77	119,760
1740–41	42,720	1177–78	108,312
1741–42	38,400	1778–79	98,208
1742–43	44,112	1779–80	95,688
1743–44	42,120	1780–81	10,152
1744–45	40,536	1781–82	96,792
		1782–83	102,480
1745–46	34,392	1783–84	111,336
		1784–85	nd
1746–47	39,312	1785–86	75,024
		1786–87	83,328
1747–48	37,344	1787–88	83,328
		1788–89	82,392
1748–49	40,800	1789–90	86,942
1750–51	38,472	1790–91	86,952
1751–52	39,888		
1752–53	38,400		
1753 –54	37,152		
1754–55	37,032		
1755–56	36,216		
1756–67	32,040		
1757–58	31,632		

Years	Pounds Troy	Years	Pounds Troy
1758–59	44,034		
1759–60	86,592		
1760–61	87,528		
1761–62	42,101		
1762–63	37,130		
1763–64	58,608		
1764–65	20,519		
1765–66	35,081		
1766–67	36,039		
1767–68	37,802		
1768–69	40,198		
1769–70	n.d.		
1770–71	n.d.		
1771–72	n.d.		
1772–73	93,360		

OS=Old Sterling 92.5% Standard; NS = New Britannia 95% Standard

Source: Court Books of the Company of Goldsmiths, Goldsmiths' Hall, London (see note 8).
I am grateful to Susie Mayhew for manuscript research in the Goldsmiths' Library, and
to David Mitchell for his advice and help.

**Table 6.2: Use of silver by the Tower Mint, the Goldsmiths and
the East India Company.**

Years	Mint output, Troy lb	Goldsmiths' output, Troy lb	EIC exports of money (silver lbs)
1610	7,332	n.d.	19,200
1611	6,748	n.d.	17,675
1612	6,485	n.d.	1,250
1613	2,071	n.d.	18,810
1614	4,953	17,040	13,942
1615	581	14,760	26,660
1616	3,974	16,716	52,087
1617	472	15,972	
1618	69	15,996	298,000 (1617–1619)
1619	151	13,872	
1620	–	20,700	62,490
1621	95	19,416	12,900
1622	6,694	17,172	61,600
1623	10,942	19,692	68,720
1624	15,265	21,192	n.d.
1625	33,387	21,192	n.d..
1626	23,330	23,119	60,000 + rials
1627	16,625	22,656	n.d.
1628	3,201	n.d.	n.d.

Years	Mint output, Troy lb	Goldsmiths' output, Troy lb	EIC exports of money (silver lbs)
1629	1,559	27,228	200,000
1630	1,171	31,476	
1631	1,629		16,500
1632	21,788		
1633	49,676		115,900
1634	61,189		20,000
1635	88,089		100,000
1636	42,417		65,000
1637	129,573		
1638	169,387	13,520	20,000
1639	119,455	18,973	
1640	134,693	24,561	40,000
1641	160,487		
1642	529,808		
1643			
1644		341	
1645	703,609	823	
1646	266,357		
1647	242,293		
1648		4,946	
1649	31,411	4,790	
1650		8,881	
1651	10,183	14,851	
1652		18,229	
1653	113,460	23,085	
1654		40,792	
1655		31,580	
1656		32,062	
1657	108,041	27,142	
1658		28,275	
1659	4,190	26,131	
1660	6,690	28,507	
1661	7,484	37,295	
1662	160,218	33,827	
1663	98,412	32,331	
1664	14,301		Silver lbs 5-yearly
1665	19,910		88,319
1666	11,982		
1667	17,131	25,825	
1668	40,303	3,206	
1669	14,291		
1670	46,142		50,402
1671	38,645		
1672	86,673	39,147	
1673	101,064	39,947	

Years	Mint output, Troy lb	Goldsmiths' output, Troy lb	EIC exports of money (silver lbs)
1674	10,286	41,002	
1675	1,856	39,805	98,621
1676	101,836	42,273	
1677	146,034		
1678	7,366	46,204	
1679	87,313	34,159	
1680	58,204	42,251	394,354
1681	30,782	43,467	
1682	12,759	36,144	
1683	69,851	11,013	
1684	17,309	19,810	
1685	30,572	84,728	530,094
1686	19,294	61,796	
1687	80,848		
1688	24,590		
1689	31,152	46,613	
1690	643	44,940	67,247
1691	1,203	42,314	
1692	1,341	52,866	
1693	2,992	43,859	
1694	51	45,412	
1695	20	46,422	16,911
1696	876,127	29,743	
1697	1,179,003	20,781	
1698	149,170	38,393	
1699	19,498	46,931	289,324
1700	4,806	44,623	
1701	37,447	46,130	
1702	114	48,899	
1703	718	51,033	
1704	4,007	52,551	
1705	430	49,435	367,147
1706	932	53,957	
1707	1,174	45,891	
1708	3,751	52,924	
1709	24,423	51,046	
1710	817	48,021	382,542
1711	24,768	43,676	
1712	1,784	43,736	
1713	2,333	44,425	
1714	1,567	50,197	
1715	1,643	51,357	367,516
1716	1,650	51,649	
1717	948	50,898	
1718	2,295	52,845	

Years	Mint output, Troy lb	Goldsmiths' output, Troy lb	EIC exports of money (silver lbs)
1719	1,756	52,371	
1720	7,832	64,358	551,872
1721	2,313	35,981 OS	
		10,797 NS	
1722	1,983	15,632 OS	
		23,789 NS	
1723	48,099	21,510 OS	
		17,697 NS	
1724	1,652	25,776 OS	
		11,580 NS	
1725	2,495	32,159 OS	636,567
		9,278 NS	
1726	836	30,972 OS	
		7,623 NS	
1727	661	32,719 OS	
		4,604 NS	
1728	852	36,244 OS	
		3,638 NS	
1729	2,055	32,394 OS	
		2,328 NS	
1730	1,122	30,642 OS	575,082
		1,503 NS	
1731	703	40,313 OS	
		1,591 NS	
1732	845	3,601 OS	
		1,508 NS	
1733	1,153	35,815	
1734	1,590	35,112	
1735	1,174	35,280	572,224
1736	1,713	36,856	
1737	1,200	34,240	
1738	0	33,396	
1739	3,396	33,264	
1740	0	n.d.	572,832
1741	3,060	42,720	
1742	0	38,400	
1743	2,400	44,112	
1744	2,528	42,120	
1745	600	40,536	567,340
1746	44,010	34,392	
1747	1,500	39,312	
1748	0	37,344	
1749	0	39,624	
1750	0	40,800	805,838
1751	2,614	38,472	

Years	Mint output, Troy lb	Goldsmiths' output, Troy lb	EIC exports of money (silver lbs)
1752	19	39,888	
1753	19	38,400	
1754	19	37,152	
1755	19	37,032	875,690
1756	39	36,216	
1757	5,359	32,040	
1758	20,189	31,632	
1759	34	44,304	
1760	43	86,592	425,607

Sources: for Mint Output - C. E. Challis (ed.), *A New History of the Royal Mint* (Cambridge and New York: Cambridge University Press, 1992), Appendix 1, converted from pounds sterling to Troy lbs. For Goldsmiths' Output - See Table 6.1. For EIC - K. N. Chuadhuri, *The Trading World of Asia and the English East India Company, 1660–1760* (Cambridge: Cambridge University Press, 1978), p.177, and *The English East India Company: The Study of an Early Joint-Stock Company 1600–1640* (London: Routledge, 1999), p.115n2.

7 THE BURDENS OF TRADITION: DEBASEMENTS, COINAGE CIRCULATION AND MERCANTILIST PUBLIC POLICY DEBATES IN SEVENTEENTH-CENTURY ARAGON

José Antonio Mateos Royo

The gradual depreciation of national currencies in pursuit of fiscal and monetary goals, a practice inherited from the late medieval period, was a key feature of monetary policies so often pursued by states in early-modern Europe. Recent studies have highlighted the decisive importance of monetary objectives for these decisions. In 1988, Glassman and Redish, citing the experiences of England and France, contended that the successive depreciations carried out in early-modern Europe – either through enhancements or physical debasements of the currency – were designed to avoid the difficulties and costs generated by progressive undervaluations of the coinage.[1] Meanwhile, the shortage of legal gold, silver and billon money itself created the conditions for this process, encouraging the parallel use of counterfeit and clipped coins. More recently, Sargent and Velde have argued that medieval and early-modern coinage debasements were essentially a rational defensive policy to remedy periodic shortages of 'small change', especially when circulating coins became worn over time.[2] Given the need for petty coins in everyday transactions, these debasements were absolutely necessary to avoid economically damaging price deflation.

Both of these arguments implicitly assume the emergence of an ever more coherent monetary policy in the leading European states of this era. However, these states were still in the process of formation, and the authority of the monarch and government differed widely in the various territories under their control. The limited nature of royal power is revealed in the coexistence of two kinds of coins in many seventeenth-century states. Thus, the monarchy would usually issue the principal coinage associated with the state in the regions that were more directly under its control, and from which it obtained the majority of its tax revenues. Other subordinate regions, however, enjoyed greater political autonomy and a separate institutional framework, so that they conserved the right to issue their own domestic coinage, which usually coexisted in the market alongside the principal currency. In these states and regions, the monarchy had to negotiate its monetary policies, as it did its fiscal policies (taxes) with the local public institutions. When the monarchy was forced to negotiate debasements for fiscal rather than purely monetary purposes, and thus usually under far more difficult conditions, depreciation was either postponed or failed to be implemented, for lack of consensus. If debasements were finally introduced, usually in exchange for tax concessions, their efficacy in stimulating economic recovery depended on the interest of the elites who had agreed with the monarchy to implement the reforms.

This chapter seeks to examine, in the light of these political-economic realities, the monetary policies pursued in seventeenth-century Aragon, one of the kingdoms that was integrated with other Spanish territories under the crown of Aragon. Thus the crown was itself a federation of realms that had coalesced in the late medieval period, including Aragon itself, Catalonia, Valencia and the Balearic Islands, and various Italian provinces. Situated in the north-east of the Iberian peninsula, these lands had gradually increased their economic links with Castile in the sixteenth century, following the unification of the two Spanish crowns under a single dynasty, by the 'Catholic Monarchs' (Isabella of Castile and Ferdinand of Aragon) in the late fifteenth century. Although the petty coins of Castile never circulated in the crown of Aragon in the sixteenth and seventeenth centuries, these political links prompted the use of Castilian silver and gold, from the sixteenth century, in trade throughout the crown lands – and to the detriment of the domestic currencies created in the medieval period, subsequent issues of which became increasingly rare.

We shall also see that the kingdom of Aragon underwent other significant changes in coinage circulation from the early 1600s. Market demand for monetary instruments came to be more for coins having a lower intrinsic value than the current Aragonese coinage, for coins whose value was more closely aligned with those for gold and silver, and for forms of money that would better facilitate commercial and financial transactions. This need was in fact met through a rising influx of foreign, counterfeit and debased coins in Aragon, whose circulation had adverse effects on the economy, even though they often did benefit commerce. This situation sparked a serious debate in the second half of the seventeenth century, between the various public institutions on the need to increase the seigniorage and thus reduce the intrinsic value of the local coinage. The debate that arose between 1674 and 1702 also reflected a modest influence from current Castilian mercantilism, along with a considerable knowledge of monetary developments in Catalonia and Valencia. In contrast to such developments in Catalonia and Valencia, the inability of public institutions in Aragon to introduce necessary monetary reforms not only hampered economic recovery but also, eventually, ended any further attempts to forge an autonomous monetary policy for Aragon in the early modern era.

Coins and Monetary Circulation in Seventeenth-Century Aragon

The main feature of monetary circulation in seventeenth-century Aragon was the chronic shortage of local coins, a problem already identified in the medieval period, with the consequent misalignment between market demand and market values for coins.[3] This problem was particularly acute for the petty coinage, or what is now deemed to be 'small change'. The gold florin, which was common throughout the crown of Aragon, was first introduced in the mid-fourteenth century; and it was subsequently debased several times in the late medieval period: or more precisely, the monarchy debased those gold coins that it struck in its other territories, such as Catalonia and Valencia. In Aragon itself, however, the nobility was more successful in preventing the king from reducing the weight and fineness of the *jaquesa* petty coin or *dinero* in the fourteenth and fifteenth centuries.[4] Since this coin was the benchmark unit for the official money of account system in this kingdom, the nobles were interested in maintaining its value in order to protect their earnings derived from the export of raw materials, such as wheat, meat, oil and wool. The kingdom of Aragon lacked a silver coin similar to those of Catalonia and Valencia, while commercial transactions were further constrained by the meagre supply of Aragonese petty or billon (*vellón*) coins, whose relatively high intrinsic value prompted their export abroad. As a consequence, market demand encouraged counterfeiting and debasement, and the illicit use of foreign silver coins, even though their circulation was strictly forbidden by the Aragonese Parliament.

Faced with these endemic problems, various governments introduced monetary reforms – in John II's reign (1458–79) and especially under Ferdinand II the Catholic Monarch (1479–1516) – that transformed monetary circulation in Aragon during the sixteenth century.[5] These reforms sought to bring the intrinsic value of the Aragonese coins into line with gold and silver market prices, and to align their metal content with the coins struck in the neighbouring kingdoms in Spain and western Europe. As one of the first measures, from 1477, the government abandoned the traditional florin because of its relatively low fineness – 18 carats – and replaced it with a more prestigious gold coin, with a higher intrinsic value: the *ducado*, which was based on the Venetian coin with a fineness of 23.75 carats and a weight of 3.5 g. Ferdinand also introduced this coin (*excelente*) in Castile in 1497. Secondly, in 1484, after several attempts in the reign of John II, Parliament introduced a series of silver coins (*reales* and *medio reales*) with a fineness of 11 *dineros* or 22 carats. Finally, Parliament, in authorizing new and subsequent issues of the *jaquesa* billon coins, reduced their fineness from a silver content of 25 per cent to just half that, 12.5 per cent.

This debasement of the *jaquesa* petty coin was needed to retain the kingdom's circulation of local fractional coins. The *dinero* was thus kept as a base coin for the official accounting system, together with its multiples, the *sueldo*, equal to 12 *dineros*, and the *libra*, equal to 20 *sueldos*. However, after this monetary reform, the silver *real* coin replaced the billon coin as the benchmark unit for the realm's money of account, i.e. as the 'link' coin for accounting purposes. For such purposes, 1 *real* was always equal to 2 *sueldos* or 24 *dineros*, during the sixteenth and seventeenth centuries. The adoption of the purities and weights prevailing in Castile's silver and gold coinages, by Aragon's Parliaments in 1519 and 1528, certainly favoured both commercial transactions with Castile and the penetration of Castilian coins into the realm of Aragon, both of which factors helped to restore economic growth from the middle of the sixteenth century.[6] Then, in 1564, the *ducado* was replaced by the *escudo*, based on the French model with a fineness of 22 carats. All other regulations that Parliament had enacted, in 1519 and 1528 were maintained for all issues of all other Aragonese coins for the rest of the century (see Table 7.1).

Table 7.1: **Main units of the Aragonese coinage system under the Habsburg monarchy.**

Name	Metal	Issue	Fineness		No. of coins/*marc*	Weight
ducado	gold	1518–56	23.75 carats		67	3.5 g
escudo	gold	1564–76	22.00 carats		68	3.15 g
real	silver	1518–1652	22	carats (11 *dineros*)	67	3.425 g
dinero	billon	1518–98	3	carats (1.5 *dineros*)	288	0.81 g
dinero	billon	1611–80	3	carats (1.5 *dineros*)	360	0.65 g

One Aragonese *marc* = 233.571 g

Sources: Mateu, 'El sistema'; Archive of the Crown of Aragon, Council of Aragon, file 91.

But some rules and decisions governing these coin issues became gradually inefficient, in adapting the monetary units to market requirements during the second half of the sixteenth century, in accordance with market changes in the prices for gold and silver. Thus, the supply of Aragonese billon coins responded well to moderate domestic demand until the end of the sixteenth century, chiefly because of the alignment of the weight and purity of coins to these fluctuations, and the greater frequency of their issues compared to gold and silver coins during this period.[7] At the same time, however, a combination of the infrequency and low volumes of outputs of both gold and 'full-bodied' silver coins, their high intrinsic values and a consequent chronic export of such high-valued coins, both Castilian and Aragonese, to France, from the mid-sixteenth century, began to undermine the monetary economy of Aragon.[8] Furthermore, the legislation of the Aragonese Parliaments, from 1563 to 1585, to remove the customs duties on exports of gold and silver coins to Catalonia served only to promote further coin exports to France, to aggravate their domestic scarcities and to encourage an influx of counterfeit and otherwise debased coins, thus leading to a further deterioration in Aragon's monetary economy.[9]

During the early seventeenth century, Aragon's coinage circulation would be greatly and adversely transformed, as a consequence of changes in the money supply throughout the crown lands. Rising prices for both gold and silver fuelled the market demand for coins with intrinsic values lower than those of the official established coins. Thus, early attempts to debase silver coins in Catalonia and Valencia were a response to two related factors: first, the relatively low official exchange values of their coins – lower, in the Iberian peninsula, than were their market values in other European countries and in Asia – and second, the growing appreciation in the value of gold in relation to silver (reflecting the growing relative abundance of silver within Europe in general). Those conditions finally forced the monarchy to raise the bimetallic ratio (the legal parity) in favour of gold, at least within Castile.[10]

In the crown of Aragon, its public institutions pressed their demands for a coinage debasement: both to protect their territory from the incursion of foreign coins and to correct their trade deficit. Other declared or implied motives for debasement were to earn higher seigniorage profits on the coinages, or, more exceptionally, to improve market functions and stimulate the economy. The need for reform became increasingly acute with continued depreciation of the petty coinage, rising trade deficits and the growing financial weakness of the Castilian monarchy, all of which factors aggravated the exodus of gold and silver coins from the Spanish realms, chiefly to France.

In addition to these problems, the Castilian economy was unable to supply the crown of Aragon with low value currency because Castilian petty coins (*maravedís*) were not accepted as either legal or market-value tender in these territories, while Castile's own silver coins (*reales*) preserved their traditional fine-metal content between 1497 and 1686. With this decision, the Spanish monarchy sought to defend the high market price and prestige of the Castilian *real* in international trade in order to finance Spain's costly foreign policy by more and more loans contracted from merchants and bankers.[11] Thus, the crown of Aragon received only large numbers of Castilian *reales* of below-legal fineness struck in Peruvian mints between 1650 and 1654. As we shall see, when the Castilian *real* was debased in the 1680s during the reign of Charles II (1665–1700), its presence in the crown of Aragon had already been supplanted by low-value coins (in both weight and purity) from Catalonia and Valencia.

As a part of this process, the consolidation of a more outward-looking economy in Aragon favoured a greater influx of coins that had a lower intrinsic value than did the local currency. The virtual extinction of Aragonese mercantile capital in the late sixteenth and early seventeenth centuries[12] (which would only recover in the form of *rentier* capitalism in the second half of the century) and the sharp decline in local manufacturing output[13] after 1650 produced a long-lasting trade deficit, which in turn also promoted a continuing exodus of gold and silver. The primary destination for the high-value Spanish coins was again France, whose merchants controlled major transactions in Aragon, facilitating French imports of raw materials such as Spanish wool and exports of French manufactured goods, which were more competitively priced than Aragonese products.[14] Assisted by the greater openness of this economy, which was increasingly specialized in the production of raw materials, successive invasions of low-quality foreign coins, whether legal currency or local and alien counterfeits, flooded the kingdom.

Coins from neighbouring Valencia were the spearhead of these foreign currency incursions. The Diputación, which acted as a standing committee of Aragon's Parliament to protect the realm's rights, observed this penetration during the early seventeenth century with alarm. This process gathered pace around 1650 because of the favourable trade balance between southern Aragon and the kingdom of Valencia, one that was based in particular on a strong demand for wheat and meat.[15] Silver and petty coins from Valencia had been used in Teruel since the late medieval period,[16] entering southern Aragon to offset the deficit, often through the trade of merchants attending the main fairs. The use of the Valencian *real* or *dieciocheno* took hold and spread in Aragonese markets after reaching a parity of 16 *dineros*, which was a lower rate than its face value of 18, but higher than its intrinsic value of 11 or 12 *dineros*. Driven by these factors, silver and billon coins from Valencia became common in the south of the Aragonese kingdom during the second half of the seventeenth century, and were widely used even in Saragossa, the capital of Aragon.[17]

Meanwhile, billon formed the core of the coins arriving from Catalonia, which coins had a smaller, more local impact in Aragon.[18] At times associated with invasions of French (e.g. Béarn *vaquettes*) and Valencian coins, Catalan currency first entered Aragon around 1611 and their influx grew rapidly between 1620 and 1640. Their continued influx was halted, however, by the war of Catalan secession (1640–52), which temporarily terminated commercial transactions with the Principality, while the presence of a Castilian army and the court in Aragon attracted silver coins into the kingdom, temporarily facilitating payments and trade. Even though some low-quality Catalan billon coins did circulate in Aragon during this conflict, their role was very limited compared to that of coins from Valencia, which squeezed Aragonese and Castilian coins out of the market.[19] Two orders issued by the Diputación in 1689 and 1695 banned the use of Valencian billon, recognizing in passing that this coinage was entering Aragon not only from Valencia but also from Catalonia and other frontier kingdoms.

Associated with the penetration of such foreign currency, various counterfeits of low-value domestic coins also appeared in Aragon during the seventeenth century.[20] Thus, the incursion of Valencian coins in the early seventeenth century coincided with fraudulent debasements of Aragonese *reales*, local counterfeiting of silver and petty coins and the arrival of false Aragonese and Castilian *reales*, struck in Béarn in 1611–12 and known as *bosqueteros* or *bosquejos*, imported by both Gascon and Catalan merchants. New counterfeits of Aragonese petty coins were detected after 1620, especially between 1626 and 1632, along with an influx of French, Catalan and Valencian coins into Aragon. In 1660, counterfeit Aragonese coins struck in France and Navarre would spread throughout the kingdom. A new billon issue in 1677–80 again stimulated counterfeiting in Saragossa.

In principle, the presence of this coinage in Aragon had the virtue of expanding the money supply, which was hamstrung by the scarcity of Aragonese and Castilian coins (particularly in the southern part of the kingdom) and the misalignment of the legal currency with market prices for gold and silver. As had occurred in the late medieval period, this was a response to market demand and it again had the beneficial effect of stimulating trade. The modest increase in the premium paid by parties receiving silver instead of billon on these transactions, compared to the situation in Castile,[21] where it ballooned, is a clear indication of these positive outcomes. The premium estimated by the Diputación in the course of the 1626 Parliament for the preceding ten years was 1–2 per cent of the transaction values.[22] This increased to 3 per cent around 1650, staying at that level throughout the second half of the seventeenth century.[23] Though many of the Aragonese institutions blamed this increase in the premium on the influx of foreign and counterfeit billon, as well as on the circulation of other coins with lower intrinsic value than local issues, the continuous absorption of Valencian *reales* into the Aragonese economy probably helped to moderate this phenomenon.

Nevertheless, this currency also had a range of adverse effects on the economy. Thus, it displaced both Castilian and Aragonese coins with higher intrinsic values, in transactions, in accordance with Gresham's Law. Together with the trade deficit with France, the influx of low-quality *reales* also exacerbated the exodus of gold and silver coins. As one obvious consequence, the fairly large issue of Aragonese *reales* struck in 1651–2 swiftly vanished from the market. In response to the increasing scarcity of good coin, people began hoarding gold coins, whose values thus appreciated sharply against local silver: rising by 8.7 per cent against the Castilian *doblón* and 7.7 per cent against the Aragonese *escudo* in the last quarter of the seventeenth century.[24] These flows also frequently led to restamping Aragonese petty coins, also frequently debased, and to striking counterfeits or legal tender coins with a lower metal content. Those strategies were frequently employed by the profit-seeking Valencian mint in the later seventeenth century.[25] The growing circulation of these debased and defective coins soon undermined confidence in the Aragonese currency, an effect that was compounded by the disappearance of good local coins (Gresham's Law), and complicated conversions between Aragonese and foreign coins. In the absence of any regulations, the rapid spread of these low-value coins sometimes fuelled inflation, as revealed by the prices of manufactured products during the mid-seventeenth century.[26] Worsened by the decline of the Aragonese economy, and its increasingly foreign orientation, these problems came to vex the kingdom's authorities, because they seriously impaired public control over the market. These problems thus proved to be decisive in shaping monetary debates and monetary policies in the final quarter of the seventeenth century.

Minting in Seventeenth-Century Aragon: Legislation and Public Policy

During the seventeenth century, the increasing circulation of debased, counterfeit and otherwise low-quality coins brought about acute market changes in Aragon: in particular, as a consequence of the inherent and intractable difficulties in attempting to establish a monetary policy that was more in tune with current economic developments. The scarcity of new coin issues combined with an unwillingness to debase the higher-valued coinage had been typical features of the late medieval Aragonese currency. [27] Unfortunately, they would be replicated in the seventeenth century, especially in comparison with the other kingdoms in the crown of Aragon.

Table 7.2 presents all of the legal issues of seventeenth-century Aragonese currency. The decisions, on the part of Aragon's monetary authorities, not to mint new issues of gold and to retain a scarcity in the issues of higher-valued silver and low-valued bill coins were intended to meet two different objectives.

In 1626, the Diputación and the learned Doctor Francisco de Arpayón estimated the total value of silver circulating in Aragon at somewhat less than 500,000 *libras*. This amount was increased, during the War of Catalan Secession (1640–52), by the presence of the royal army and the court and then it evidently declined once more in the second half of the seventeenth century.[28] In this context, the issue of *reales* was not intended to increase the total money supply but rather to replace the low-quality counterfeit Castilian coins, *reales bosquejos* (1611–12) and *reales peruleros* (i.e. from Peru: 1651–2), which had entered the kingdom and were then, when received by public authorities, melted down as bullion for the mint. The monarchy permitted these new issues to be minted, without seeking approval from the Aragonese Parliament, even though such approval was necessary for minting any new gold and silver coins. This royal privilege (to by-pass Parliament), which the Diputación first cited in 1482 and which the monarchy strictly respected during the first sixty years of the sixteenth century, provided the kingdom's government with the ideal mechanism for conserving the intrinsic value of the recently created silver *real*.[29] As an expression of the same interest on the part of the elites and the monarchy for the preservation of the weight and fineness of the Aragonese currency, the royal mints of Aragon continued to strike silver coins during the seventeenth century in accordance with the Castilian models as stipulated by the Parliaments of 1519 and 1528.

Issues of Aragonese petty coins were also few and far between, occurring only in 1611–18, 1655–7 and 1677–80. These three issues were designed to expand the supply of local petty coins, in view of the evidence, presented in 1655–7 and 1677–80, that most of the earlier issues had become seriously worn, debased or had been restamped. In contrast to the minting of high-valued silver coins, these billon issues were not struck from bullion that came from demonetized illegal or foreign coins. The crown's main concern was to limit the amount of billon coined, with a low weight and fineness, to the quantity that the market could absorb without producing inflation, an increased silver premium or other trade-related problems. These new issues, with an estimated maximum value of 100,000 or 120,000 *libras* in the second half of the seventeenth century, represented a respectable part of the total billon circulating in Aragon; and that estimate may provide some indication of the kingdom's current coinage scarcity.[30] In 1655, Juan Antonio Costas, an adviser to the Supreme Tribunal of Justice or Real Audiencia, estimated that the total amount of billon was over 500,000 *libras*; but in 1702, a more prudent report that a committee of minor nobility presented to Parliament estimated a figure of just 350,000 *libras*.

Table 7.2: Aragonese coinage minted in the seventeenth century.

Period	Metal	Unit	Amount of issue	Fineness	Weight
1611–2	silver	*real*	100,000 libras	11.00 *dineros*	3.425 g
1651–2	silver	*real*	454,000/470,000 libras	11.00 *dineros*	3.425 g
1611–8	billon	*dinero*	150,000 libras	1.25 *dineros*	0.650 g
1655–7	billon	*dinero*	70,000/88,000 libras	1.50 *dineros*	0.650 g
1677–80	billon	*dinero*	100,000/112,000 libras	1.50 *dineros*	0.650 g

Notes: In the case of the billon issues of 1655–7 and 1677–80, the lowest estimates reflect the initial issue established by the monarchy, while the higher amounts include the increases permitted by the master of the mint in order to use up residual and surplus metal, thereby increasing profits.
Each libra issued = one Aragonese *marc* = 233.571 g

Sources: Archive of the Crown of Aragon, Council of Aragon, file 91; Municipal Archive of Saragossa, box 7805.

If the silver contents of the *reales* and other higher valued coins remained unaltered, the precious-metal content of the Aragonese billon was reduced in the very late sixteenth and seventeenth centuries. In contrast to the medieval period, debasements of petty coins became feasible from the final decades of the sixteenth century because these issues did not require approval from Parliament, benefiting from a legal loophole. After the intrinsic value of *jaquesa* coins was reduced under John II and Ferdinand II, the weight and fineness of sixteenth- and seventeenth-century issues were no longer established by law. These amounts were either set by committee, as occurred in 1519 and 1528, on Parliament's initiatives, or referred back to correspond with established traditions.[31] This rather vaguely defined regulation, which required a weight of 0.81 g and a fineness of 1.5 *dineros* (Table 7.1), permitted a reduction in intrinsic values, especially during the reign of Philip II (1555–98).[32] Both this reduction and the significant issues of billon *dineros* towards the end of the sixteenth century were accommodated by the Valencian market; and the success of those issues may be interpreted as an acceptable means of generating seigniorage revenues, after the decline in gold and silver issues in Aragon during the last three decades of the sixteenth century.[33] Supported by Catalan and Valencian precedents, debasements of these billon coins grew in intensity during the seventeenth century.[34] The fineness of those billon coins minted in 1611–18 was reduced from 1.5 to 1.25 *dineros* and their weight from 0.81 to 0.65 g. This latter reduction was maintained in the following issues of 1655–7 and 1677–80 (see Tables 7.1 and 7.2). Though this reduction in the billon coin's intrinsic values was much less than those those was made in Valencia and Catalonia, it led to significant changes in the metallic parity between silver and billon coins that Parliament had established in 1519 and 1528. To the extent that this modification abandoned traditional conversions between Aragonese *dineros* and the Castilian *reales,* with exchange rates that had defined commercial transactions throughout the entire sixteenth century, these billon issues provoked strong criticisms from the kingdom's different elites and institutions.

The reasons for the scarcity of local money in Aragon were rooted in the legislation governing minting, which ensured that the monarchy had little financial interest in promoting new issues. In the first place, the king was not entitled to seigniorage on the currency, having given up this right in medieval Parliaments in return for a coinage tax (*impuesto del maravedí* or *del monedaje*), similar to the surrender of royal rights over the coinage in neighbouring Castile (1474, 1497).[35] Again, in order to guarantee the intrinsic value of the coinage, the 'brassage' income granted to the master of the Saragossa mint was very modest. Thus, in 1593 the viceroy of Aragon established a rate of 5 *reales* per marc of gold, 1 *real* per marc of billon and just 2 *dineros* per marc of silver.[36] A second major difficulty came from the economic evolution of Castile and the role of its monarchy in the seventeenth century. When the Parliament or other institutions did resolve issues concerning gold or silver coins in Aragon, the Saragossa mint had to acquire the metal required in Castile, either in the form of coins or ingots. Apart from meeting demands from other territories lacking access to gold and silver from the America, the Spanish monarchy found it increasingly difficult to provide the necessary precious metals, since ever more quantities of gold and silver were being committed to military ventures and repayment of bank loans. At the same time, the chronic trade deficits led to a growing outflow of gold and silver from Castile, while debasements of the petty billon (*vellón*) coinage for fiscal reasons encouraged hoarding and thus rising values for precious metals during the seventeenth century. Finally, the need to maintain or reduce minting costs in preserving the weight and fineness of the Aragonese currency led both the monarchy and the Diputación to waive customs duties on precious metals (including coins), levied on the border between Castile and Aragon.[37]

In addition to these difficulties, the Saragossa council, serving as the main public institution with the ability to issue coins, was constrained by its need to obtain royal licences and to negotiate profits on billon issues with the influential Lanuza family; for that family, thanks to royal privileges granted in Philip III's reign (1598–1621), held the office of master of the mint between 1600 and 1658.[38] As a consequence of such problems, the Saragossa city council chose not to issue petty coins in 1611–18 and 1655–7, although it did make concessions to undertake minting silver coins. From 1658, anxious to avoid any further such conflicts, the council petitioned for royal privileges during the reigns of Philip IV (1621–65) and Charles II (1665–1700) to grant it the office of mint master in perpetuity and the right to mint coins under terms similar to those that Barcelona had received from James I and Peter III in the thirteenth century, terms subsequently confirmed by later Aragonese monarchs.[39] Despite the support of the viceroy Juan José de Austria, Saragossa never did gain such freedom to mint coins, even though Charles II, in May 1677, did grant it the office of master of the mint in perpetuity, in consideration of the services that the city had rendered. As a result, the issues that the monarchy had authorized in the last quarter of the seventeenth century were confined to just 112,000 *libras* of billon, in 1677–80, to pay for military services in Catalonia. Isolated petitions to mint small amounts of billon from other councils, such as Teruel in 1678, were in vain.[40]

Monetary Debate in Aragon (1660–1702)

Significantly, the Habsburg monarchy's own interest in regulating local issues opened the way for the monetary debate that took place in Aragon in the last quarter of the seventeenth century. Shackled by the monarchy's deficit, Philip IV seized on Saragossa's requests, in 1660, for permission to engage in minting as an opportunity for the crown to generate seigniorage revenues through fresh billon issues. The Council of Aragon, an administrative and judicial institution that helped the monarchy to govern, requested this year's reports on the seigniorage and intrinsic value of their domestic petty coins. In contrast to the seigniorage of 20 per cent levied on billon in Valencia, despite the poor quality of its copper and its weight reductions, the master of the Saragossa mint received an income that was only 6 per cent of the face value of the 1655–7 issues. This amounted to 20 *dineros* per marc (233.571 g).[41] In a report submitted to the Council of Aragon in 1660, the Real Audiencia, composed of royal officers, contended that the lower intrinsic value of local billon had promoted both the circulation of counterfeit petty coins in the kingdom and the export of silver coins from the realm as their premium against billon increased. However, the viceroy of Aragon admitted in another report that any higher precious-metal content in the billon coins would reduce the crown's seigniorage.

Despite such objections from the Real Audiencia, which were linked to *rentier* attitudes and to the jurists' attachments to the legal system (as petty nobles and burgers), the institutions closest to the king continued with their demands for aggressive debasements, increasing their pressure between 1669 and 1676, after the accession of Juan José de Austria as viceroy of Aragon. Thus, in 1663 the governor of the kingdom ordered certain municipalities to test the acceptance of new lower-quality silver *reales* (*pilares* coins) among the population.[42] The presence of *reales* minted in 1669 and *dineros* struck in 1670, 1673 and 1676, which were nevertheless not legal tender, was the result of similar attempts.[43] As a touchstone for the prevailing climate of opinion, the jurists of the Real Audiencia, in their reports to the Council of Aragon in 1675–6, supported the new issue of billon coins without seeking Parliament's approval, but they cautioned the government against engaging in any excessive degrees of debasement.[44]

In light of this institutional interest in debasing the domestic coinage, Aragonese mercantilists began debating monetary reforms. In 1674, Viceroy Juan José de Austria set up the Junta de Comercio (Trade Council) to seek solutions for the kingdom's current economic problems, such as the control of commercial transactions by French merchants, the decadence of manufacturing, the currency shortage and depopulation. The numerous letters addressed to the Trade Council reveal two opposing lines of economic thought that clashed particularly on trade policy.[45] The advocates of protectionism enjoyed the support of the municipal councils, especially in Saragossa, which were influenced by those guilds that were lobbying against foreign competition. The free trade party was backed by the Diputación in order to boost transactions and protect the customs duties, which were the main source of its revenues. While protectionist arguments won the day in the Trade Council, the adoption of specific measures was reserved for the Aragonese Parliament of 1677–8, which generated a flood of new proposals.

This economic debate sparked the first calls for a debasement of the local coinage. The main benchmark was Valencia, where the Spanish monarchy extended the seigniorage on silver coins to other coins towards the end of the sixteenth century, and would even increase it significantly on billon coins during the seventeenth century.[46] This process led to frequent issues of silver and billon coins from the very end of the sixteenth century and to aggressive debasements in 1607–11. A substantial reduction in weight and fineness of these coins persisted in the important mint issues undertaken in the first half of the seventeenth century and was increased in the modest coinages that took place in the second half.[47] Those measures in turn prompted a restriking of Castilian *reales* and Aragonese *dineros* into Valencian coins in order to increase mint profits.[48] Commercial transactions spread these pieces throughout the crown of Aragon, especially during the second half of the seventeenth century.

Aragonese writers of this period, even though evidently well versed in current economics, showed little knowledge of Castilian thinking – with the exception of Manuel Lasheras – and did not cite the main proponents in their writings.[49] These *arbitrists* concentrated their efforts on the silver coinage, in line with contemporary bullionist thinking that prevailed in the medieval and early modern eras: i.e. the classic views that associated a country's economic prosperity with its possession of precious metals. Their scant interest in gold not only indicates its scarcity in an inland region like Aragon, but also highlights the essential role of silver coins in dominating economic activity, and in serving as the essential link to the money of account (i.e. in establishing commercial values). They paid far less attention to the petty billon coinage, since Aragon's billon coins had suffered less alteration of their face and intrinsic value than had Castile's *vellón*. Proposals for debasing the Aragonese *real* thus frequently ignored the necessary modifications of face values on billon and silver coins in order to maintain their equivalences as moneys of account.

Monetary reform was indeed continuously subordinated to commercial policy. For example, some *arbitrists*, while proposing an increase in customs duties or the ban on imports of foreign manufactures, also advocated a defensive debasement of the Aragonese *real* in order to reduce the export of coins to France and thus to correct the trade deficit.[50] In 1674, in an address to the Trade Council, Antonio Cubero Sebastián proposed a 25 per cent reduction in the weight of the *real*, while, in 1678, Pedro Borruel recommended that Parliament should require that *sueldos or* half *reales* be henceforth minted with a fineness of not more than 9 *dineros* compared to the 11 previously established. As late as 1684, José Tudela Tarazona, addressing the Council of Aragon, contended that issues of numerous *reales* with a low intrinsic value in Valencia had not only prevented the flight of that currency to France, but also attracted supplies of Castilian silver, while it also created more favourable terms of trade.

Although the Parliament of 1677–8 did adopt firmly protectionist measures in foreign trade, it continued to maintain the traditional ban on the debasement of the local currency. However, monetary measures adopted in Catalonia did contribute to reawakening debates among the Aragonese mercantilists. In 1674, the viceroy granted the city of Barcelona the right to apply a reduction of 26.47

per cent of the intrinsic value of Castilian *real* prior to its 1686 debasement in the weight of local coins. The depreciation of these new coins or Catalan *reales* was maintained in the issues carried out in 1674–7, 1682 or 1693 and even was extended to 40 per cent of this intrinsic value in the 1698 issue. The monarchy did not obtain any seigniorage in exchange, but the implicit cooperation of the city in the defence of Catalonia during the wars between Spain and France (1673–8, 1683–4, 1689–97).[51]

Two monetary reforms implemented in Castile also had an effect on the Aragonese *arbitrists*.[52] The first was Charles II's nominal debasement of the Castilian petty *vellón* coinage in February 1680, in order to reduce the high premiums on the silver currency. According to the Council of Saragossa in 1683 and to Manuel Lasheras in 1684, this decision was accompanied by a surreptitious issue of *reales* and *medio reales* with a weight reduction of 16.65 per cent for use as legal tender in the domestic market.[53] The new intrinsic value of this Castilian *real* was equal to 20 Aragonese *dineros* and was constantly referred to after 1680 by writers such as Manuel Lasheras and Miguel Azores, who wished to see the Aragonese silver coinage brought into line with the coins struck in Castile and other neighbouring territories. The second measure was the official debasement of the Castilian *real* in October 1686, when Charles II chose to maintain the silver purity of the coin but to reduce its weight by 25.37 per cent. The number of *reales* struck from one silver *marc* in Castile thus increased from 67 to 84, approximately in line with the recommendations made by various Castilian *arbitrists* in the early seventeenth century.[54] This reform was extended to all silver minted in peninsular Spain, while the former intrinsic value of the coins issued in Spanish America was maintained for use in international markets.

Against this background, monetary reform took its place on Parliament's agenda in 1684–6, provoking a very heated debate on the issue of maintaining the protectionist policy adopted in 1677–8, for it had evidently failed in its goal of reactivating the economy.[55] Despite the repeal of this legislation, Parliament still refused to change the intrinsic value of the Aragonese currency. Discussion of the problems caused by the debasement of the Castilian *real* in 1686 was entrusted to a Council formed by some delegates of the four estates or social groups with representation in Parliament: citizens, the clergy, high and petty nobility. This Council of the Four Estates undertook various consultations between 1686 and 1687, but without reaching any definitive conclusions.

The most original contribution to this debate was made by Manuel Lasheras, who appeared before the Council of the Four Estates in April 1684 to expound his *Memorias históricas sobre el valor de la plata y oro*.[56] Lasheras returned to the early seventeenth-century arguments of the Castilian *arbitrists* Tomás de Cardona and Alonso de Carranza, stressing the role of undervaluation as an explanation for the flight of gold and silver from Aragon and Spain. As several Castilian *arbitrists* had suggested from 1665, and particularly in 1677–84,[57] Lasheras concurred with both authors in proposing an enhancement of monetized silver and gold in order to prevent their export. He recommended increasing the official values of the *escudo* by 28.5 per cent, of the *real* by 17.65 per cent and the values of lower quality silver ingots by 18.75 per cent. In order to gain the necessary political consensus, Lasheras advised splitting any profits generated by minting silver between the royal treasury and the Diputación. Opting for the free trade line that triumphed in the Parliament of 1684–6, he argued that the return of this issue to the hands of the Diputación could be used to cancel its debt, repeal customs duties and strike lighter *reales* in order to align their intrinsic value with the coinage of Catalonia, Valencia and Castile, thereby preventing both hoarding and export of good coins, while also facilitating trade.

Despite Saragossa's interest in minting money to aid the municipal treasury,[58] these reforms were firmly opposed by the Diputación.[59] This position was the result of the control that the nobility (high and petty) exercised in the Diputación, and the presence of the clergy among its members.[60] These social groups were not represented on the Saragossa city council, and their interest in the defence of a stable intrinsic value for silver money to guarantee its face value had been established in the medieval period, because these coinage values determined the value of their tax yields and land rents.[61] Aragon's increasing exports of raw materials to France, Valencia and Catalonia at the end of the seventeenth century served only to reaffirm this policy, which was intended to maximize profits on transactions by defending the prestige and hence the value of the Aragonese *real* abroad. The Diputación thus opposed any debasement of the Aragonese currency or even any large issues of petty coins on the grounds that such measures would be harmful to trade by producing a revaluation of silver against billon, raising premiums on silver, and by promoting the outflow of silver.[62] Accordingly, the Diputación financed numismatic studies and legal works as well as submitting reports to the Council of Aragon in the 1680s: in order to defend its right to participate in any new Aragonese issues and to preserve the intrinsic values of coins established by law and customs, unless the Parliament authorized any changes, in accordance with medieval legislation for the *jaquesa* billon coinage.

Institutional opposition to monetary reform in Aragon eventually received support from the monarchy, when at the end of the seventeenth century the crown ceased its efforts to reduce the intrinsic value of the issues. As a result, in 1686–9, the Real Audiencia once more supported the principle of conserving the traditional weight and fineness of the coinage.[63] There were three reasons for the monarchy's volte-face in its monetary policies. In the first place, while Catalan silver debasements had been aided by institutional consensus,[64] political conflict in Aragon had prevented any similar reforms. Second, the increasing export orientation of Aragon's economy, toward the end of the century, consolidated the commercial and monetary flows that were associated with restructuring trade in the seventeenth century. Third and finally, the coins minted in Valencia provided the monarchy with a higher seigniorage profit, and it therefore preferred to conserve the already established system of monetary circulation for conducting trade between the two kingdoms. Thus, at the same time that it had allowed continuous issues of billon and silver coinages in Valencia, from 1681 to 1699, it rejected minting coins in Aragon or any reduction in their intrinsic value.[65]

Clearly reflecting these adverse circumstances, monetary *arbitrism* gradually faded away in Aragon during the 1690s. At the same time, the Aragonese Parliament ceased to be convoked. This was the only political forum that could overcome the legal obstacles to the monetary reforms and impose these decisions on all public institutions in the kingdom. The last Parliament held in the early modern period, at the beginning of Philip V's reign (1700–46), allowed the estate of the petty nobility, in 1702, to submit to Queen María Luisa de Saboya a report in support of a defensive debasement of the Aragonese currency. This petition sought to prevent the flight of local *reales* and *dineros* by recommending the issue of coins with an intrinsic value closer to those of the Valencian and Catalan coinages.[66] Despite having recognized the monarchy's right (either in perpetuity or until a new Parliament might be held) to issue coins with a lower metal content and retain the resulting profit, this petition was not well received.

The failure of voices favouring debasement to make themselves heard meant that Aragon was deprived of the stimulus to its economy that might have come from issuing a local currency that was regulated by its own authorities to be more closely aligned with market demand. In response to such demands for an adequate coinage, the invasion of foreign and counterfeit coins continued throughout the early modern period, and its adverse effects could not be even partially offset. In contrast to the autonomous leanings of both individuals and institutions in seventeenth-century Aragon, the monetary policy of the eighteenth-century Bourbon monarchy clearly shifted to a state-wide conception of monetary and economic affairs. After the billon issue of 1710–19 and its nominal debasement in 1718, no new Aragonese currency was issued. Instead, the more-centralizing Bourbon state began to promote a slow process of harmonizing the coinage minted in peninsular Spain, a coinage based on the Castilian system, with particular emphasis placed on billon, and with the ultimate aim of eliminating local coins in order to establish a fully national currency.[67]

Conclusions

The crown and kingdom of Aragon underwent far-reaching changes in monetary circulation in the seventeenth century, chiefly as the result of market demands for a coinage with a lower intrinsic value than that indicated its official face value, and thus one that would have been better aligned with the current market prices for gold and silver. The failure of the existing Aragonese and Castilian currency to meet the market's needs for legal tender led to both widespread debasement and counterfeiting, and to the continual influx of low-quality foreign coins: debased, worn and counterfeit. Though such coins facilitated transactions, their unrestricted circulation had a damaging impact on the market, in promoting exports of gold and silver and the disappearance of good local coins, as well as in reducing confidence in the local currencies and in generating inflationary processes. In other words, Aragon was a chronic victim of classic Gresham's Law. These problems, aggravated by the continued decline of the Aragonese economy – all too clear in its trade deficits with France – became a matter for concern among the public authorities, who were predominant in shaping the monetary debate.

In contrast to the situation in both Catalonia and Valencia, where elites and institutions could agree with the monarchy on debasements of local coins in exchange for fiscal cooperation, the adverse effects of the monetary situation in Aragon were intensified by seriously deficient economic policies. Hampered by the crown's legal inability to exact seigniorage revenues and by difficulties in obtaining gold and silver, any changes in the weight and fineness of the coinage required a wide-ranging institutional consensus.[68] The possibility of achieving ay such consensus was further undermined in the second half of the seventeenth century by an institutional divergence of economic ideas. The traditional policy, represented by the Diputación, was to conserve the intrinsic value of the currency in order to guarantee its face value. This policy was defended by the social groups that were most concerned about receiving rents in cash or in kind in order to maximize their real incomes, and this concern gained ground as the economy became more and more oriented to foreign trade, with rising raw material exports. Those institutions closest to the monarchy (i.e. the viceroy, the Real Audiencia and the city of Saragossa) advocated debasements, from the 1660s, in order to generate higher revenues; but their advocacy was not sufficient to overcome this deeply entrenched opposition, which relied on Parliament's historic approval (from 1372) for any change in the intrinsic values of the coinage. Meanwhile, the monarchy was patently uninterested in repairing the institutional breach during the last quarter of the seventeenth century, since it could readily earn a higher yield on coins minted in Valencia where the parliamentary writ did not run. This attitude nullified any possibility of minting local coins as debased moneys that were better aligned with the needs of the market, even though this reform could well have stimulated an economic recovery. This decision ensured a perpetual recourse to influxes of foreign and illegal coins in Aragon for the early modern period, without any mechanisms in force to mitigate the harm that such a coinage circulation did to commercial transactions and foreign trade.

Driven by the monarchy's interest in aggressive debasements of local coins after 1660, monetary debate intensified in Aragon, especially in the Parliaments held in 1677–8 and 1684–6. Initially linked to protectionist thinking and strongly emphasizing the precedent of Valencia, opinions in favour of coinage debasements (especially of the silver coinage) took firm root when Charles II adopted a similar measure in Castile in the 1680s. These defensive debasements were mainly aimed at preventing the export of gold and silver from the kingdom in order to correct the trade deficit. In this context, Manuel Lasheras stands out for his defence of monetary reform (for high-valued local silver coins) in order to stimulate economic recovery: through both the alignment of the intrinsic values of the coinage with those of neighbouring territories and the elimination of customs barriers. Though well adapted to the political and legislative framework of the kingdom, the proposals of the *arbitrists* failed to overcome the institutional rift in order to reduce the intrinsic value of the local currency; and that failure led to the decline of the monetary debate in the later seventeenth century.

Acknowledgements

This work is included in the research projects HAR2008-05425 and HAR2011-29036-C02-01. Both projects have been financed by the Spanish Ministry of Science and Innovation.

8 MONEY OR EXPORT COMMODITY FOR ASIA? AMERICAN SILVER IN THE MARKETS OF MEXICO, CASTILE AND AMSTERDAM FROM THE SIXTEENTH TO THE EIGHTEENTH CENTURY

Renate Pieper

The monetary regimes of the early modern Atlantic have usually been described as based fundamentally on a bimetallic system of precious metals.[1] Nonetheless, there are some cases that seem to contradict this general assumption. During the whole colonial period, that is, almost three centuries, Mexicans continually complained about chronic shortages of petty coins, notwithstanding the very large outputs of their world-renowned silver production and the Spanish colony's absolute monetary stability.[2] Despite all complaints and petitions to the Spanish crown there was almost no legal copper coinage, not even in the eighteenth century – even though large volumes of copper coinage had been struck within Spain (Castile) itself, since 1599. Thus current token money for everyday payments consisted of different materials, such as lead, playing cards, cocoa (cacao) beans and the like, along with different forms of credit.[3] At the same time that the Mexican colonists were complaining about chronic shortages of small coins, monetary complaints within Spain were directed instead at shortages of gold and silver. Copper coins and fractionary money were, however – as just indicated – always available, sometimes in overwhelming quantities, because of Spain's erratic monetary policies.[4] In the eighteenth century, since copper or *vellón* coinage no longer presented a problem for the Spanish economy, a debate ensued instead about the possible utility of adopting paper money.[5]

In Amsterdam the monetary situation differed considerably from that found in Spain (Castile) and in Mexico. In the seventeenth century, Amsterdam had emerged as the major financial centre for the Atlantic economies, in part because of the operations of its new Wisselbank (founded 1609), especially in utilizing a money of account 'bank money' whose value remained fixed in its fine silver contents (as shown in Herman Van der Wee's chapter in this volume).[6] But in

Amsterdam, in contrast to both Mexico and Spain, no chronic complaints about monetary shortages were to be found, despite the concerns of Dutch merchants about obtaining licences to export silver from the Spanish realms (to Amsterdam and then to various foreign regions).[7] Therefore, we may conclude that the monetary functions of the two precious metals in Mexico, Castile and Amsterdam differed from each other and often varied in their forms and goals over the course of the seventeenth and eighteenth centuries.

When the influx of American silver into Western Europe began in the mid-sixteenth century, various scholars almost immediately engaged in disputes about its economic effects, especially in terms of the readily detectable rise in prices.[8] From the early eighteenth century, however, and especially in the second half of the century, Spanish American silver outputs, principally in Mexico (Zacatecas and then Guanajuato), greatly expanded, but without inciting any discussion similar to that of the sixteenth century. We are thus led to inquire whether the differences in those reactions to the much increased influxes of Spanish American silver may have been due to the changing monetary functions of silver in the early-modern Atlantic economies. Possibly some useful insights may be gained by an examination of the relationships between silver production and prices in the markets of Mexico, Castile and Amsterdam during the seventeenth and eighteenth centuries.

For the purpose of such a comparison, we require long-term series of silver production and prices. The tax records of the Spanish American mining industry will be our starting point. The period under consideration finishes with the Coalition Wars against France (1792–7). The entrance of French troops into Amsterdam, the disruption of the Spanish American Atlantic trade and the massive issues of royal notes, the *vales reales*, in Spain put an end to the strong connections between the Dutch Republic and the Hispanic world. The present study will analyse the relationship between silver production and price levels in Mexico, Castile and Amsterdam from 1550 to 1800, to provide a better understanding of the changing monetary functions of silver in these markets during this period.

A now rich historiography has dealt in considerable depth with the economic impact of Spanish American silver production on the European and global economies in the early-modern era, though in a variety of ways. The mining outputs really became significant only from the 1540s; and then, with the introduction of the mercury amalgamation process for silver ores in Mexico in the 1550s and in Peru in the 1570s, those outputs rapidly exceeded those from the silver-copper mines in South Germany and Central Europe (which had peaked by about 1540). From the mid-sixteenth century, the Spanish government maintained regular accounts of royal taxes on silver production, accounts that are well preserved. Thanks to considerable research on Spanish American finances, we now have at our disposal reliable estimates of the registered bullion production.[9] Although both smuggling and tax evasion were obviously a constant threat to the reliability of these estimates, their general validity can be substantiated by comparing them with the royal accounts of mercury consumption (financed with credits from the royal treasuries).[10] At the same time, however, we must acknowledge that some bias remains in these data, because the actual amount of silver refined in the smelting processes was not verified by the treasury controls. Nevertheless, we may conclude that the available data do provide a good proxy for total Mexican silver production. Along with the numerous studies on the Mexican mining industry of this era,[11] we can also utilize much published research on the monetary regime of New Spain (the official name for Mexico). Overall, our focus will be on the later eighteenth century and end of the colonial period, while the seventeenth century and the period of and just following the War of the Spanish Succession (1701–14) will receive less attention.

In order to examine the role of silver on the Mexican market, we should compare the data on silver production with subsequent changes in the price level. We must also admit, however, that these silver-output data are not necessarily a reliable proxy for the aggregate money supply; and further admit that we cannot estimate the amount of token money, credit facilities and treasury bills in circulation, because we have only qualitative and institutional studies on these forms of money.[12] Studies of the long-term Mexican price level are essentially based on the evolution of maize prices for what was the basic foodstuff in this Spanish colony; and these prices commence only in 1577. Even if they certainly reflect the vagaries of the harvests and effects of demographic changes, we have no choice but to use these prices series as an indicator of changes in the general price level, simply because no other long-term commodity price series are available.[13]

For these monetary and price analyses, we must also utilize another group of historical studies that deals with the monetary situation in Spain and the kingdom of Castile. While in Mexico (New Spain) the domestic coinages (chiefly the peso) remained unchanged, the metropolitan Spanish economy experienced several monetary disturbances. When issuing a new and strong silver coinage in 1497, the Catholic Monarchs (Ferdinand and Isabella) had promised the Cortes of Castile that they would never again debase the gold or silver coinages, nor take any seigniorage beyond the traditional amount, without its consent; and the monarchy kept that promise until the next authorized change of 1686 (under Charles II). That promise did not, however, include the largely copper petty *vellón* (billon), which had always contained at least some silver. In 1599, Philip III (r. 1598–1621), having just ascended to the Spanish throne, commenced debasing the *vellón* coinage, which now became for the first time a purely copper coinage. Subsequently it was also debased (by a reduced weight), with increased seigniorage, in a futile attempt to finance Spain's European wars. For Earl Hamilton these issues of debased *vellón* coins were the single most important factor fuelling inflation in the second half of the seventeenth century, until finally (with the coinage changes of 1686) radical deflationary measures had to be undertaken.[14] Thus, Castile experienced extreme monetary instability that lasted until the end of the War of the Spanish Succession, in 1714. At the same time, Castile experienced a rise in its gold:silver ratio: from 1:10.6 in 1550 to 1:15 in the mid-seventeenth century. During the eighteenth century, however, the Bourbon kings maintained an almost perfect stability of the monetary system, applying only minor devaluations. But when the Coalition Wars against Revolutionary France began (1792–7), such stability was no longer possible, so that currency debasements and massive issues of paper money followed.

For the monetary situation and the price level in Spain one can still rely on the careful investigations of Earl J. Hamilton, who went through monastery and hospital accounts on the eve of the Spanish Civil War. His edition of price series for Castile starts in the fourteenth century.[15] Apart from various recent local price studies, for short periods of time, there has been no further attempt to continue Hamilton's price history on a larger scale.

Finally, we must also consider studies dealing with relationships between Mexican silver and the Dutch economy. This connection is analysed in several investigations into Spanish American commerce and smuggling. But many of these works focus on trade with the British, who emerged as the most important trading partner of Spanish America after the Seven Years War (1756–63), or certainly by the end of the eighteenth century.[16] The role of Dutch traders, pirates and smugglers who dealt with Spanish America, has been chiefly studied for just Brazil.[17] Dutch trade with Spain itself has been the subject of many investigations for the Golden Age; but for the eighteenth century, our knowledge of Spanish American precious metals, silver especially, in Amsterdam is very limited. Even the role of such silver in Dutch trade with Asia during the seventeenth century has been obscured by the attention devoted to the English East India Company, despite the fact that many London-based merchants in this trade were Dutch or continental in their origins, as were their networks and their merchandise.[18]

Nevertheless, the commercial and monetary relationships between the Spanish Americas and Amsterdam are vital for this study. We commence with the gold:silver ratio, which was considerably lower in Amsterdam than it was in Castile. It rose from 1:13 in 1620 and reached a peak (for this era) of 1:15, only in the mid-eighteenth century. Price indexes for Amsterdam are available from the beginning of the Thirty Years War (1618–48), when the Beurs commenced its regular price quotations. For the Amsterdam market itself, we have the well-known price series of Nicolaas Posthumus.[19] Prices recorded for Amsterdam, in contrast to the Mexican and the Castilian consumer prices, were wholesale prices established at the Beurs.

The purpose of this study is to offer a hypothesis concerning the use of silver as a monetary basis in the early-modern Atlantic economies by comparing the relation between Spanish American silver production – especially in New Spain (Mexico) – with the development of commodity prices in the markets of Mexico, Amsterdam and Castile.[20]

We must also, however, take into consideration (as far as is possible to do so) the role of credit and banking systems. In New Spain the Banco de Avío Minero was founded in 1784 but it lacked the support of the leading commercial and mining families and therefore went bankrupt in 1792.[21] Even if there was no public bank, credit was still widespread in New Spain. Besides deferred payments and credit activities of merchant houses, different sorts of treasuries as well as private bills circulated. In addition, some ecclesiastical institutions and indigenous-Indian municipalities offered various forms of credit.[22] In Spain private bankers moved from Seville to Madrid at the beginning of the seventeenth century.[23] In 1782, the Banco de San Carlos, the first public bank, opened in Madrid in order to redeem public promissory notes, the *vales reales*. From 1794, when another tranche of *vales reales* was issued in order to finance the Coalition Wars against France, the *vales* rapidly lost their value. The bank notes of the Banco de San Carlos also found little acceptance.[24]

Amsterdam's Wisselbank (1609) operated on a money of account whose value remained fixed in terms of its silver content; but operating solely as a giro bank and not as a credit bank, the Wisselbank was legally unable to assist in financing the warfare and public debt of the Dutch Republic.[25] Furthermore, Dutch colonial efforts were not formally financed and organized as a state affair.[26] Thus in examining the economic histories of Spain, New Spain and the Dutch Republic, we are attempting to compare three very different economic systems: two with a stable monetary policy (New Spain and the Dutch Republic) and one with a very unstable monetary system (Castile: from 1599 to 1713); and we are also comparing two systems without a public bank with one that has such a bank, but not a modern-style 'lender of last resort' bank (as the Bank of England, founded in 1694–7, later evolved to be).

In estimating the aggregate money supplies of New Spain, we should consider, in addition to possible supplies of credit, Spanish American gold production, even though its aggregate value was considerably lower than that of silver. Throughout the seventeenth century, New Granada (modern Columbia) supplied some gold for the Atlantic markets; but from the 1690s until the mid- to later eighteenth century, Portuguese-Brazilian gold exports became far more important. Even so, those gold exports were not sufficient to alter the gold:silver ratios in the Atlantic and Asian markets.

Volume of Silver Production in Mexico and Peru

In order to discern the monetary influence of Spanish American silver outputs on the economies of these three regions – New Spain, Spain, and the Netherlands – we need to begin with the production cycles of Mexican and Peruvian silver (Figures 8.1 and 8.2). One may distinguish three different periods. The mid-sixteenth century was the starting point for the massive outputs of Mexican silver. Those outputs reached their initial peak in the first decade of the seventeenth century when, for several years, more than 6 million pesos were registered for taxation at the royal offices. Mexican mined silver production was then overshadowed by that of Peru and Alto Peru, in which more than 8 million pesos of silver were declared in 1610. From the 1590s the mean value of the Peruvian silver outputs was about 6–7 million pesos a year. In 1628, when the Dutch corsair Piet Heyn captured the Mexican silver fleet, he had just missed much richer Peruvian silver shipments.

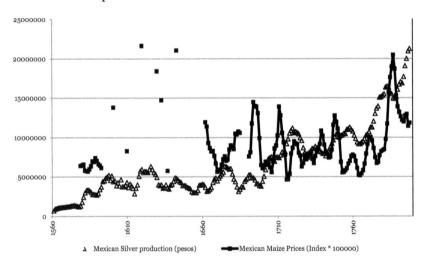

**Figure 8.1: Mexican Silver Production and Mexican Maize Prices (1561–1798)
(5 years moving averages).**

During the second period, and especially from 1628, a permanent decline in registered silver production in Mexico may be observed. In Peru and Alto Peru (modern-day Bolivia), mined silver production remained at a high level for another decade. In Mexico, the nadir of silver production was reached in 1663, with a registered output of just 2 million pesos. In Peru, the value of registered silver dropped even more – to less than 1 million pesos per year during the War of the Spanish Succession (1701–14). In and from the later seventeenth century, Mexican silver production achieved a notable recovery and surpassed the

Peruvian mined outputs. By the beginning of the eighteenth century, registered Mexican silver outputs had reached and surpassed their previous maxima, and continued to grow through much of the century. Severe fluctuations characterize the Mexican silver output, while the rise and then decline of silver production in Peru were much more regular and indeed steady.[27]

Between 1592 and 1634 Mexican and Peruvian silver production together reached their first maximum, with an annual mean value of 10 million pesos; and sometimes the aggregate outputs reached 13 million pesos. By the mid-1660s, however, those aggregate outputs had fallen to just half that amount. In the following and final decades of the seventeenth century, aggregate Spanish American silver output had become stabilized at around 8 million pesos.

During the third period, in the early eighteenth century, Mexican production surpassed its previous levels, as just indicated, and reached 7 million pesos a year. New mining and refining techniques, in particular the use of gunpowder in blasting rock, led to a new upward trend. By the 1730s, Mexican silver production had stabilized at around 9–10 million pesos a year, remaining at that level until the early 1770s. After the Seven Years War (1756–63), silver production was fostered by even newer techniques and the Spanish crown that reduced the price of mercury – in two stages – to just half its former cost. Thus, during the final quarter of the eighteenth century, Mexican silver production increased until it reached a new peak, with a mean value of 21 million pesos in 1796–1805. Although the same mining reforms were in operation in Peru, the results were much more modest in both absolute and relative numbers, so that the mean value of the first boom period was attained only in the 1780s. Between 1796 and 1805, total Spanish American mining output reached almost 30 million pesos per year.

As indicated earlier, the renewed Spanish American silver mining boom, and exports to Europe did not elicit anywhere nearly the same public interest as did the silver influxes of the sixteenth-century Price Revolution era, possibly because of the reduced influence of silver on the eighteenth-century economy. In order to obtain a better insight into the importance of such silver inflows for the eighteenth century, we should compare the newly obtained data on Spanish American silver production with changes in the price levels (i.e. the Consumer Price Indexes for this era) in Mexico itself, Castile and Amsterdam.

Relation between silver production and monetary supply in Mexico

In Mexico, the price level, as measured in maize (corn) prices, more than doubled by and at the beginning of the seventeenth century (Figure 8.1). The Mexican price index attained in 1600–3 was, in fact, maintained for the next 60 years. Thereafter, Mexican maize prices fell to almost their former position, so that from 1667 until 1783, this price index was generally at a level only half that of the early seventeenth century. In the years following the Treaty of Paris (1783), however, maize prices increased once more and roughly doubled, but without reaching the level of the first half of the seventeenth century.[28]

A comparison of these maize prices with the data for Mexican silver production shows no statistically significant relationship. Between 1577 and 1598, when Spanish American silver production increased at least four-fold, maize prices rose by only a third. From 1628 to 1663, when silver production and Mexico's population were both steadily falling, Mexican maize prices reached their maximum for the colonial period. Prices still remained stable when Mexican population and silver production stopped declining and then increased substantially from 1700 well into the eighteenth century. Only during the last quarter of the colonial period did both maize prices and silver production rise, but with opposing fluctuations. Thus both the calculation of the correlation coefficient and Figure 8.1 show very clearly that there was no connection between changes in the Mexican price level and silver outputs in New Spain.

The available information suggests that, in New Spain, the silver peso was a general unit of account but that the silver coin itself was also considered to be an export commodity like dyestuffs or sugar. The commodity function of the silver peso was strengthened by the legislation stipulating that indigenous 'Indian' communities had to pay their annual taxes (*tributo*) according to their old customs, region by region. A variety of items, such as textiles, dyes, cacao beans could be delivered along with or instead of silver. This was a sharp contrast to the obligations of the Spanish communities in New Spain and to the situation in Europe where tax payments to the crown always had to be made in coins. Thus in Mexico, the silver peso did not serve always as a monetary basis and was not used on every occasion as a means of payment, even if it always served as a money of account unit.[29]

Complaints from colonial contemporaries about shortages of small coins reaffirm this impression, and also confirm that the actual colonial domestic monetary system, for day-to-day transactions, was based fundamentally on petty credits and regional token moneys (*tlaco*). Such moneys consisted of such objects as copper, lead, wood, leather, paper or glass and in some region on old traditional, pre-Hispanic means of payment such as cacao beans in particular.[30] Larger and interregional transactions made extensive use of credit.[31] We may conclude that, in the short run, the price level in New Spain depended on climate and harvest fluctuations, which led to often severe oscillations in grain prices. In contrast, the longer term shifts in the Mexican price level may be explained by transformations of New Spain's economy and changes in its commerce with the Caribbean and eastern Asia (via the Philippines). These influences appear to have been far more important for the monetary supply and thus the price level than the changing outputs of the silver mines.[32] Token money and credit were offered only on demand and on a small scale by different public, private and religious institutions, so that prices remained stable until the 1780s. Only from the Peace of Paris, in

1783, and to the very end of the colonial period, did this situation undergo any significant changes. When trade with both northern Europe and the new republic of the United States of America became more intensive, the monetarization of silver on the home markets of New Spain seems to have increased.

Relation between Silver Production and Monetary Supply in Spain

While silver, in Mexico, chiefly fulfilled the role of an export commodity, the situation in Spain and especially in Castile and Andalusia was quite different (Figures 8.2 and 8.3). Between 1551 and 1621, the general price level in terms of fine silver was largely determined by the officially declared imports of American silver, as the correlation (in terms of the coefficient of determination R squared = 0.66 and R = 0.81) indicates. The relation between taxed American production and Castilian prices was less intense than with silver imports. According to these regressions, total American silver production was responsible for 62 per cent (R = 0.79) of the changes of the Castilian price level. Mexican silver output alone was responsible for 49 per cent (R = 0.70) of the changes in Castilian prices, while Peruvian influence was somewhat higher, with an R-square value of 0.59 (R = 0.76) (These correlations were calculated for n = 63 and the probability of the t-test was 0.995). These data suggest that, during the sixteenth and early seventeenth centuries, the monetary basis of the Castilian economy depended heavily on the supply of American precious metals, in spite of the fact that most of the currency that actually circulated in Castile consisted of billion and copper coins (from 1599). The divergence between the impact of taxed silver production and taxed silver imports on the Castilian price level might have been due to different distribution and information channels. The amounts of specie embarked on the *flotas* and *galeones* were well known in advance, even before the departure of the fleets from Havana. But as Atlantic weather conditions and privateering represented a considerable risk, Sevillian brokers of precious metals (*compradores de oro y plata*) traded with the specie only after its safe arrival on the Andalusian-Atlantic shores. Since both American silver ingots with a fixed weight and fineness and American pesos had no official value in Castile, the specie should have been sent to the mint at Seville. But a large part of the silver was never disembarked and thus not (re)coined, being exported directly to other European realms without any physical transformation. Nonetheless, on its arrival on the Andalusian coast American silver influenced the monetary supply of the Iberian peninsula. This was chiefly due to the credit circuits that were based on the American deliveries connecting Seville with its Iberian hinterland and with other European centres of manufacturing.[33] Thus, until the Thirty Years War (1618–48), and in sharp contrast to the situation in Mexico, the monetary situation at Seville and in the interior of the Iberian peninsula was determined to a considerable degree by the silver ingots and American coins that were traded by the Sevillian brokers.

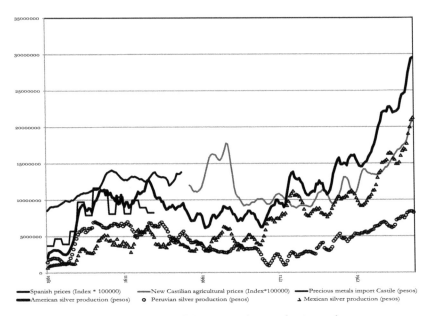

Figure 8.2: Spanish American silver production and Spanish prices (1561–1798) (5 years moving averages).

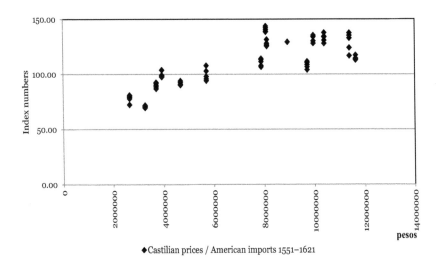

◆Castilian prices / American imports 1551–1621

Figure 8.3: Correlation between Castilian prices and imports of Spanish American silver, 1551–1621.

In the 1580s the sudden influx of large quantities of American silver changed the ratios between the uses of specie and credit within Europe's interregional trade. Manufacturers and merchants from foreign countries increasingly demanded payment in silver and were more reluctant to offer Andalusian commercial houses credit. This had negative effects on the European and especially the Castilian fairs.[34] Thus, at the end of the sixteenth century, silver was distributed far more quickly than before across European manufacturing centres.

The effects were even felt in Central Europe. In Styria, where the quicksilver (mercury) mines of Idrja produced an important export commodity, noble inventories recorded a sharp increase in the possession of coins and in credit from that of the mid-sixteenth century. Yet the value of the high-valued coins rose even faster than did the amount of credit. In the mid-sixteenth century the relationship between coins and credit was about 1:56, whereas in 1635 the value of the coins had continuously risen, in comparison to credit, to about 1:11.[35] The change of the ratio between coins and credit in European commerce, fairs and probate inventories thus attenuated the inflationary effects of the Spanish American bullion influxes, and thus possible supplies of precious metals, at the end of the sixteenth century.

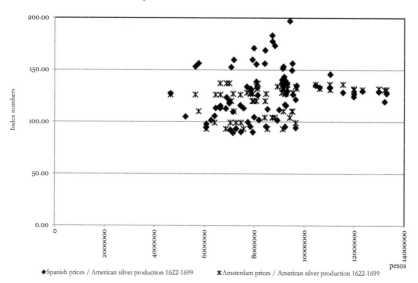

♦ Spanish prices / American silver production 1622-1699   ✖ Amsterdam prices / American silver production 1622-1699

Figure 8.4 : Correlations between Spanish American silver production and Castilian and Amsterdam prices, 1622–99.

The entry of Spain in the Thirty Years War, from 1621, changed the situation completely. For the rest of the seventeenth century, the data on American silver exports or on silver production registered at Mexico and Peru had no discernible, statistically significant effect on the Spanish monetary economy (Figures 8.2 and 8.4). Whether prices were calculated in fine silver or as money of account (in copper coins), the price level was not affected by the changes in supplies of Spanish American silver. Prices computed in silver remained rather stable until the mid-seventeenth century; but from 1664 to 1680 they experienced a sharp increase in the range of 30–40 per cent, and then fell somewhat below their former level.[36] At the beginning of the eighteenth century, the Castilian price level was lower than it ever been during the seventeenth century.

Two factors may have been responsible for nullifying the former relationships between Spanish American silver production and the behaviour of Castilian prices. First, European warfare led to disruptions in mercury production, producing frequent shortages, so that fewer silver ores were refined by mercury amalgamation, and as a consequence more of the silver produced (by melting) escaped the taxation. At the same time, the European wars – and the piracy that such wars promoted – also disrupted commerce between Spain and its overseas American colonies. One major consequence was a marked shift in oceanic trade routes involving these colonies, so that, for New Spain in particular, much more of its silver was exported across the Pacific, from Acapulco to Manila in the Philippines, though that traffic was also promoted by a growth of trade with China, especially in silks.

We therefore lack sufficiently reliable information about the actual quantities of silver produced in the Spanish Americas and the amounts expected to be delivered to Spain, though clearly such deliveries were frequently interrupted. From the Thirty Years War (1618–48) until the War of the Spanish Succession (1701–14), Castile's money supplies depended only to a very small extent on American silver, and consequently they then depended far more on copper, treasury bills and other forms of paper credit.

Subsequently, during the eighteenth century, the influence of Spanish American silver production once more became important and certainly more visibly evident for the Castilian economy (Figures 8.2 and 8.5). Though at first Castilian prices did remain stable, at a relatively low level, from the 1750s they experienced a steady growth, so that the Castilian price level had doubled by 1800.

Several factors combined to promote the increased silver flows to Spain. Trans-Atlantic commercial connections improved considerably with the end of war-promoted Caribbean piracy. At the same time, the crown's mercury supplies for refining the silver ores improved so that the proportion of silver obtained through amalgamation greatly increased. Therefore, after the Treaties of Utrecht concluding the Wars of the Spanish Succession (1713–14), information on Spanish American silver outputs became far more predictable and reliable, so that the production records of American tax officials could once again be used for commercial, financial and monetary purposes (including speculation). During the eighteenth century the correlation index – R-squared (coefficient of determination) – between declared total American silver production and Castilian agricultural prices, as recorded in the account books of urban monasteries and hospitals, reached 0.75 (R = 0.86), exceeding the levels of the sixteenth and early seventeenth centuries. Mexican silver production accounted for 68.4 per cent (R = 0.83) of that relationship with the Castilian price index, even if very few silver coins circulated within Castile, so that the use of copper and credit remained dominant during the eighteenth century. In this century, in contrast to the monetary situation in the sixteenth century, the most important silver-related data were no longer the official declarations of silver imports into Spain but rather those for the quantities of silver brought to the royal mints in New Spain. Furthermore, in contrast as well to the current situation in Mexico itself, the quantities of silver recorded in the Spanish American treasuries had an evidently significant monetary impact on the Spanish domestic economy, since the price indexes for agricultural goods in Spanish internal markets correspond closely with the Spanish American treasury data – at least until the outbreak of the Napoleonic Wars (1799–1815) and the consequent disruption and destruction of the Spanish Empire.

Relation between Silver Production and Monetary Supplies in Amsterdam

In Amsterdam, the relationships between Spanish American silver outputs and prices resembled those in Spain during much of the seventeenth and eighteenth centuries (Figure 8.6). During the early seventeenth century the prices recorded at the Amsterdam Beurs remained stable and at a high level, until the Treaty of the Pyrenees (between France and Spain, in 1659). From then until the 1680s, Amsterdam prices experienced a steady decline, finally reaching a level of just two-thirds of the previous peak in prices. From the later 1680s and 1690s, a very uneven recovery in prices – with many oscillations upwards and downwards – can be observed until finally, by the end of the Seven Years War (1756–63), the price level of the mid-seventeenth century was once more attained. From then until the end of the Dutch Republic (1792), prices on the Amsterdam stock exchange rose, on average, by 50 per cent. A comparison of these Dutch price movements with Spanish American silver production produces no signification correlation (R-square of 0.11, R = 0.33) during the seventeenth century (Figure 8.4). During the eighteenth century, however, we find a very marked contrast, with a very close relationship detected between the data for registered Mexican silver output and Amsterdam prices (with an R-square of 0.69, R = 0.83). This relationship was just as strong as the previously observed dependence of Spanish prices on the same data for declared Mexican silver production (Figures 8.5 and 8.6).

The correlation between total registered American silver production and the Amsterdam wholesale prices was also very strong (R-square = 0.66, R = 0.81), but the correlation between Peruvian silver production and the Amsterdam market was much less pronounced (R-square = 0.46, R = 0.68). (For the eighteenth century, the correlations for Castile and Amsterdam were calculated for n = 101 and the probability of the t-test was 99.5 per cent).

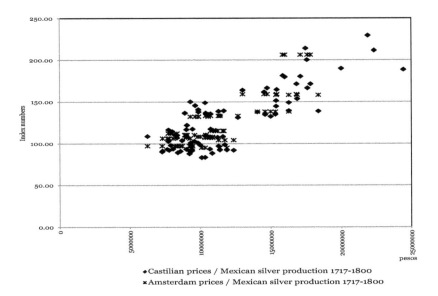

◆Castilian prices / Mexican silver production 1717-1800
✕Amsterdam prices / Mexican silver production 1717-1800

Figure 8.5: Correlation between Mexican silver production and Castilian and Amsterdam prices, 1717–1800.

Thus during the seventeenth-century Dutch Golden Age, changes in both the production of Spanish American silver production and shipments to Europe were of no great importance for the Dutch money supply and for the prices at the Amsterdam stock exchange – even though the Wisselbank's bank money was silver-based and American silver was the only source of specie for the European markets. As in both Mexico and in Spain, during the seventeenth century, other monetary elements, especially credit, were evidently much more important for Holland's monetary supplies and for Dutch trade.

The interdependence between the American economies – especially its silver production – and the European markets was the weakest during the seventeenth century. Caribbean privateering, which should have improved Dutch access to the American riches, did not alter the situation but only worsened it. The Dutch and English merchants, using the official Spanish trade monopoly with the

American colonies, for their own ends,[37] undoubtedly suffered seriously from the assaults of corsairs and freebooters. Those attacks probably provide the main reason why the uneven influx of American silver via Spain to the Amsterdam markets did not have any discernible consequences on the behaviour of monetary flows and price changes in the Dutch Republic.

During the eighteenth century, after peace had been restored in the Caribbean, restoring smoother economic connections with Mexico, independently of European warfare, the improved information about Mexican silver production seems to have provided a valuable asset for Dutch merchants. Thus silver was clearly considered as a monetary commodity on the Amsterdam exchange, and variations in the Dutch money supply more evidently reflected the fluctuations in Mexican silver production. Even more remarkable is the minimal time-lag between silver production in Mexico and changes in the price level on the Dutch market; and that is in striking contrast to the behaviour of prices in New Spain itself.

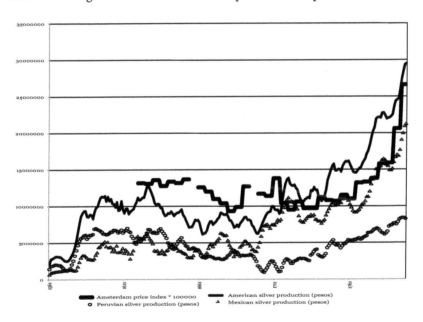

Figure 8.6: Spanish American Silver Production and Prices in Amsterdam (1561–1798) (5-year moving averages).

The commercial and monetary connections between Amsterdam and Mexico were much more intense than those between Peru and the Dutch Republic. This was due to two factors: first, the now tremendous volume of Mexican silver outputs, which clearly overshadowed the Peruvian silver outputs; and, second, the very strong Dutch presence in the Caribbean. Even if only a small fraction of Mexican silver production in fact entered Amsterdam's harbour, this small volume did not prevent the establishment of a strong correlation, with small time-lags, between registered production in faraway Durango and Guanajuato on the one hand and wholesale prices in Amsterdam on the other. One possible explanation may be that the summary accounts of silver taxed in America, which were sent to Spain, provided a basis for future estimations of prices. Copies of these summaries were published (with major errors) by European merchant gazettes, from the early seventeenth century.[38]

In the eighteenth century, these summaries became much more reliable because an increasing proportion of silver produced with mercury (quicksilver) had been presented for taxation in Mexico. Accordingly, the correlation between annual Spanish quicksilver deliveries and Amsterdam prices was high as well (R-square = 0.56, R = 0.75), even if the connection between registered Mexican silver production and Amsterdam wholesale prices was considerably higher (R-square = 0.69, R = 0.83).[39] At the beginning of the nineteenth century, Alexander von Humboldt also used the official summaries of silver production issued by the Mexican fiscal bureaucracy.[40] The monetary foundations for the operation of the Amsterdam stock exchange thus may have been determined by the official synopsis of legal (i.e. taxed) silver production in Mexico and to a lesser extent those of Peru as well; and the uses of such fiscal records were not dependent on whether the Spanish American silver was actually disembarked at Amsterdam. The direct connection between New Spain and Amsterdam is even more astonishing in view of the fact that an increasing amount of Mexican silver was exported to Asia via the Trans-Pacific trade, silver that at least in part was previously recorded in the tax registers. Moreover, the amount of silver that was smuggled varied in both absolute and relative numbers. These effects did not affect the influence of officially registered precious metals on the monetary economy of Amsterdam. Thus, although smuggling may have been crucial for the actual transfer of specie either within the Caribbean basin, or within the Atlantic and Pacific trading zones, it had no discernible impact on the price levels recorded on the Amsterdam stock exchange during the eighteenth century.

Conclusion

Comparing the monetary situations in these three different markets – New Spain (Mexico), Castile (Spain) and Amsterdam – one may conclude, first, that silver had relatively unimportant monetary functions within New Spain (Mexico) itself, during the early modern period. Second, in Castile, on the other hand, American silver served as a monetary basis during the periods of a relatively stable monetary system: during the second half of the sixteenth century, during the early seventeenth century, before the Thirty Years War (1618–48) and again during the eighteenth century. During these two periods, reliable records of silver imports or silver production in Mexico had become regularly available to the merchant community. When warfare and piracy interrupted the flow on this information on silver, various credit instruments and copper coinage (*vellón*) then provided the basis for the Castilian monetary system.

Third, in Amsterdam, the steady flow of trustworthy information from the Spanish American centres of silver production proved to be crucial as well, but again only in the eighteenth century. For such regular and reliable information was lacking at Amsterdam for much of the seventeenth century, despite the publication of various merchant gazettes that announced the arrival of American silver fleets, as these lacked precise and reliable information. Therefore, during this period, the production of Spanish American silver had no discernible effects on the money supplies available in the Amsterdam market. Subsequently, however, during the eighteenth century, the changing levels of wholesale prices on the Amsterdam stock exchange, recorded in a stable money of account (the Wisselbank's guilders of account) defined in terms of fine silver, much more clearly did depend on Mexican records of silver production. It should be stressed that the influence of the American bullion did not depend on the physical deliveries of silver but rather on the information on bullion production that was transmitted to Amsterdam. The rapidity of those information transfers also reduced the time-lag, by at least one year, between the production of the Mexican silver and its effects on Amsterdam money supplies and prices on the exchange.

In summary, we may conclude that, within Europe, Mexican silver did perform expected monetary functions both before the era of the Thirty Years War and during much of the eighteenth century (at least after the Wars of the Spanish Succession, 1701–14).

In New Spain (Mexico), however, and in striking contrast, the locally mined silver served more as an export commodity, for the European, African and Asian markets, than as a domestic medium of exchange. Indeed, the costs of producing silver in Mexico were paid for in part in cocoa beans (cacao) and in paper money, while in both Madrid and Amsterdam the production of paper and the consumption of cocoa beans had to be paid for with silver coins – with silver that had come primarily from Mexico.

9 CACAO BEANS IN COLONIAL MÉXICO: SMALL CHANGE IN A GLOBAL ECONOMY

Arturo Giraldez

Introduction

In the early nineteenth century, the German scientist Alexander von Humboldt visited New Spain, then still part of the Spanish Empire but soon to become the independent nation of Mexico. His book about the economy of Mexico contains a wealth of information about the general economy of the viceroyalty, including an extensive study of silver production with detailed observations about mining operations, production figures, taxation, coinage at the mint and global silver trade. Mexico was at the time the largest silver producer in the world and the Mexican peso was an international currency. Along with the precious-metal coinages, introduced by imperial authorities, cacao or cocoa beans facilitated exchanges of lesser values, and could thus be called 'small change', in terms of modern economies. But this form of 'small change' was of considerable antiquity, because cacao beans had been used for this purpose by the Aztecs and Mayans, long before the arrival of the Spanish conquerors. Indeed Humboldt himself observed how, in the old Aztec market of Tlatelolco, cacao beans were used as money 'like the shells in the Maldives islands' (i.e. cowrie shells). He also indicated that 72 cacao beans were currently exchanged for the smallest silver coin (*medio real*) minted in Mexico.[1]

The Imperial Monetary System

The monetary system of the Spanish Empire from the fifteenth century to the independence of the American colonies was far from being a unified set of coins under a common institutional framework. In 1497, the Catholic Monarchs, Isabella of Castile and Ferdinand of Aragon, issued a decree (*Ordenanza de Medina del Campo*) establishing the basis of the Castilian monetary system that would last for centuries. Aragon itself was divided into three kingdoms, each with a somewhat different monetary system. Because Spain was located in the Venetian ducat area Ferdinand minted a similar gold coin in Valencia in 1481 under the name of *excellent*. In Catalonia a similar gold piece, the *principat* appeared in 1493 and in 1497 the *excelente* of Granada or ducat was issued for the kingdom of Castile. By 1500 these three main gold coins of the Spanish realm had the same value. In 1537, Charles I (who was also the Emperor Charles V) ceased minting the gold ducat and, in its place, he substituted the *escudo,* of lower fineness, to maintain parity with similar European gold coins.

In addition to these gold coins, the Catholic Kings minted the silver rial (*real*) and their multiples. Of particular importance was the 8 rial coin, the famous peso or piece of eight. As J. Regla has rightly commented, the peso had become, by the reign of Philip II (1556–98), 'the Spanish coin par excellence'.[2] Silver and gold coins of different denominations were related by two moneys of account: the *maravedí,* and the ducat with a value of 375 *maravedís*. In the kingdom of Aragon the Castilian *maravedí* was the equivalent of the Catalonian *diner* (1.30 *maravedís*), the Aragonese *sou* (1.42 *maravedís*) and the Valencia *lliura* (1.65 *maravedís*).

Of particular economic and political importance, as we shall see, was the *vellón,* which the Catholic Monarchs first issued as a largely copper coin, though it still contained 2.43 per cent silver.[3] In 1599, Philip III (1598–1621) authorized a new *vellón* coinage of pure copper (debased again, by half, in 1602); and from that date Spain's 'small change' was in the form of this copper coinage.[4]

Compared with the Iberian peninsula, the Spanish American territories lacked a unified monetary system. The history of the diverse coins and moneys of account used in the New World is beyond the scope of this chapter, so that a brief summary will suffice to indicate the extent of that monetary diversity. The use of coins in the American lands was prevalent only along the more important trade routes and in large cities. In areas distant from the mining fields, local products became the effective means of exchange with which to pay tribute and to make like payments: such as the *hierba mate* in Paraguay, bundles of tobacco leaves, or pieces of cotton cloth. Precious metals were also employed as means of exchange, by weight, in the Spanish colonial mining regions and areas engaged in substantial trade. Commercial transactions were also transacted by various means of credit; and, when the time came to smelt the precious metals, debts were often settled by paying any differences with silver bars, gold ingots and nuggets.[5] Silver wedges – *piñas* in Spanish documents – were also used in international trade along with silver bars or coins. In 1637, Thomas Gage, an English traveller in Portobello, before returning to London from Chiapas, observed that merchants bought commodities 'not paying in coined pieces of money, but in wedges of silver and nothing else'.[6]

Gold coinage was represented by the *peso de oro* (also called *castellano* and *peso de minas*): a gold coin gold of 22.5 carats fineness, weighing 4.6 g, which circulated from about 1525. The *peso de tepuzque* of much lower fineness appeared

in Mexico about 1536. Not until 1675 did the crown permit any gold minting. Nevertheless, gold coins did circulate, though not as legal tender, in certain
American regions during the seventeenth century. In Mexico, shortly after 1675,
and in Lima, by the end of the century, gold coins were being issued by the local
mints. In the viceroyalties, in addition to the ducat and *maravedí*, other units
of account were used, such as the *tomín de oro* or units under the names of *peso
común, peso de chafalonia, peso de plata ensayada*, though only for shorter periods
of time.[7] During the sixteenth century, gold coins were predominant in Nueva
Granada (modern-day Colombia). The seventeenth century marked a transition
to silver coins, but not until the eighteenth century did the peso or 'piece of eight'
enjoy a wide circulation.[8] A rather different monetary structure prevailed in the
Canary Islands, a commercially important archipelago, close to Spain itself, that
served as a necessary way station for Spanish fleets carrying the precious metals
from the American viceroyalties to Seville. There only silver coins circulated.[9]

The seeming diversity of monetary regimes in Spanish America masked a *de
facto* basic monetary uniformity: one provided by the peso of 8 rials, a coin with
25.56 g of almost pure silver. During the seventeenth century, the peso was produced in the Americas by using a hammer to stamp fragments of silver with the
royal shield. Each coin had different shape, size and weight, so that only the most
defective ones were resmelted. In cases of excessive weight, a fragment was cut
from the coin and circulated in that irregular shape. Circular pieces with clear
symbols and legends appeared only after the introduction of a new minting technology in the eighteenth century. Previously, coin manufacturing was therefore
highly deficient, but the sheer volume of these pesos or 'pieces of eight' made
them globally acceptable. Antonio-Miguel Bernal observed that the Spanish
crown 'created for the era the most efficient and complex framework concerning
monetary policy known until then ... and that Spain was, for almost three unin-
terrupted centuries, the minting house of the world'.[10] If we include the Spanish
Empire, then Bernal certainly is right on both counts.

Cacao and the Monetary System in Mesoamerica Before the Conquest

The name Mesoamerica designates the geographical area occupied today by
Mexico, Guatemala and parts of Honduras, Nicaragua and El Salvador. The word
cacao, originally pronounced *kakawa*, has a Mesoamerican origin. It was from
the Mayas that the Spanish conquerors obtained their knowledge of cacao.[11]

According to Bletter and Daly, the universal search for both stimulants and
sweet substances explains the conversion of cacao seeds into a food, because
the chemical components in cacao are not only neuroactives and antioxidants
but also stimulants. They also note that there is a 'glaring' lack of stimulating
substances in Mesoamerica, 'given that this area has one of the highest concentra-

tions of non stimulant psychoactive plant uses in the world';[12] and they further observe that 'the combination of sugar and fats in chocolate stimulates the brain's release of natural opiates'.[13] Discussing the chemical properties of cacao, Sophie and Michael Coe state that the alkaloids present in chocolate 'have physiological consequences on the animals that ingest them', and that 'human animals pursue at least some of them with passion', in explaining why this plant was domesticated in the New World and was promoted 'to a position near the center of the Aztec state ideology, and then, continued with the conquest of Spain and other European countries by cacao'. Their observation is accurate but we should note that cacao also crossed the Pacific to reach the Philippines, where Spanish colonizers and Muslim potentates of the southern sultanates drank chocolate.[14]

Remains of spouted vessels with cacao residue that have been recovered in archaeological excavations indicate that its consumption as a beverage began in the Maya lowlands. Such vessels were in use between 1000 BC and AD 250. During these same centuries, states, hierarchical societies and urban centres emerged in these areas, with local markets and long-distance trade. Such social processes required a uniform unit of exchange, a need that cacao beans readily fulfilled. Thus Aztec, Mayan, and other peoples used cacao beans for commercial transactions, so that cacao beans became a widely used form of money in Mesoamerica, from Central Mexico to Yucatan, south of the region of modern-day Nicaragua, by the time of the Spanish conquest.[15]

Cacao (*Theobroma cacao*) was not grown everywhere in Mesoamerica. The plant requires a large amount of labour and considerable agricultural knowledge. A small broad-leafed under-story tree, it needs shade and minimal fluctuation in climate; under those conditions, the young trees become productive by the third or fourth years. It grows usually between 20 degrees north and 20 degrees south of the Equator and requires a temperature warmer than 16 degrees Celsius and year-round moisture because the flowers are pollinated by a midge which requires a humid environment. The most important place for its production is the Chontalpa, a territory on eastern Tabasco, 'the homeland of the Chontal Maya, also known as the Putún' whose cacao plantations allowed them to engage in long-distance trade, particularly in a coastal circuit around the Yucatan Peninsula that extended its reach to the Gulf of Honduras.[16]

According to R. F. Millon, 'The almost universal demand for cacao in ancient Mesoamerica played a major role in the development of trade in aboriginal times.' Indeed the essential goal in the military strategy of the Aztec Empire was to acquire cacao. According to Diego Duran, in *The History of the Indies of New Spain* (1588), Emperor Ahuitzotl (1486–1502) extended the Aztec territory to encompass the central region of Mexico, large areas of the states of Guerrero, Veracruz, Puebla, Oaxaca and some portions of Chiapas, reaching the border with Guatemala.[17] When the inhabitants of Telooapan (modern-day Guerrero) were accused of fomenting rebellion, they were subjected to an 'excessive trib-ute'. Every 80 days, some 400 loads of cacao (10 tons) were to be paid, because, the Emperor 'was extremely fond of the cacao, cotton, and all kinds of fruit from orchards that existed in that region'.[18] After the regions of Alauiztlan and Oztoman were destroyed, and 'all their fruit, cacao, and cotton plantations were deserted, their fields made barren', colonists were sent there with the admonition that the ambassadors and envoys from Tenochtitlan 'were to be treated especially well when they went to collect the cacao harvest that was to be set aside for the royal crown of Mexico'. The cacao was to be sown collectively, each group con-tributing whatever labour it could, according to the number of its people. The cacao was to be sent to the capital city in lieu of tribute.[19]

In 1499 Ahuitzotl added the province of Xoconochco, located 965 km from Tenochtitlan, on the border with Guatemala. To avoid the fate of other conquered places, according to Duran, 'the people of Xoconochco however surrendered and offered allegiance to Mexico-Tenochtitlan before the Aztecs could carry out all this destruction, all this disaster that had been their plan'.[20] 'Instigated and abet-ted by the *pochteca,* the long-distance merchants', the Aztec war machine had extended the empire to its furthest frontier, and 'ensured a steady flow of premium cacao and other elite goods into the imperial storehouses'.[21] The tribute levied was 200 loads of cacao (5 tons) every six months.[22] The load (*carga* in Spanish) had three indigenous units called *Xiquipilli* of 8,000 cacao beans, totalling 24,000 cacao beans per load. The cacao of Xoconochco was highly appreciated by the Aztec emperors and also by their successors the Spanish kings. Ulloa noted that 'it was the responsibility of the Viceroys to send bags of this cacao for the use of his Majesty and of the Royal Persons and to send it as a present to other places, particularly to the Princes of the Royal Family living outside Spain.'[23]

This policy of territorial expansion allowed the Aztecs to control important areas of cacao production in Tabasco, northern Oaxaca, Veracruz, southern Chiapas, Guatemala and Honduras in addition to some areas of Nicaragua and El Salvador. There was also the area of Xoconochco – Soconusco in the Spanish documents – and Cihuatlan in the state of Guerrero. In fact, three of the major cacao-producing areas were under the control of Tenochtitlan.[24] Another large production region was under the independent Maya to the east of the Empire whom the Aztecs never tried to rule.

The *pochteca,* the aforementioned long-distance traders, played a crucial role in the Aztec economy. They followed two main trade routes: one leading to the Xicalanco in the coast of Mexico to acquire the cacao from Chontalpa and products from Yucatan, Honduras and the Caribbean Islands; and the other one reaching the coast of the Pacific in Chiapas to acquire quetzal feathers, jade, precious metals and cacao from Soconusco.[25] In addition to engaging in long-distance trade, merchants of Tenochtitlan also operated a large, well-regulated urban market with abundant goods. One companion of Cortes, Bernal Díaz del Castillo wrote in his famous treatise that: 'when we arrived at the great market place, called Tlatelolco, we were astounded at the number of people and the quantity of merchandise that it contained, and the good order and control that was maintained, for we had never seen such a thing before'.[26] There were numerous similar markets in the Aztec Empire. The monetary units employed in its economic transactions were then quite diverse. The diligent Jesuit historian Francesco Saverio Clavigero, in his *History of Mexico*, mentioned five kinds of 'real money' used by the Aztecs: cacao beans, small cotton cloth, *patolcuahtli*, gold dust contained in goose-quills, pieces of copper shaped in a T form and small fragments of tin.[27]

The *Pocthecayotl* (the art of trading), a document translated from the Nahuatl by Angel María Garibay, and the *Florentine Codex* of Bernardino de Sahagún, provide the prices of three different kinds of 'small cloths of cotton' equal to the price of 185 and 65 cacao beans.[28] In addition to the different moneys used among the Aztecs in the Yucatan Peninsula, sixteenth-century documents indicate that native people also used red beads.[29]

Accounting systems among the Mayans and Aztecs were similar, both being related to cacao. Diego de Landa, a sixteenth-century bishop of Yucatan, wrote about the Mayan numerical system, using Roman numerals: 'The count is from V to V until XX and from XX to XX until C. and from C. until CCCC and from CCCC to CCCC until VIII thousand and they use this way of accounting for the cacao trade.'[30] The Aztec numerical system was vigesimal and they 'used a flag to indicate twenty, repeating it for quantities up to four hundred, while a sign like a fir tree, meaning numerous as hairs, signified four hundred (20 × 20); the next unit, eight thousand (20 × 20 × 20), was indicated by a bag, referring to the almost innumerable contents of a sack of beans'.[31] Toribio de Motolinia, one of the first Franciscan friars in Mexico and a famous chronicler, recorded the units of the cacao trade. In his *History of the Indians of New Spain,* he observed that cacao 'is commonly used in place of money and is current in all the land. A *carga* of it has three numbers and each number, called *xiquipilli* by the Indians, amounts to 8,000. A *carga* contains 24,000 grains of cacao-beans.'[32] A *carga* – the amount one man could carry with a tumpline – weighed about 50 lb.[33] Such an important currency and commodity could not escape human skulduggery. Indigenous informants of Sahagún reported elaborated procedures to deceive cacao buyers:

> The bad cacao seller, [the bad] cacao dealer, the deluder counterfeits cacao. He sells cacao beans which are placed in [hot] ashes, toasted, made full in the fire; he counterfeits by making fresh cacao beans whitish; he places them in [hot] ashes – stirs them into [hot] ashes; then he treats them with chalk, with chalky earth, with [wet] hearth; he stirs them into [wet] earth. [With] amaranth dough, wax, avocado pits [broken into pieces which are then shaped like cacao beans] he counterfeits cacao; he covers this

over with cacao bean hulls; he places this in the cacao bean shells. The whitish, the fresh cacao beans he intermixes, mingles, throws in, introduces, ruins with the shrunken, the chilli-seed-like, the broken, the hollow, the tiny. Indeed he casts, he throws in with them wild cacao [*Theobroma bicolor*] beans to deceive the people.[34]

In Nicaragua, a sixteenth-century historian, Gonzalo Fernández de Oviedo, explained the particular procedure used to distinguish counterfeited cacao beans.

> Even with those almonds there exist fraudulent practices such as including a portion of hollow almond shells which have been filled with dirt or some other substance and cleverly sealed so as to appear whole. To avoid this fraud, it is a common practice, upon counting the almonds, to hold each one between the thumb and index finger so that the touch can detect those which feel different and are noted to be inferior to the good almonds.[35]

Chocolate and Cacao after the Conquest

The first encounter between Europeans and cacao occurred on 15 August 1502 when Christopher Columbus ordered the capture of a large Mayan trading canoe. The account came from his second son Ferdinand. In addition to cotton garments, war clubs, bells and small axes made out of copper, they carried 'many of these almonds which in New Spain are used for money'.[36] Although Columbus's sailors were the first to see cacao beans, Juan de Grijalva's men were the first to drink chocolate. They reached San Juan de Ulua, an island facing Veracruz in Mexico in 1518. It was there that the Aztecs first encountered the Spaniards and an exchange of food and drinks from the Old and New Worlds took place with some intoxicating consequences. Two Aztecs, Teuctlammacazqui and Cuitlalpitoc, sent by Moctezuma to investigate the truth of alarming sights on the coast, were invited on board the Spanish ship. They brought their food to offer to the newcomers. This was the first gastronomical Columbian exchange in history, a portent of events and processes of fundamental consequences. According to the chronicle of Diego Duran:[37]

> The two men tasted the different foods and when the Spaniards saw them eating they too began to eat turkey, stews, and maize cakes and enjoy the food with much laughing and sporting. But when the time came to drink the chocolate that had been brought to them, that most highly prized beverage of the Indians, they were filled with fear. When the Aztecs saw that they dare not drink, they tasted from all the gourds and the Spaniards then quenched their thirst with chocolate and realized what a refreshing drink it was.

On 21 April 1519 Hernán Cortés arrived at the same place. As soon as Moctezuma received news about the arrival of the expedition, he sent large quantities of provisions 'and cacao that had been ground to make a beverage'.[38] Soon the Spaniards 'found out that the beans could be used to buy things, and to pay the wages of their native labourers, such as the all-important porters'.[39] Consequently, before Cortés destroyed the capital of the Aztecs, he requested land from Moctezuma to establish a plantation in what is now the state of Oaxaca.

The new arrivals soon became acutely aware of the dual uses of cacao and all of the requirements to grow it successfully. The *Anonymous Conqueror*, an unknown soldier who accompanied Cortés in the conquest of the Aztec capital, published a narrative in Italian with details about New Spain including the uses of cacao:

> They make various classes of wine, but the beverage which is the most excellent and which they use principally is one which they call *Cachanatle* [chocolate]. ... These trees are held in great esteem because the said grains are the principal money that passes in the land and each one is the value of half a marchetto of our money. Inconvenient as this money must be, it comes after gold and silver and is the one most used by everyone in this land.

Another important observer was Peter Martyr D' Anghera (or Pedro Martir de Anglería), an Italian humanist, who was the first to apply the name New World to America, and the author of the famous *De Orbe Novo: The Eight Decades of Peter Martyr D' Anghera*. In the *Fifth Decade*, dedicated to Pope Adrian VI (r. 1522–3), he wrote that 'I am well aware that people of feeble imagination will accuse me of being fantastic when I speak of trees bearing money. These trees are planted in but few situations, for they require a climate both warm and damp, and a relatively fertile soil'; and he further comments: 'O blessed money, which not only gives to the human race a useful drink, but also prevents its possessors from yielding to infernal avarice, for it cannot be piled up, or hoarded for a long time.'[40] He clearly wished to convey this information to his European readers, because similar details appear in one of his letters written on 7 March 1521.[41]

As early as 1538, at a banquet to celebrate a peace treaty between Charles V and Francis I of France, Spanish ladies were served chocolate.[42] Motolinia, one of the first to write about life in Mexico, commented about the presents to the friars who baptized the natives: 'They offered many roses and flowers and sometimes also chocolate, which is a favourite beverage in this land, especially in hot weather.'[43] In 1590 the Jesuit Jose de Acosta in his *Natural and Moral History* wrote that: 'Both Indians and Spaniards, and especially Spanish women who have grown accustomed to the land, adore their black chocolate.'[44] Alonso de Zorita, a judge (*oidor*) in the Audiencia of Mexico in the sixteenth century, calculated that from Guatemala came 30,000 loads (*cargas*) of cacao, and more than 40,000 came from Soconusco and the Pacific coast. He observed that in Mexico City and New Spain 'there is a large trade [of cacao] and that is the livelihood of many Indians and Spaniards'.[45] A good example was the region of Izalcos currently located in El Salvador, which soon became popular with merchants, royal officials and priests, leading him to comment that: 'The dynamic cacao industry based in the Izalcos towns soon led to the establishment, in 1553, of the Spanish merchant-town of La Trinidad de Sonsonate, which became a magnet, drawing outsiders to the region.' Population losses changed the cacao commercial map over the centuries. During the first decades after the conquest, cacao arrived from Soconusco, Colima and southern Mexico. Major population decline during the 1540s shifted the importation sites to Guatemala and El Salvador. Three major waves of epidemic disease from 1552 to 1577 affected the aforementioned areas and cacao plantations soon collapsed.[46]

In the early seventeenth century, the main areas exporting cacao to Mexico were in Venezuela (Caracas and Maracaibo), Guayaquil in Ecuador and Cartagena de Indies (Colombia).[47] So important were cacao exports from Venezuela that, by 1640, it was incorporated into Mexico's economic orbit.[48] During the eighteenth century, Mexico, being unable to cultivate much cacao, had to import from abroad most of the quantities consumed. The beans arrived from the same places as in the previous century; but the disposition of 1777 permitted much larger imports from Guayaquil into Acapulco than in previous years. The legendary Soconusco cacao was, however, too expensive for Mexico, so that most was exported to Spain.[49] .

Alexander von Humboldt attributed the quality of Mexican chocolate to its geographical origins, 'because the trade from Veracruz and Acapulco bring to New Spain the famous cacao from Soconusco (Xoconochco) in the Guatemala coast; the one from Gualan in the gulf of Honduras and the one from Uritucu near San Sebastian in the provinces of Caracas; the one from Capiriqual in the Nueva Barcelona and the one from Esmeralda in the kingdom of Quito'.[50] For centuries the places providing the Mexican market evidently remained substantially the same, though with some additional changes.

In the middle of the seventeenth century, Thomas Gage observed in his chronicle 'Chocolate being this day used not only over all the West Indias, but also in Spain, Italy, and Flanders, with approbation of many learned doctors in physic'.[51] Notwithstanding this strong endorsement from eminent 'doctors in physic', the product was not in fact uniformly appreciated. For Gage also observes that when Dutch or English pirates seeking silver or gold encountered 'a ship laden with cacao, in anger and wrath' not only did they throw all the cacao overboard but added insult to injury by called it 'in bad Spanish *cagarruta de carnero* or sheep dung in good English. It is one of the necessariest commodities in the Indias, and nothing enricheth Chiapa in particular more than it, whither are brought from Mexico and other parts the rich bags of patacones only for this *cagarruta de carnero*'. Priests received among other items cacao beans for administering the sacraments. Gage remarked that a friar received as offering for All Souls' Day, 'four zontles of cacao, every zontle being four hundred beans, among other items.'[52] With such presents, Gage himself accumulated 'near nine thousand pieces of eight', during the twelve years that he lived in Guatemala as a Dominican priest. The Indians used to leave cacao beans as offerings in front of a sixteenth-century image called the 'Christ of the Cacao' located in the cathedral of Mexico City. But Gage commented that 'the true beneficiaries of these offerings would have been the priests at the cathedral'.[53]

Money in Colonial Mexico

The Nahuas adopted the Spanish currency system without any particular effort because their society had long participated in both local and long-distance trade employing a variety of different currencies. According to James Lockhart, 'the word *tomín*, signifying a coin, gold weight, and standard of value equal to the *real* of eight or the peso, is one of the first attested Spanish loanwords in Nahuatl, and "peso" itself was not far behind (1548). Both, as well as *medio*, half a tomín or *real*, were an indispensable part of the Nahuatl vocabulary from the mid-sixteenth century forward.'[54] Large transactions required rials and pesos, but cacao beans were employed for smaller transactions. Prices were given in beans, as attested in the well-known *List of market prices established by judge Tlaxcala, 1545*, a document translated from the Nahuatl. The first item establishes the equivalence between 1 rial of silver (tomín) and cacao beans respectively to quality. It follows some of the list's prices.[55]

> -One tomín is worth 200 full cacao beans, or 120 shrunken cacao beans.
> -One good turkey hen is worth 100 full cacao beans, or 120 shrunken cacao beans.
> -A turkey cock is worth 200 cacao beans.
> -A grown Castilian hen is worth 40 cacao beans.
> -A rooster is worth 20 cacao beans.
> -A young chicken is worth 15 cacao beans.
> -A hare or forest rabbit is worth 100 cacao beans each.
> -A small rabbit is worth 30.

By his testament of 1566, Julián de la Rosa bequeathed to his wife the rents of his fields, which included among other items 200 cacao beans to be given at Christmas and Easter and Corpus Christi and the Assumption of Mary, and on St Peter's day.[56] In Nicaragua during the same century, Fernandez de Oviedo presented the following prices in cacao beans: a rabbit was worth 10 beans; a piece of fruit called *munoncapot* 4 beans; a slave could have been bought for 100, depending upon the price, and the *guatepol* – that is 'women who sold their bodies' – asked 8 or 10 almonds.[57] According to J. Lockhart, a new monetary system soon emerged that amalgamated the coinages of the Aztec and the Spanish colonizers, 'for the two became integrated. The tomín/*real* and its multiple the peso quickly replaced the quachtli for larger transactions, but for items worth under a tomín or half a tomín, cacao beans continued in use'. The tribute imposed on native populations required the adoption of the imperial monetary system.[58]

The later sixteenth century witnessed a significant conversion of tributary and tax payments to the Spanish rulers. By 1570, the Spanish crown had eliminated the large *encomiendas* in the Valley of Mexico, converting the diverse commodity contributions into payments in money and maize. Widows and widowers, bachelors, and independent unmarried women paid half-tribute and old people, children, the blind and crippled, and unmarried people living with their parents were exempted from any payment. Royal regulations determined the quantities reserved for the Spanish authorities and for the town government. In the seventeenth century a tributary paid the following: 8 rials and one-half *fanega* of maize, another rial for 'Fabrica and Ministros', and 4 rials of Service. He also contributed to his community's treasury according to his land, paid the sales taxes (*alcabala*), legal or illegal fees and special local taxes. This tributary also was expected to provide occasional work for local authorities and in certain towns he received payments for the mandatory labour called *servicios*. For most of the seventeenth and eighteenth centuries, royal tributes in maize were commutable at the rate of 9 rials per *fanega*. In the mid-eighteenth century 'a normal total payment per tributary' was 17½ rials per year.[59] Outside the central area of New Spain, cacao was paid as tribute in places of cacao production.

The following cases are only a small sample of exceptions to royal regulations. Reports to the crown about the Yucatan region, called *Relaciones*, show a quite diverse range of tribute products. For instance, the *Relación de Cotuta y Tibolon* of 1579 indicated that 'the tributes paid by the naturals are cotton blankets and chicken and maize and wax and honey and frijoles and other things'.[60] In the Province of Tabasco, in the same year, the *encomendero* Melchor Alfaro wrote that the natives 'pay their tributes in cacao'.[61] In 1660, the tributaries of Tabasco paid about 1,644 *xiquipiles* to the *encomenderos* (1 *xiquipil* was equivalent to 8,000 cacao beans). As one exception, the village of Xicalango, subjected to the direct administration of the crown, paid only '44 pesos de minas in rials' without any other contributions.[62] In its *Relacion,* the City of Valladolid reported that natives paid the tribute in cotton cloth, maize, chicken and wax.[63] In El Salvador, according to Fowler, 'thirteen of the fifteen towns of the Izalcos region paid tribute in cacao. ... Both Izalco and Caluco paid 1,000 *xiquipiles* (about 18,000 lb.), Naolingo paid 685 *xiquipiles* (about 12,330 lb.), and Tacuscalco paid 400 *xiquipiles* (about 7,200 lb.) in cacao tribute each year'.[64] According to Gasco, the famous region of Soconusco in 1548 gave 200 *cargas* of cacao, the same amount that the Aztecs received, and for the next 200 years, 'the indigenous residents of

Soconusco paid cacao as part of their annual tribute assessment, although the amounts changed from year to year'.[65]

Ilarione da Bergamo, an Italian friar in Mexico from 1761 to 1768, collecting alms for the Franciscan mission to Tibet, was a careful observer of everyday life who left us important information about monetary matters in New Spain, in his treatise on *Miscellaneous Topics and Disasters*, as did Gemelli Carreri, another Italian traveler. According to the latter, the Mexican mint coined 16,000 pesos each day; but Da Bergamo thought that figure to be 'somewhat exaggerated'. Da Bergamo also observed that manufacturing coins by hammering chunks of silver had been superseded by a new minting technology, so that 'at the present time they no longer produce those poorly minted pieces'. He described the different types of silver coins that were minted in addition to the pesos of 8 rials: 'they coin half, quarter, eight, and half-eighth pesos, which are the only coins used in the realm, all of the very finest silver. ... The lowest coinage of those lands is the half-real, or half of an eight of a peso'. To all of these details he adds important observations about problems with small change, and the solutions implemented:

> Because they cannot divide it up [the half-real] and there are no copper coins, they have devised the method of further dividing this into four parts, using certain small pieces of round wood, like counters in the game of backgammon – pieces they call *clacos* [i.e. *tlacos*]. In every store they have a number of these *clacos*, all of them with the store's special mark. Whenever a customer goes to a store like this with his own *clacos*, the storekeeper is obliged to accept them. They have, as well, another method of dividing the real or the half-real – with cacao beans, sixty and even eighty of which they offer for a real. But this number increases and diminishes depending on whether there is a greater or lesser abundance of cacao in the city, and consequently its price remains relatively high. With these beans they can make purchases in any store and in the plazas, where everyone accepts them in exchange for coins, but always at a rate more favorable to the seller.[66]

Manuel Romero de Terreros, a Mexican numismatist, wrote that this private money was also made of copper, crystal, leather and, in some cases, soap and pieces of wood. The *tlacos* carried the names of the shop and the owner of it. The word *tlaco* derived from the Aztec language *tlahco*, which means half.[67]

The problem of equivalences of cacao beans with the silver *real* or rial depended on the prices of both commodities. Motolinia had already perceived two of the factors affecting the price of cacao: distance from the production area and size of the crop. For, 'where it is gathered a *carga* is worth five or six *pesos de oro*; when it is carried inland, the value increases, rising and falling according to the year's crop, because in a good year it multiplies greatly. Heavy frosts cause the yield to be small, the plant being very tender'.[68] Charles Gibson provided equivalencies between 1 rial of silver and cacao beans, in noting that 'the ratios of cacao beans to reales declined from 200 to 1 and 180 to 1 in the middle sixteenth century to 150 to 1, 100 to 1, and 80 to 1 in the late sixteenth century. Rates of 140 to 1, 120 to 1, 80 to 1, 60 to 1, and 50 to 1 were reported in the seventeenth century and 80 to 1 at the end of the colonial period.'[69] In addition to these data, there is some spotty information derived from various sources concerning exchanges between cacao beans and European currencies. Thus, as early as the sixteenth century, the Italian *Anonymous Conqueror* wrote that a cocoa bean was 'the value of half a *marchetto* of our money' and Gemelli Carreri in the last years of the seventeenth century, compared 1. 5 *carlino* of Naples to sixty or eighty cacao beans, depending upon whether 'the price of cacao is high or low'.[70]

Mexico, like the other Spanish colonies in the Americas, had no copper coinage. Acosta asserts that 'although it is true that in some islands in the Indies, such as Santo Domingo and Puerto Rico, they use copper money, the coins have value only in those islands, for there is little silver there and, although much gold exists, there is no one to refine it'.[71] Minting such copper coins in mid-sixteenth-century Mexico produced such a hostile public reaction that indigenous 'Indians' refused to accept it; and, in response, they were fined and submitted to corporal punishment, but without any positive results. Thus, in 1565, the copper coinage was discontinued. Subsequently, two centuries later, on 24 October 1767, Charles III, in prohibiting the *tlacos*, ordered the viceroy of New Spain to consult the colonial authorities 'as to the desirability of coining [copper] *vellón* for New Spain'. In response, the Consulado (the merchant guild), insisted 'that the coinage of vellon in New Spain would injure the king, the businessmen, the general public, the Indians, and the poor whites'. As a consequence, no *vellón* coinage was introduced.[72]

In Santa Fe (Colombia), the merchants and all social sectors similarly rejected the circulation of *vellon rico*, an alloy of copper and silver with a predominance of the precious metal, as soon minting commenced on 20 June 1622. The only place in which copper circulated was the small island of La Española, during the second half of the sixteenth century. In the words of Fernando Serrano-Mangas, 'it caused tremendous turmoil and it was the direct precedent of the seventeenth century peninsular perturbations'.[73]

In Spain itself, in seeking to obtain indispensable financial resources, the crown resorted to collecting copper coins and then reissuing them at a higher nominal value – a form of debasement; and doing so immediately produced a premium on silver and thus raised prices. An extensive inflation ensued in the years 1634 to 1656. The first part of this period encompassed the government of Philip IV's favourite, the count-duke of Olivares, renowned for his aggressive foreign policies. Deflationary measures finally brought about the fall of Olivares, in 1643; but in 1651 Philip IV, seeking to finance his wars, again resorted to inflationary measures, which had to be corrected the next year, in 1652. The period from 1656 to 1658 was 'a monetary catastrophe'. After the peace with

France in 1659 (Treaty of the Pyrenees), deflationary measures were implemented (in 1664), but again without success. From 1665 to 1680 inflation as measured in the debased copper coinage reached an astonishing level, in that the premium on silver reached 275 per cent. In response, the crown imposed a drastic deflation in 1680, one that led to a fall in prices of about 45 per cent.[74] Elena García Guerra has enumerated the years of inflationary coinage measures: in 1603, 1636, 1641, 1651, 1654 and 1661. In contrast, deflationary measures were undertaken in 1628, 1642, 1652, 1658–9, 1664 and 1680.[75] As was so often the case in both Spain and early-modern Europe, foreign policies and consequent warfare provided the essential causes for almost all these monetary manipulations, economic upheavals and concurrent misery. Serrano Mangas summarized well the monetary and financial history of seventeenth-century Spain: 'Without Castile would never have been able to prolong its death throes ... the *vellón* which, in reality, was the credit provided to their king by the poorest and most helpless strata of society.'[76]

The American colonies contributed heavily in taxes and other exactions to the military machine of the Spanish Empire. The financial activities of the Viceroy Don Lope Diez de Armendáriz, Marques de Cadereita, demonstrate the importance of cacao in New Spain's economy, in the years 1635–50, when he was required to raise 'funds in the order of 500,000 pesos per annum' to build and maintain a fleet. The quarrels and misfortunes of the previous years had created discontent among the Creoles – descendants of Spaniards born in Mexico. To avoid further conflict and to ingratiate himself with the merchants and other financial powers, the viceroy appointed a committee of viceregal authorities to consider their demands. Among the many requests, one of them 'asked that a cacao exchange be established in Mexico City in order to stabilize the market and reduce the scope for racketeering in that basic commodity'.[77] Cacao was almost always uppermost in the minds and interests of the Mexican elites.

The American subjects of the Spanish Empire were willing to contribute to the common enterprise, but wanted to retain as much control as possible over the monetary system so as to avoid the outrageous economic distortions that the crown's *vellón* manipulations had produced in Spain itself. While they did have a seeming abundance of silver and gold, most of those precious metals were continually being exported. Confirming other views expressed in this volume, Céspedes del Castillo, a noted historian of colonial America, has contended that 'there was a chronic scarcity of coins in the markets of the Indies because it was constantly drained; when the fleets leave Portobelo or Veracruz, it is more difficult to find coins in Mexico or Lima than to find the proverbial needle in a haystack'.[78] Fortunately for the colonists in New Spain, that dire shortage of 'small change' was usually remedied by supplies of cacao beans, through various local arrangements made with indigenous institutions.

Just as the prices for silver and gold were determined by global demand, so too were the prices of cacao beans. The aim of producers of and merchants trading in both silver and cacao beans was to make the largest possible profit from selling them. That explains their frequent use of credit and 'fictional currency', instead of resorting to such valuable merchandises as silver and cacao.

The monetary systems of Spanish America were not, however, immune to royal intervention. For example, while the Spanish kings attempted to maintain the purity and stability of the silver coinages in the sixteenth and early seventeenth century, their ministers were less likely to respect these 'strong money' policies. Thus, for example, the reign of Philip III (r. 1599–1621), his minister Tomás de Cardona recommended a devaluation of silver coinage by 25 per cent in the Empire. But strong, deeply entrenched opposition thwarted such debasement plans, because a strong silver coinage was considered to be 'the sinew of commerce'.[79]

The crown was equally rigorous in maintaining the purity of the peso in the colonies. A particular problem arose in the middle of the seventeenth century when counterfeiting in Potosi grew to such alarming proportions that the fraudulent pieces of eight were rejected globally. The monarchy punished the culprits without mercy. In the eighteenth century changes in the quality of the silver coin were again met with swift reaction. Richard von Glahn has noted how sensitive the Chinese market, and by extension, global markets, were to any changes in the silver peso. Thus, in 1772, when new pesos of eight rials were coined with a slightly reduced fineness – of 90.2 per cent rather than the standard 91.6 percent – Chinese merchants rejected the new peso and after long negotiations it was accepted at a discount.[80]

Such was the reputation of the Spanish imperial coins, that 'long after merchants had adopted the Mexican republic dollar as their official monetary standard (1853 in Hong Kong, and 1857 in Shanghai), the Carolus dollar and its Chinese imitations continued to prevail in retail trade, down to the early years of the twentieth century'.[81]

Kuroda Akinobu has also observed that 'complementarity (non integral) among monies in history reveals that some assortments of monies with moving exchange rates could offer flexibilities to make supply meet demand in actual markets'. During the colonial centuries, the integration of the Spanish with the indigenous monetary systems proved highly efficient for three centuries, especially in adopting new monetary devices (the case of *tlacos*) to meet local and global market needs. The observation of Kuroda proves to be correct in the Mexican colonial case.[82]

10 PRECIOUS METALS, DEBASEMENTS AND COWRIE SHELLS IN THE MEDIEVAL INDIAN MONETARY SYSTEMS, *c.* 1200–1575

John S. Deyell

How did a pre-modern government sustained largely by agricultural revenue maintain a viable monetary system when it lacked indigenous sources of precious metal? Importation was key, but supply constraints induced different responses. This chapter examines the early medieval Indian context, where both debasement and coinage substitutes were attempted. A case study is examined: the coastal Bengal sultanate, which maintained for almost four centuries a monetary system based on imports of silver and cowrie shells. This system is contrasted with the monetary situation in the inland Delhi sultanate, which progressively lost its capacity to sustain precious metal coinage, coincident with its loss of sovereignty over coastal connections.

India's Monetary Context

To summarize several millennia of monetary history for a place as populous and diverse as India is manifestly impossible. Yet there is still considerable value in providing a 'gloss' of these pre-modern Indian monetary issues in order to compare the Indian experience with pre-modern European monetary history. As in pre-modern Europe, the monetary systems of the various Indian economies were dependent on the highly variable availability of precious metals for coinage. For most of the pre-modern era, however, western European countries differed in experiencing a loss of coinage metals through export beyond their continent. Indeed, for much of this era, European commentators have commonly identified India as the ultimate destination for European precious metals, through the nexus of international trade with intervening regions (such as the Levant).[1] Within India, however, there is no such overall concern with a slow drainage of metals elsewhere. Rather, the ever-present promise of imported metals (to the extent that a polity was linked into external trade routes) is a constant refrain in Indian monetary history.[2]

Situated in a distinct geological province of great antiquity, the Indian subcontinent has been blessed with significant sources of gold mineralization (narrowly distributed in veins in the south and alluvially in the north-east), but only modest sources of silver (mostly as a minor component of lead/zinc ores in Rajasthan) and plentiful copper deposits (moderately well-distributed geographically).[3] The prolific and renowned issue of a silver fiat coinage by the ancient Mauryan Empire (fourth–second centuries BC), which was probably based on indigenous silver sources, proved to be unsustainable because those sources were ultimately exhausted. In the succeeding Kushan and Gupta Empires (second to fifth centuries AD), those silver coinages were succeeded by gold issues that were probably derived from gold workings within the Kushan realm.[4] In the latter half of the first millennium, debased silver fiat coinages once again became the norm throughout northern and western India, based on new silver mines in the nearby Indo-Afghan borderlands.[5] In contrast, Bengal proper, in eastern India, had no such silver access, and thus resorted to using imported cowrie shells for all monetary purposes.

Subsequently, from the late twelfth century, the Muslim invasions and progressive conquests in northern India exposed India to the universal tripartite Islamic system of gold *dinars*, silver *dirhams* and copper *falus*. While the lessons of tri-metallism endured, the indigenous metrological standards were soon reasserted. Indeed, briefly in the fourteenth century, almost all India underwent a period of political and monetary integration under the Khalji/Tughluq sultanate of Delhi, not to be experienced again until the seventeenth-century Mughal Empire. This short-lived experiment in integration extended Delhi's tri-metallic system throughout the subcontinent. For a short period, coins of gold, silver, billon and copper were struck from mints in most geographic regions. Most historians contend that this prolific coinage was based upon the de-thesaurized treasuries of conquered and looted kingdoms, so that the ensuing monetary system was actually a product of conquest itself.[6] In the event, neither the universal conquest kingdom nor its universal monetary system survived the century's end.

Given the polyglot nature of the immigrant invading ruling classes, political unity could remain only a temporary phenomenon at best.[7] Probably the strongest disincentive against unity was the difficulty of communication and transportation over large distances. This was exacerbated by (or perhaps characterized by) the proliferation of indigenous and mutually unintelligible regional languages, which fed regional cultural identities and a preference for regional political structures. By the fifteenth century, India had once again fragmented into regional kingdoms (see Figure 10.1), each of which had a coinage system that reflected local preferences and available metal supplies. Thus, for example, peninsular Vijayanagara had a prolific gold coinage derived from the Kolar goldfields; the Bahmanid sultanate of the Deccan utilized a plentiful copper coinage based on abundant local sources and a silver coinage based on bullion imports from the west coast maritime trade; the landlocked north Indian Delhi and Jaunpur kingdoms relied almost exclusively on billon (silver alloy) or copper coins, while the coastal kingdoms of Gujarat in the west and Bengal in the east managed to sustain relatively pure silver coins. Only the west coast Gujarat sultanate and its close neighbour the Malwa sultanate, both astride major West Asian trade routes, managed – virtually alone in India – to retain the tradition of simultaneous issues of gold, silver and copper coinages.

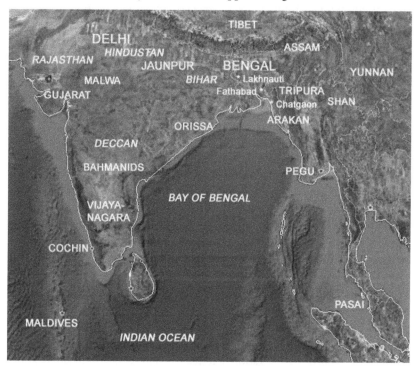

Figure 10.1: Places mentioned in the text. Overlay by the author. Base data ©2010 Google; © 2010 Tele Atlas; © 2010 Europa-Technologies; © 2010 Mapabc.com.[8]

Thus, by the early pre-modern era, India had established a pattern of regional states in which each had its own distinctive coinage. Perhaps the only significant remnant of ancient Indian traditions was the Hindu state of Vijayanagara in southern India, which relied on small (3 g) gold and copper coins. Otherwise most of India comprised Muslim sultanates, whose monetary disparity developed in spite of very strong contextual similarities. They were almost exclusively dependent on agricultural revenue supplemented by customs duties; they were ruled by foreign elites supported by immigrant military and administrative cadres; and their armies were highly dependent on the steady import of horses. The coinage systems that arose had to function efficiently to service all these needs.

Among those disparate kingdoms ruled by immigrants, a few common traditions survived, notably in the tendency to issue gold and silver coins of about 10 g weight (or its half-unit), copper coins of about 20 g, and mixed-metal coins of about 8 g.

There remained, however, a few smaller indigenous states outside this pattern, most notably in Rajasthan. These vestiges of Hindu rule tended to rely on pastoralism for their more modest state revenue, feudal relations to provide armed force, and often had no coinage to speak of. Notable exceptions were the Hindu kingdoms on Bengal's borders (Assam and Tripura) and the coastal kingdom of Arakan, all of which had functioning silver coinages by the sixteenth century. These places, however, lay on trade routes known to have been conduits for silver bullion.[9]

The Role of Circulating Media in Medieval Indian Economies

By the fifteenth century, a more clearly discernible economic, essentially agricultural, pattern had also been established in India. Thus, for example, much of the great Gangetic monsoon forest had now been cleared for arable agricultural settlement.[10] Further west in dryland Rajasthan, pastoralism had become the norm; further south, in the still great forests of Gondwana, forest products provided the basis of subsistence. Agriculture, however, generated the greatest marginal surplus per family, so that the agricultural regions were the ones that gave rise to great empires.

The sultanates of Delhi, Jaunpur and Bengal were conquest states with a graft of the foreign governing classes on the indigenous cultivator root. Agriculture was the basis of government revenue for which land taxation systems had become highly articulated and administratively intense. A variety of legal categories were applied to the taxation of different types of land, different localities and different governance traditions. Taxation was recorded in various ways, but grain and money were the most common measures. The Kashmir sultanate, for example, reckoned its revenue and expenditures (notably government salaries) in multiples of cowrie shells, although its officials actually collected and disbursed paddy-rice, while settling some accounts in copper coins based on local mines.[11] In contrast, the Bengal sultanate recorded its revenues in a notional 'ancient coin cowrie', the *kapardaka purana*, as the money of account, while rendering payments in both cowries and silver coins.

This focus of monetary usages for facilitating revenue collection and government expenditure reflected the main economic activities of government: court, military, administration and religion. Historical and archaeological evidence indicates that the governments of the sultanates were structured to undertake a broad range of expenditures, from salaries to public works; from regal display to pious endowment. Eaton has catalogued the evolution of such expenditures, linked closely to the needs of the ruling classes for security, luxury, religious validation, cultural articulation and rulership symbolism. That was manifested not only through ceremonial pageantry but through sponsorship of imposing architecture, fortifications and public works.[12] While at first glance much of this medieval infrastructure seems to be related only to state purposes, we must recall Dale's dictum that in India, 'Rulers constructed religious monuments and civic institutions that simultaneously functioned as commercial centers.'[13] He points out that shops and markets were often attached to religious institutions as a form of endowment (*waqf*) that ultimately generated revenue for the state.

Quite clearly, therefore, physical moneys played an important role in the revenue collection and public expenditures of the many kingdoms of India in the medieval (pre-Mughal) period, as well as trade and commerce. Yet an important distinction should be made between coinage circulation during the periods of imperial unity – the fourteenth-century Delhi sultanate and the seventeenth-century Mughal Empire – and during the intervening period of regional fragmentation, from the fifteenth to early sixteenth centuries. As might be expected of the local coinage of the regional kingdoms mentioned earlier, their coins circulated within a tighter circuit: by and large, within the political boundaries of the state. Malwa sultanate coins are found in Madhya Pradesh; Gujarat sultanate coins in Gujarat; Bengal sultanate coins in Bengal, etc. Prior to the Suri era (*c*.1538), very few of the sultanate copper or silver coins travelled very far.[14] Hence their role in government transactions was more tightly circumscribed, and governments had commensurately greater control over the money supply, not only in its volume but also in the shape and form of the money. Shape was indeed important, for the Malwa coinage was square (gold, silver and copper), while Gujarat coinage was round but small-sized (less than half the standard 10.5 g *tanka*). Differentiation of design tended to help conserve and retain the money supply within the kingdom, by limiting its acceptability elsewhere. That was certainly true in the case of Delhi and Jaunpur, whose billon coinage was of uncertain (not readily detectable) precious metal content. This latter characteristic, of course, is reminiscent of the products of the 'coinage wars' that resulted from competitive debasements in contemporary Europe.

What remains to be studied for India in the medieval era is the role of physical moneys in inter-regional trade in the subcontinent. So far, little historical research has been devoted to tracing patterns of coin movements between these Indian regions; but undoubtedly specific coinage elements of one kingdom influenced the monetary systems of neighbours. We might mention, for example, the adoption of the Delhi/Jaunpur 'large billon *tanka*' format by both Malwa and Gujarat, although neither suffered any shortage of coinage of silver or the other metals. Clearly the mimicry was influenced by fiscal and commercial preferences rather than by political or economic necessity.

Nor, in fact, can we find much literature on the functioning of the mints, beyond what can be inferred from the coins themselves. There is no detailed historical testimony comparable to that for the records of the later Mughal mints, which worked on the principle of free coinage of bullion, thereby encouraging a financial industry as well as vibrant trade and commerce throughout the Indian subcontinent. Such studies for the earlier sultanate period are yet to be undertaken.

A Tale of Two Moneys: Delhi and Bengal

Delhi: the Decline of Robust Tri-Metallism and Birth of Debasement

If we take the apogee of imperial Delhi (*c.* 1325–51) as a logical starting place, we find that the state-issued money was quite appropriate for a great imperial structure. The sultanate had been established as a centralized autocracy, and built through expansion with only a modest adjustment of its centralized structure, which radiated outwards from the authority and person of the sultan. Each new kingdom or region absorbed through conquest was placed under the authority of a governor and other officers that the Delhi sultan appointed and made directly accountable to him. A treatise on minting left by the Delhi mint master of *c.*1318 describes in some detail the highly regulated gold, silver, billon and copper coinages of the Empire.[15] It also records in great detail the immense variety of coinages of subject provinces and kingdoms received at the central mint for assay and refining, demonstrating that the Delhi monetary system had absorbed a large number of local monetary systems during the period of imperial expansion.

Nowadays, it is difficult to grasp fully the high degree of political control that the Delhi sultan had established over the broader economy. Much has been written, for example, about the extensive price regulation of the public markets, undertaken during a period of extreme military threat from Mongol invasion.[16] Equally clear is the highly articulated nature of the land revenue system, in which taxation was levied according to well-defined criteria of field size, crop yield, nature of soil, etc.[17] All of this was in support of a massive and centrally administered army, composed of paid cavalry and soldiers. This huge military was necessary for the triple purposes of maintaining the security of the sultan, expanding the realm and defending it against external invasion. Up until the late fourteenth century, all three functions were frequently put to the test, placing considerable strain upon the administration in general and the monetary system in particular.[18]

As indicated earlier, the source of this plentiful tri-metallic coinage was treasure captured in the ongoing conquest of southern India. One early indication of the limits of the capacity of dishoarded wealth to sustain a 'full service' coinage system was Delhi's renowned 1330s flirtation with token coinage. For a period of several years, Sultan Muhammad bin Tughluq authorized the issue, throughout his empire, of brass tokens of various weights and denominations (corresponding to existing silver, billon and copper coins), decreeing that they pass as current coin.[19] This sovereign, well-known for his experimentation in affairs of state, was considered either innovative or foolhardy by contemporary observers. He may well have been acquainted with the Chinese use of paper money.[20] In the event, the fiat coinage was an attempt to mobilize financial resources to overcome an imbalance between reserves of gold and silver.[21] The immense Delhi army was paid in silver, which was in increasingly short supply, while the bulk of the imperial treasury held gold.[22]

Richards and others have given much thought to the strikingly different political and economic situation which prevailed in the Delhi sultanate by the late fifteenth century.[23] By the period of the Lodi sultans (1451–1526), much of the agricultural land was no longer under central control but had been granted as fiefs to the great nobles and others in the administrative echelons. Many layers of increasingly local nobility (rather than administrators) absorbed much of the land revenue. The sultan directly collected taxes only from the *khalisa* or crown lands. The salaries of soldiers were no longer paid by the sultan, but were financed the great landed nobles through their levies. Thus, in the later Delhi sultanate, the role of coined money in revenue-gathering was increasingly constrained. This adverse situation was reflected in the much reduced 'menu' of coins put in circulation by the government. The rich feast of tri-metallism was over, to be replaced by a sparse diet of billon (heavily alloyed silver) and copper coins.

The situation sounds strikingly like that pertaining in contemporary areas of still-feudal Europe. It came about in the first instance because a tribal oligarchy of Afghan origin gained power and brought elements of their tribal governance to bear in much of northern India. Also responsible were the shocks of *realpolitik:* the invasion and devastation of northern India by Amir Timur in 1399, which shattered much of the centralized state apparatus; the latter did not fully recover in the subsequent confusion. As well, the successive irruptions of the Mongols and the Timurids on India's north-west frontier destroyed the silver mining activities of that region, and sporadically interrupted the long-term trade flows of central Asian silver to India.[24] Simultaneously, the opportunistic secession from central authority of all of India's coastal regions left Delhi isolated and landlocked.

By the mid-fifteenth century, the coinage of the Delhi sultanate, and indeed of its neighbour in Hindustan, the Jaunpur sultanate, was reduced to a thin layer of ceremonial gold coins that supplemented the actual bulk of the working coinage comprising billon *tankas*, called *bahlolis,* of 9 g and some 80 per cent copper, as well as pure copper coins.[25] A temporal trend of debasement was clear: the billon *tanka* contained 30 per cent silver *c.*1340, 20 per cent silver in the 1360s, 15 per cent *c.*1460, and only 5 per cent *c.*1500.[26] The economy cannot be said, however, to have become demonetized: for these coins are still found in treasure trove hoards, albeit in somewhat smaller quantities than later Mughal coinages.[27] There was necessarily an element of fiat or fiduciary function in this billon coinage. Once written into the accounts of revenue collection and royal expenditure, the coins passed at nominal, not intrinsic, value.[28] In these circumstances, there was some incentive for the governing power to cheat.

The progressive yet slow debasement of the *bahlolis* is so consistent over time that it cannot have been due to accident or random effect. Some of the blame for this situation no doubt rests on the impoverished local sources of silver and the poor or irregular supply through trade channels.[29] Whatever the case, it is not likely the average coin user would ever have been able to determine the actual precious metal content of the *bahlolis*. Since the *bahlolis* in general show no evidence of 'shroff marking' (counter-stamping by money-changers), it is clear they were not discounted in circulation because of age or poor metal content. Hence we may conclude that they were largely a fiat coinage, passing by authority and sanction rather than by virtue of their metallic soundness. We may further conclude that the progressive devaluation benefited the issuing authorities.[30] So the Delhi case study is resonant with those of contemporary Europe discussed elsewhere in this volume.

This brief review begs the question, of course, as to the active – as opposed to passive – role of money in the medieval political dynamic. Did the changing political situation result in monetary contraction, that is, did the introduction of a feudal model reduce the role of coinage in the economy? Or was the opposite true: did the ever-contracting money supply weaken the powers of those defending a strong central authority, and enhance the powers of those less reliant on a revenue/financial system based on coin? The question is obviously very important, but there is yet to be a consensus amongst historians of the period.[31]

A more detailed regional analysis of the monetary economies of medieval India is now necessary.

Bengal: Coined Silver Introduced into the Existing Cowrie System

For much of its existence, the Bengal sultanate encompassed what is now modern Bangladesh as well as the Indian states of West Bengal and Bihar. Much of Bengal proper comprised the subtropical deltaic floodplains of the Ganges River in the west, and of the Brahmaputra River in the east (the two did not join prior to the mid-sixteenth century).[32] This hot riverine environment permitted both rain-fed and irrigated agriculture, which yielded up to three crops a year. Throughout the historical period, governments in Bengal have been sustained by highly articulated revenue systems that have drawn on this surplus agricultural wealth.[33]

Deltaic Bengal has no metallic mineralization. Since time immemorial, metals have had to be imported. To service the needs of state and trade, the Bengal sultanate (1205–1576) had a dual monetary system based on silver coins and cowrie shells, although neither commodity was produced locally. In effect, the currency was mono-metallic and bi-denominational.[34]

In 1205, the Turkish invaders of Bengal found in place an advanced and well-developed agricultural revenue-gathering system that was defined and recorded in monetary units. Yet, despite this system, Bengal still had *no metallic coinage*. Both archaeological excavations[35] and contemporary accounts[36] affirm that the principal circulating medium was the cowrie shell, *cypraea moneta*, called *kauri*. While each one had a tiny value, when packaged in large pre-counted lots, cowries were used for large payments.

Sagaciously, the Turks left intact this indigenous monetary system based on *kauris*. To supplement the *kauris*, they instituted the coinage of a silver *tanka*, a coin with distinctive physical properties, and one that, for this era, was relatively heavy (11.0 g), wide (25–30 mm) and pure (96–8 per cent). Although completely Islamic in idiom, the silver *tanka* physically resembled the traditional silver coinage of south-east Asia, which had circulated in the first millennium from Cambodia to Burma, flourishing in south-east Bengal as late as the eleventh century.[37] Since this system of *kauris* or cowrie shells had long proven sufficient for revenue and expenditure purposes, the new government evidently created this new silver coinage for its own purposes, namely to strengthen its rulership by attracting military and administrative cadres from countries further west that were using silver coins.

On the other hand, no copper coinage was issued or used in medieval Bengal prior to the sixteenth century (not according to any available evidence). Rather, this function was again filled by the cowrie shells. As I recently observed in a related publication:

> Cowries were the small change of Bengal since ancient times. Originating in the Maldive Islands, cowries were brought in trade to Bengal in large quantities. There is no evidence of state involvement in, or regulation of, this trade. Indigenous and foreign references confirm that in both the pre-Muslim and sultanate periods, the cowrie acted as the exclusive small-value circulating medium of Bengal.[38]

The value of the cowrie as money was dependent on normal market forces, and therefore varied considerably over time and place. The further inland the cowries travelled, the higher they were valued, reflecting transportation costs from the port of entry, as well as commercial risks.

Like silver coins, cowries were subject to changes in supply and demand over time. Hence the relative exchange ratio of cowries to silver was in flux, varying over seasons and year to year. The important issue, however, is that both functioned fully as monetary instruments, suffering no more exchange variability than was the case with gold–silver exchanges (and bi-metallic ratios) elsewhere.

In this manner the two dissimilar currency commodities – silver and seashells – were integrated into a single functioning monetary system. The state provided 'big money' and the market provided both 'big money' and 'little money'. In effect, Bengal had anticipated and solved the 'big problem of small change', so famously articulated by the late Carlo Cipolla.[39]

If we refer to Cipolla's four-part formula for maintaining a successful fractional coinage,[40] the cowrie either met or satisfied each criterion:

'to issue small coins having a commodity value less than their monetary value'	Cowrie shells were an imported commodity whose monetary value at any moment, in any particular place, was exactly equal to their commodity value expressed in silver *tankas*. By definition, the commodity value could never exceed the monetary value.
'to limit the quantity of these small coins in circulation'	Since the shells came from the Maldive Islands, in effect the quantity of cowries available at all times was constrained by their rate of import, which was sensitive to demand and price.
'to provide convertibility with unit money'	By all accounts, the free market provided a vigorous exchange function, which made the cowrie shells a relatively liquid asset in terms of the formal metallic *tanka* currency. If the buy/sell spread or exchange commission was too high, it would reduce the frequency of exchange or the exchange of large quantities.
'fractional money cannot be legal tender in payments over a certain amount'	While no legal constraint on the convertibility of cowries into *tankas* is discernible, the large mass and volume of high values of cowries imposed both transaction costs (counting or weighing, bagging and sealing) as well as transportation costs. This limited their utility as legal tender.

Two such disparate money forms could co-circulate only if they were interchangeable. There is no evidence that government facilitated this exchange, except to the extent that revenue obligations could be settled in either currency. This need only happen a few times per year. In trade, however, it was important for the two moneys to be exchanged on a daily basis.

References well into the early modern period indicate the silver–cowrie exchange was undertaken by money-changers who attended each market from the lowliest village weekly gathering to sophisticated city bazaars. On traders' demand, they changed coins into cowries at the start of business, and converted the cowries back into coins at the end of trading.[41] In the port cities, this network was linked with merchants who imported cowries from the Maldives. Indeed, in the cowrie trade there may have been no boundary between mercantile and banking functions; and the same may be said, of course, of later medieval western Europe.

Two Sides of the Coin: Consistent Quality, Debasement Avoided

Bengal's new money, the silver *tanka*, was initially produced in modest quantities, but by the 1500s it was manufactured and circulated in the millions. At the birth of the sultanate, silver was a supplementary coinage to the universal cowrie money; but by the twilight of the sultanate these roles had reversed, so that the cowrie had become a subsidiary coinage to silver. Launched with a mean weight of 10.8 g, the same as the contemporary Delhi *tanka*, the Bengal *tanka* underwent a long and gentle decline over the next two and a half centuries, losing 5 per cent of its weight (and net precious metal content) overall. This decline was not arrested until 1538 when Sher Shah fully increased the weight, by 10 per cent by replacing the *tanka* denomination with the *rupiya* denomination. This rate of weight-reduction was quite modest, a mere 1.5 per cent diminution per century. It is unlikely this represents an intentional effort to assure that new coins matched the weight of coins in circulation, as often happened elsewhere (e.g. in medieval Europe). This would be possible only with a very modest velocity of circulation, which is flatly contradicted by the evidence of very vigorous circulation (wear and tear and countermarking), exhibited by coins in so many hoards.

The *tanka*'s precious metal content was consistently high, with very minor debasement noticeable, remaining within a narrow band of 95–9 per cent silver, alloyed with copper.[42] Indeed, the Bengal coinage was intended to be virtually pure silver. As I have noted elsewhere, the predictability and reliability of the precious metal content was a key factor in its acceptability.

Bengal's silver coinage was not a fiat currency, as the term is generally understood, although the presence of less than 5 per cent of copper does indicate a modest fiduciary element which was likely the mint's seigniorage and brassage (see Chapter 1 above). There is no doubt that money-changers closely monitored and verified the coins' precious metal content: this is evident from the plethora of banker's marks found on surviving specimens. Some coins were so severely marked by bankers that they may have been demonetized and thus traded as bullion.

This consistently high quality of the coinage stood in stark contrast to the debased silver moneys mentioned above as current in contemporary Hindustan (Delhi and Jaunpur) from the late fourteenth century until the establishment of the Suri Empire in 1538 (see Figure 10.2). The major reason to explain this marked difference lies in the accessibility of silver in trade channels. After the independence of Bengal and Gujarat, upper India lacked direct access to Indian Ocean trade, which throughout this period had conveyed silver bullion as a major commercial commodity.

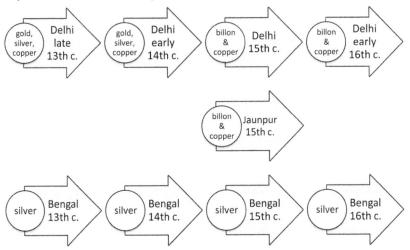

Figure 10.2: The predominant coinage metals in the inland kingdoms of Delhi and Jaunpur, and the coastal kingdom of Bengal. Note that in the late thirteenth/early fourteenth century, Delhi encompassed several coastal kingdoms, subsequently lost. Dates approximate. Source: see Appendix. below, Table 10.1 p. 194.

Some differences were also due to the political and economic factors of governance. While Delhi lost its centralized political character, Bengal continued to be a highly centralized realm to the very end of this period. The use of high-purity metal money in revenue and administrative systems, far from falling into decline as in Delhi, was only strengthened in Bengal.[43] The importance of a high-purity coinage in finance and trade is not, however, to be denied. The close inspection by bankers of Bengal's coins from the mid-fifteenth century onwards indicates how important metal content was to the coin's acceptability in trade. We are reminded of Chilosi's finding for late medieval Europe, that 'when monetary policy was driven by the interests of merchants and members of the nobility, rather than by those of princes, silver currencies were comparatively stable'.[44]

In Bengal, as in other Indian sultanates (and as in later medieval and early-modern Europe), control of the minting process was a jealously guarded government prerogative. Mints were operated by the state directly or by close regulation of contractors. Either way, they levied a seigniorage or fee for their own profit (while covering costs in the 'brassage' component). In this manner mints not only created the circulating medium, but contributed to the state's revenue, as may well be observed in late medieval western Europe. As might be expected, during the earliest years of the young sultanate (*c.* 1204–1300), all the coinage of the kingdom was manufactured in a single mint at Lakhnauti, the capital. This centrality of minting reflected not only the modest quantities of new silver coinage, but also the modest territory that the new rulers controlled. As the sultanate expanded in the fourteenth century, especially after its absorption of Vanga, the south-east delta region, more mints were created in other parts of the kingdom.[45] Finally, at the apex of the sultanate in the fifteenth and early sixteenth century, the growing volume of the silver coinage, and its important function in the taxation system justified the opening of mints in most of the major revenue districts of the kingdom.[46] While trade by this time was also heavily dependent on coined money, it was clearly a secondary factor in the selection of minting places.

Although many mints were in operation by the Husainid period (1494–1538), it cannot be said that all were equally productive.[47] By my estimate, about a fifth of the sultanate's coinage was struck at a city named Fathabad (modern Faridpur), a major port on the Padma River below its confluence with the Jumna (in those days not the main channel of the Brahmaputra). It was well located to be the principal entrepot between Chatgaon (Chittagong) on the ocean and the inland capital Husainabad/Lakhnauti. During the sixteenth century, Chatgaon served as the maritime entry-point for silver bullion arriving in Bengal by sea. Shahnaj Jahan notes,

> The fact that in 1569 Caesar Frederick travelled from Pegu to Cattagrama in a ship laden 'Silver and Gold ... and no other kind of Merchandize' indicates that the port was the most important centre in Bengal for importing bullion (Purchas 1905: 136).[48]

Fathabad's favourable situation enabled it to regulate the river traffic in imported silver, which probably explains the strong activity of the Fathabad mint. Tellingly, the Portuguese merchant Tome Pires observed the high customs duties that foreign merchants paid on clearing their goods into the sultanate at the port of entry.[49] This heavy tariff was extracted in imported bullion or coins, resulting in a steady flow of silver into the treasury.

The Source of Bengal's Silver for Coinage

Bengal's plentiful natural resources unfortunately did not include an indigenous supply of silver. So like the cowrie, use of the silver *tanka* was ultimately dependent on commodity supplies from sources elsewhere. Once launched, the circulating medium itself was the primary source for fresh coin production. In a sense, the governments that depended on old coinage to produce new coinage were operating in a closed-loop system. Certainly this often seemed to be the case in later medieval Europe, as many of its historians have observed. Indian rulers shared with their European counterparts a number of practical options to secure supplies for the minting process. The first source was the old coinage itself. When circulating coins were clipped, sweated, discounted and demonetized, they became in effect bullion suitable for reminting. The second source was the tribute payments exacted from subordinate kingdoms, often in the form of silver bullion. Indeed, the inscriptions on Bengal sultanate coins themselves indicate they were often minted from silver received from the neighbouring states. The third source was de-thesaurization, otherwise known as 'loot and plunder'. In Bengal's case, military campaigns were a more important source of silver during the early years, with the exception of the expansionist phase at the start of Husain's reign in 1494. These campaigns were redistributive in the sense that most of the conquered kingdoms lay on the trade routes between Bengal and its most important sources of silver.

These of course were all forms of internal recycling; the ultimate source of all this silver was external trade. Only by securing reliable sources through trade to replenish this fixed supply could a regime escape this tyranny of the 'closed loop'. This situation essentially explains why Bengal was so successful in perpetuating a pure silver coinage over almost four centuries, while contemporary Delhi, and many other governments (Asian and European) were not.

Counterbalancing the Fluctuating Trade in Silver and Cowries

The two commodities (silver and cowries) formed a fully functioning monetary system in Bengal, but their relative importance changed over time. In the early period the cowrie was predominant in all affairs public and private, while the new silver *tanka* served a subsidiary role in terms of limited circulation in the immigrant community. As time passed, this relative importance was reversed, so that by the late sixteenth century the silver coin had become predominant. But silver never eclipsed the cowrie, which continued in an important subsidiary role in the central provinces, and actually retained its dominant role in some peripheral areas well into the modern (colonial) period.

The long slow evolution was not, however, a smooth one; for the supply of both commodities was subject to much variance over time. Thus, for example, Yunnan's mines experienced periods of strong production as well as periods of relative decline, between the thirteenth and sixteenth centuries.[50] As well, other regions, in China especially, underwent episodes of fluctuating demand for silver that seriously affected the supply of Yunnanese silver for trade to the west.[51] Similarly, Blanchard has shown how the Indian Ocean experienced sustained periods of climatic change, when wind systems and ocean currents departed from the norm, with significant economic (and monetary) consequences.[52] The Maldivian cowrie was extremely sensitive to variations in temperature and salinity, and although there have not as yet been detailed studies of the phenomenon, production evidently varied considerably over decades and centuries, depending on climatic and oceanic conditions.[53] As well, its use ebbed and flowed in other kingdoms. For example the demand for its use in the economies of both the Yemen and Gujarat periodically affected its availability for the Bengal trade.

In this respect, Bengal's reliance on two foreign commodities (rather than one), both of which were produced far beyond its borders, provided a beneficial risk-aversion strategy that reduced its vulnerability to the vagaries of supply for either of them. The relative exchange value of cowries and silver *tankas* might well have waxed and waned over time, but there was a reasonable chance that the two combined would be available in sufficient quantities to assure an adequate money supply.

Compared to the coined money, the quantities of cowries in circulation are poorly documented, but it would be worthwhile to seek proxy indicators to determine how the two moneys functioned together over long periods. In my view, periods of sharp monetary contraction resulting from external shocks were far fewer than in neighbouring kingdoms that relied on coined money alone. Indeed, the best example of this is the strong contrast in the monetary situations in Bengal, Jaunpur and Delhi in the late fifteenth century.

Conclusion

In commencing this study, I posed the question: how did a pre-modern government sustained largely by agricultural revenue maintain a viable monetary system when it lacked indigenous sources of precious metal? In the preamble, I demonstrated that in medieval and early-modern India, indigenous (Hindu/Buddhist) regimes were successful in using a variety of approaches, some of which had very low requirements for precious metals. Those requirements depended on the structure of power and administration in the state, the revenues and expenditure that could be reckoned and transacted in non-metallic commodities, in kind and in base metal coinages. But then, from the thirteenth century, the arrival of foreign-immigrant governing regimes in much of India changed this ruling dynamic. The continued success of the immigrant rulers was contingent on their ability to attract from other Islamic lands soldiers, administrators and jurists, who were accustomed to a precious metal-based cash nexus.

This study has shown that securing access to precious metals was, for these Indian governments, central to the operation of a coin-based monetary system. Military actions might have assured an episodic supply of gold and silver, but they were subject to uncertainty and failure, as well as to very high transaction costs; and indeed their armies tended to consume the loot – in precious metals – that they 'liberated' – or confiscated. Trade usually assured a more regular supply of precious metals; and, for the state if not for individual merchants, it was generally less risky. But trade, whether international or purely regionally was subject to sporadic interruptions; and maritime trade of course required ready and low-cost access to the sea. Thus, lacking local supplies, periodic shortfalls of precious metals were so often the norm.

One classic solution for this monetary conundrum was the use of a fiat or fiduciary coinage, subject to episodic or systematic debasement, when the state was faced with shortfalls in bullion supplies. Such was the fate, for example, of circulating coinages in the landlocked Delhi and Jaunpur sultanates in the fifteenth and early sixteenth centuries.

In contrast to these landlocked sultanates, the coastal Bengal sultanate successfully tackled this problem by the alternative strategy of leveraging its nodal location on both land and sea routes. It encouraged engagement, in a sustained manner, in both overland and maritime trade to secure two vital imported commodities: cowrie shells and silver bullion. The bi-denominational monetary system thus established permitted the economy to reduce the risks of supply interruption. Evidently successful, the Bengali monetary system flourished from 1205 until the absorption of the sultanate in 1576. By this latter date, the final pre-eminence of Bengal's silver coinage over its cowrie money signalled the end of silver supply constraints, coincident with the introduction of New World silver into the Indian Ocean trade matrix.

Acknowledgements

I would like to thank John Munro for his generous invitation to participate in the WEHC panel that gave rise to this book. I am also grateful to Richard Eaton, Stan Goron, Rila Mukherjee, Michael Pearson, Robert Tye and Robert Wicks for kindly commenting on the WEHC draft of this paper, and to Syed Ejaz Hussain and Andre Wink for their welcome comments on this later version. Errors and omissions remain my sole responsibility.

Appendix

Table 10.A1 shows the incidence of coin minting in all four metals in the Delhi, Jaunpur and Bengal sultanates, 1350–1550. The table indicates years in which coins of specific metals were minted in each kingdom. Mintage quantities are quantum only, in that some mintages are 'common', i.e. survive in relatively large quantities, while other mintages are 'scarce or rare', i.e. seldom survive in significant quantities. For purposes of analysis I assume that each mintage's survival rate correlates to the original minting quantities.

Table 10.1: Incidence of coin minting in all four metals (gold, silver, billon and copper) in the Delhi, Jaunpur and Bengal sultanates, 1350–1550.

(metals indicated by their initial letter, e.g. G – gold, S – silver, B – billon, C – copper; **bold** means 'common to very common'; *italic* means 'scarce to extremely rare').

Issue date CE	1350									1360										1370										1380										1390										800		
Issue date AH	751									760										770										780										790										800		
	1	2	3	4	5	6	7	8	9	0	1	2	3	4	5	6	7	8	9	0	1	2	3	4	5	6	7	8	9	0	1	2	3	4	5	6	7	8	9	0	1	2	3	4	5	6	7	8	9	0	1	2
Delhi Gold	-	G	G	-	-	-	-	-	-	-	G	-	G	-	G	G	-	-	-	-	G	-	*S*	-	G	G	-	-	-	-	-	-	-	G	G	G	G	G	-	G	-	G	G	G	-	G	G	G	-	-	G	G
Silver	-	-	-	-	-	-	-	-	-	-	-	-	-	-	-	-	-	-	-	-	-	-	*S*	-	-	-	-	-	-	-	-	-	-	-	-	-	-	*S*	-	-	-	-	-	-	-	-	*S*	-	-	-	-	*S*
Billon	B	-	-	-	-	-	-	-	B	B	B	B	B	B	B	B	B	B	B	B	B	B	B	B	B	B	B	B	B	B	B	B	B	B	B	B	B	B	B	B	B	*B*	B	B	*B*	*B*	-	*B*	-	*B*	-	*B*
Copper	C	C	-	-	-	-	C	-	C	-	-	C	-	C	-	-	-	-	-	-	-	-	-	-	-	-	-	-	-	-	-	-	-	-	-	-	-	-	C	-	C	C	C	C	C	C	C	C	C	C	C	C
Jaunpur Gold	-	-	-	-	-	-	-	-	-	-	-	-	G	-	-	-	-	-	-	-	-	-	-	-	-	-	-	-	-	-	-	-	-	-	-	-	-	-	-	-	-	-	-	-	-	-	-	-	-	-	-	-
Silver	-	-	-	-	-	-	-	-	-	-	-	-	-	-	-	-	-	-	-	-	-	-	-	-	-	-	-	-	-	-	-	-	-	-	-	-	-	-	-	-	-	-	-	-	-	-	-	-	-	-	-	-
Billon	-	-	-	-	-	-	-	-	-	-	-	-	-	-	-	-	-	-	-	-	-	-	-	-	-	-	-	-	-	-	-	-	-	-	-	-	-	-	-	-	-	-	-	-	-	-	-	-	-	-	-	-
Copper	-	-	-	-	-	-	-	-	-	-	-	-	-	-	-	-	-	-	-	-	-	-	-	-	-	-	-	-	-	-	-	-	-	-	-	-	-	-	-	-	-	-	-	-	-	-	-	-	-	-	-	-
Bengal Gold	-	-	G	-	-	G	-	-	G	-	G	-	-	-	-	-	-	-	-	-	-	-	-	-	-	-	-	-	-	-	-	-	-	-	-	-	-	-	-	-	-	-	-	-	-	-	-	-	-	-	-	-
Silver	S	S	S	S	S	S	S	S	S	S	S	S	S	S	S	S	S	S	S	-	S	-	S	S	S	-	-	S	S	-	S	-	S	S	S	S	S	S	S	-	S	-	-	S	S	S	S	S	S	S	S	S
Billon	-	-	-	-	-	-	-	-	-	-	-	-	-	-	-	-	-	-	-	-	-	-	-	-	-	-	-	-	-	-	-	-	-	-	-	-	-	-	-	-	-	-	-	-	-	-	-	-	-	-	-	-
Copper	-	-	-	-	-	-	-	-	-	-	-	-	-	-	-	-	-	-	-	-	-	-	-	-	-	-	-	-	-	-	-	-	-	-	-	-	-	-	-	-	-	-	-	-	-	-	-	-	-	-	-	-

Issue date CE			1400					1410									1420									1430									1440											
Issue date AH			803					810									820									830									840									850			
			3	4	5	6	7	8	9	0	1	2	3	4	5	6	7	8	9	0	1	2	3	4	5	6	7	8	9	0	1	2	3	4	5	6	7	8	9	0	1	2	3
Delhi	Gold		–	–	–	–	–	–	–	–	–	–	G	G	G	–	–	–	–	–	G	–	–	G	–	–	G	–	–	G	G	G	G	G	G	–	G	–	G	–	G	–	G	G
	Silver		–	–	–	–	–	–	–	–	S	–	S	S	S	S	S	–	–	S	–	–	S	–	S	–	S	–	S	S	S	S	S	S	–	S	S	S	S	S	–	S	S	S
	Billon		–	B	–	–	–	–	–	–	B	B	B	B	B	–	B	–	B	–	B	B	B	B	–	B	B	B	–	B	–	–	–	B	B	B	B	B	B	B	B	–	B	B	B
	Copper		C	C	–	C	C	C	–	C	–	C	–	C	C	C	C	C	–	C	C	–	C	C	C	C	C	C	C	C	C	–	C	C	C	C	C	C	C	C	C	C	C	C	C
Jaunpur	Gold		–	–	–	–	–	–	–	–	–	–	–	–	–	–	–	–	G	–	G	–	–	G	–	–	–	G	–	G	G	–	G	–	G	–	G	G	G	–	G	–	G	–	–
	Silver		–	–	–	–	–	–	–	–	–	–	–	–	–	–	–	–	S	S	–	–	–	–	–	–	–	–	–	–	–	–	–	–	–	–	–	–	–	–	–	–	–	–	–
	Billon		–	–	–	–	–	B	–	–	–	–	B	–	–	–	–	–	B	B	B	B	B	B	B	B	B	B	B	B	B	B	B	B	B	B	B	B	B	B	B	B	B	B	B
	Copper		–	–	–	–	–	–	–	–	–	–	C	–	C	–	–	C	C	C	C	C	C	C	C	C	C	C	C	C	C	C	C	C	C	C	C	C	C	C	C	C	C	C	–
Bengal	Gold		–	–	–	–	–	–	–	–	–	–	–	–	–	–	–	–	–	–	G	–	–	–	–	–	–	–	–	G	–	G	–	G	–	–	G	–	G	–	–	–	–	–	–
	Silver		S	S	S	S	S	S	S	S	S	S	S	S	S	S	S	S	S	S	S	S	S	S	S	S	S	S	S	S	S	S	S	S	S	S	S	S	S	S	S	S	S	S	–
	Billon		–	–	–	–	–	–	–	–	–	–	–	–	–	–	–	–	–	–	–	–	–	–	–	–	–	–	–	–	–	–	–	–	–	–	–	–	–	–	–	–	–	–	–
	Copper		–	–	–	–	–	–	–	–	–	–	–	–	–	–	–	–	–	–	–	–	–	–	–	–	–	–	–	–	–	–	–	–	–	–	–	–	–	–	–	–	–	–	–

Issue date CE		1450				1460										1470										1480										1490										
Issue date AH		854				860										870										880										890									900	
		4	5	6	7	8	9	0	1	2	3	4	5	6	7	8	9	0	1	2	3	4	5	6	7	8	9	0	1	2	3	4	5	6	7	8	9	0	1	2	3	4	5
Delhi	Gold	–	–	–	–	–	–	–	–	–	–	–	–	–	–	–	–	–	–	–	–	–	–	–	–	–	–	–	–	–	–	–	–	–	–	–	–	–	–	–	–	–	–
	Silver	–	–	–	–	–	–	–	–	–	–	–	–	–	–	–	–	–	–	–	–	–	–	–	–	–	–	–	–	–	–	–	–	–	–	*S*	–	–	–	–	–	–	–
	Billon	*B*	–	B	B	B	B	B	B	B	B	B	B	–	–	B	–	–	B	B	B	B	B	B	B	B	B	B	B	B	B	B	B	B	B	B	B	B	B	B	B	B	B
	Copper	C	C	–	–	C	C	C	C	C	C	C	C	C	C	C	C	C	C	C	C	C	C	–	–	C	C	C	C	–	C	C	C	C	C	C	–	–	–	–	–	–	–
Jaunpur	Gold	–	G	G	–	–	–	–	–	–	–	–	–	G	–	–	G	–	–	–	–	–	–	–	–	–	–	–	–	–	–	–	–	–	–	–	–	–	–	–	–	–	–
	Silver	–	–	–	–	–	–	–	–	–	–	–	–	–	–	–	–	–	–	–	–	–	–	–	–	–	–	–	–	–	–	–	–	–	–	–	–	–	–	–	–	–	–
	Billon	B	B	B	B	B	B	B	B	B	B	B	B	B	B	B	B	B	B	B	B	B	B	B	B	B	B	B	B	B	B	B	B	B	B	B	B	B	B	B	B	B	B
	Copper	C	C	C	C	C	C	C	C	C	C	C	C	C	C	–	–	C	–	C	–	–	C	–	C	C	–	–	C	–	–	C	C	C	C	C	–	–	–	–	–	–	–
Bengal	Gold	–	–	–	–	–	–	–	–	–	–	–	–	–	–	–	–	–	–	–	–	G	–	–	G	–	G	–	–	G	–	–	G	–	–	G	–	G-G-G-G	–	–	–	G	–
	Silver	S	–	S	S	S	–	S	S	S	S	S	S	S	S	S	S	S	–	S	–	S	S	S	S	S	S	S	S	S	S	–	S	S	S	S	S	S	–	S	S	S	S
	Billon	–	–	–	–	–	–	–	–	–	–	–	–	–	–	–	–	–	–	–	–	–	–	–	–	–	–	–	–	–	–	–	–	–	–	–	–	–	–	–	–	–	–
	Copper	–	–	–	–	–	–	–	–	–	–	–	–	–	–	–	–	–	–	–	–	–	–	–	–	–	–	–	–	–	–	–	–	–	–	–	–	–	–	–	–	–	–

Issue date CE	1500				1510										1520										1530										1540										950						
Issue date AH	906			910										920										930										940										950							
	6	7	8	9	0	1	2	3	4	5	6	7	8	9	0	1	2	3	4	5	6	7	8	9	0	1	2	3	4	5	6	7	8	9	0	1	2	3	4	5	6	7	8	9	0	1	2	3	4	5	6
Delhi Gold	-	-	-	-	-	-	-	G	-	-	-	-	-	-	-	-	-	-	-	-	-	-	-	-	-	-	-	-	-	-	-	-	-	-	-	-	-	-	-	-	-	-	G	-	-	-	-	-	-	-	-
Silver	-	-	-	-	-	-	-	-	-	-	-	-	-	-	-	-	-	-	-	-	-	-	-	-	-	-	-	-	-	-	-	-	-	-	-	S	S	S	S	S	S	S	S	S	S	S	S	S	S	S	S
Billon	B	B	B	B	B	B	B	B	B	B	B	B	B	B	B	B	B	B	-	B	B	B	B	-	B	-	-	-	-	-	B	-	-	-	-	-	-	-	-	-	-	-	C	C	C	C	C	C	C	C	C
Copper	-	-	-	-	-	-	-	-	-	-	-	-	-	-	-	-	-	-	-	-	-	-	-	-	-	-	-	-	-	-	-	-	-	-	-	-	-	-	-	-	-	C	C	C	C	C	C	C	C	C	C
Jaunpur Gold	-	-	-	-	-	-	-	-	-	-	-	-	-	-	-	-	-	-	-	-	-	-	-	-	-	-	-	-	-	-	-	-	-	-	-	-	-	-	-	-	-	-	-	-	-	-	-	-	-	-	-
Silver	-	-	-	-	-	-	-	-	-	-	-	-	-	-	-	-	-	-	-	-	-	-	-	-	-	-	-	-	-	-	-	-	-	-	-	-	-	-	-	-	-	-	-	-	-	-	-	-	-	-	-
Billon	B	B	B	B	B	B	B	B	B	B	-	-	-	-	-	-	-	-	-	-	-	-	-	-	-	-	-	-	-	-	-	-	-	-	-	-	-	-	-	-	-	-	-	-	-	-	-	-	-	-	-
Copper	-	-	-	-	-	-	-	-	-	-	-	-	-	-	-	-	-	-	-	-	-	-	-	-	-	-	-	-	-	-	-	-	-	-	-	-	-	-	-	-	-	-	-	-	-	-	-	-	-	-	-
Bengal Gold	-	G	-	-	-	-	-	-	-	-	-	-	G	-	-	G	G	G	-	-	-	-	-	-	-	-	-	G	-	-	-	-	-	-	-	-	-	-	-	-	-	-	-	-	-	-	-	-	-	-	-
Silver	-	S	S	S	S	-	-	-	-	-	S	S	S	S	S	S	S	-	-	-	S	S	S	S	S	S	S	S	S	S	-	-	-	S	S	S	-	-	-	S	S	S	S	S	S	S	S	S	-	S	S
Billon	-	-	-	-	-	-	-	-	-	-	-	-	-	-	-	-	-	-	-	-	-	-	-	-	-	-	-	-	-	-	-	-	-	-	-	-	-	-	-	-	-	-	-	-	C	C	C	-	-	-	-
Copper	-	-	-	-	-	-	-	-	-	-	-	-	-	-	-	-	-	-	-	-	-	-	-	-	-	-	-	-	-	-	-	-	-	-	-	-	-	-	-	-	-	-	-	-	-	-	-	-	-	-	-

Source: S. Goron and J. P. Goenka, *The Coins of the Indian Sultanates* (New Delhi: Munshiram Manoharlal, 2001).

NOTES

Munro, 'Introduction'

1. These essays are based on ten of the eighteen papers delivered to the XVth World Economic History Congress, at the University of Utrecht, in August 2009: for Session M.10: 'Monetary Problems and Monetary Policies: the World Economy Before 1800', all of which papers have been substantially revised. That some obvious topics are not treated in this volume simply reflects limits of space and the availability of suitable contributors.
2. M. Bloch, *Esquisse d'une histoire monétaire de l'Europe*, Cahiers des Annales, 9 (Paris: Annales, 1954), pp. 40–83. Bloch, founder of the journal *Annales*, and a member of the French resistance, was executed by the Nazis in July 1944.
3. Medieval England was the major exception in banning the import (and export) of *all* foreign coins, except briefly, in the 1520s, under Henry VIII. See J. H. Munro, 'Bullionism and the Bill of Exchange in England, 1272–1663: A Study in Monetary Management and Popular Prejudice', in Center for Medieval and Renaissance Studies, University of California (ed.), *The Dawn of Modern Banking* (New Haven, CT, and London: Yale University Press, 1979), pp. 169–239, esp. appendix B, pp. 221–6: statute 38 Ed III, stat. 1, c. 2 (January 1364).
4. Peel's Act of 2 July 1819 (Statute 59 George III, c. 49), which also permitted anyone to melt down gold and silver coins. See A. Feavearyear, *The Pound Sterling: A History of English Money*, 2nd rev. edn by E. Victor Morgan (Oxford: Clarendon Press, 1963), pp. 212–22, esp. pp. 220–1.
5. Statute 15 Carolus II. c. 7, in Great Britain, Record Commission (T. E. Tomlins, J. Raithby, et al.), (eds), *Statutes of the Realm*, 6 vols. (London: Parliament, 1810-22), vol. 5, p. 451, sec. 9.
6. The more complicated ancient Roman and Indian money-of-account systems are discussed in the chapters by Harl and Deyell.
7. The relationship is an obverse proportional one, defined by this equation: $\Delta T = [1/(1 - x)] - 1$, which is explained in the editor's chapter on medieval coinage debasements. Here T represents the coined value of the mint weight of fine metal, expressed in the local money of account.
8. See the example of the *denier tournois* and the *gros tournois* (originally worth 12d *tournois*) in the reign of Philip the Fair, from 1295 to 1314, in A. Blanchet and A. Dieudonné (eds), *Manuel de numismatique française*, 2 vols (Paris: Ricard, 1916), vol. 2, pp. 233-41.
9. P. Spufford, *Money and its Use in Medieval Europe* (Cambridge: Cambridge University Press, 1988), pp. 289–318.
10. One of the best examples was the circulation of Burgundian gold nobles in England, minted to be close imitations of the prized English gold noble: from 1388 to 1428. Other

examples are the circulation of French silver *gros,* minted during the 1420s in the royal enclave of Tournai (within Flanders) to be imitations of the Flemish *gros (groot, groten);* and indeed of many imitations of Flemish coins minted in various small principalities in the eastern Low Countries. See J. H. Munro, *Wool, Cloth and Gold: The Struggle for Bullion in Anglo-Burgundian Trade, 1340–1478* (Brussels and Toronto: University of Toronto Press, 1973), pp. 43–63, 75–88, appendix II, pp. 212–14; Spufford, *Money and its Use,* pp. 289–318.

11. Of numerous examples to be cited, the best documented defensive-aggressive debasements are those of Philip the Good in Flanders (1419–33) and of Edward IV in England, in 1464–5.

12. In medieval England, from 1351, the crown was bound by a similar Parliamentary statute: obeyed by Henry VI in 1411, but ignored by Edward IV in 1464 – and also by Henry VIII and Edward VI in the 'Great Debasement' of 1542–52.

13. The crown of Aragon continued to mint billon *dinero* coins that did contain some silver.

14. The initial monetary cause of inflation was in fact the earlier Central European silver-copper mining boom of *c.* 1460–*c.* 1540 and an early sixteenth-century 'financial revolution'. See J. H. Munro, 'The Monetary Origins of the "Price Revolution": South German Silver Mining, Merchant-Banking, and Venetian Commerce, 1470–1540', in D. Flynn, A. Giráldez and R. von Glahn (eds), *Global Connections and Monetary History, 1470–1800* (Aldershot and Brookfield, VT: Ashgate Publishing, 2003), pp. 1–34.

15. See also the tables in the chapters by Van der Wee, Mayhew and Pieper. Spanish American bullion imports into Seville had fallen from an annual average of 106,045.26 kg in 1626–30 to one of just 27,965.30 kg in 1656–60. Such bullion imports ceased to be recorded after 1660, simply because the Castilian government ceased taxing those imports. See E. J. Hamilton, *American Treasure and the Price Revolution in Spain, 1501–1650* (Cambridge, MA: Harvard University Press, 1934), pp. 34, 42. According to Michel Morineau, *Incroyables gazettes et fabuleux métaux: Les Retours des trésors américains d'après les gazettes hollandaises (XVIe–XVIIIe siècles),* Studies in Modern Capitalism (Paris: Éditions de la Maison des Sciences de l'Homme; and Cambridge and New York: Cambridge University Press, 1985), Spanish American imports recovered to exceed earlier amounts in the later seventeenth century. My examination of his evidence (comparing Spanish apples with Dutch oranges) convinces me that this contention is not credible, especially when compared to the Spanish American evidence on silver mining outputs and shipments to the Philippines. Mexican silver mining and silver exports to Europe did, however, recover strongly from the early eighteenth century.

16. In 1686–7, woollen textiles accounted for 74.22 per cent of the total merchandise (excluding bullion) that western countries sold in Smyrna (now Izmir), by far the most important Ottoman port; and of these woollens, the English supplied 63.27 per cent. See M. Fontenay, 'Le Commerce des Occidentaux dans les échelles du Levant au XVIIe siècle', in S. Cavaciocchi (ed.), *Relazioni economiche tra Europa e mondo islamico, secoli XIII–XVIII/ Europe's Economic Relations with the Islamic World, 13th–18th Centuries,* Fondazione Istituto Internazionale di Storia Economica 'Francesco Datini', Atti delle 'Settimana di Studi' e altri convegni, 38 (Florence: Le Monnier, 2007), pp. 519–49; M. Fontenay, 'Le Commerce des Occidentaux dans les échelles du Levant en 1686–1687', in Bartolomé Bennassar and Robert Sauzet (eds), *Chrétiens et musulmans à la Renaissance: Actes du 37e Colloque International du Centre d'Études Supérieures de la Renaissance* (Paris: H. Champion, 1988), pp. 337–70.

17. See n. 13 above.

18. T. Sargent and F. Velde, *The Big Problem of Small Change* (Princeton, NJ, and Oxford: Princeton University Press, 2002). Sargent was the co-winner of the 2011 Nobel prize in Economics.

1 Munro, 'The Technology and Economics of Coinage Debasements in Medieval and Early Modern Europe'

1. A. Rolnick, F. Velde and W. Weber, 'The Debasement Puzzle: An Essay on Medieval Monetary History', *Journal of Economic History*, 56:4 (December 1996), pp. 789–808. See also F. Velde, W. Weber and R. Wright, 'A Model of Commodity Money, with Applications to Gresham's Law and the Debasement Puzzle', *Review of Economic Dynamics*, 2:1 (1999), pp. 291–333.

2. See E. Fournial, *Histoire monétaire de l'Occident médiéval* (Paris: F. Nathan, 1970), pp. 23–7.

3. When England, after the Norman Conquest (1066), established its own monetary system, the Tower Pound of fine silver (12 oz) was similarly struck into 240 pennies and subdivisions (half pence and farthings). N. J. Mayhew, 'From Regional to Central Minting, 1158–1464', in C. E. Challis (ed.), *A New History of the Royal Mint* (Cambridge and New York: Cambridge University Press, 1992). pp. 1–82, 83–178. In the first extant mint accounts, for Henry III in 1247, 242 pence were struck from the Tower Pound of sterling silver, 92.50 per cent pure (11 oz 2 dwt silver and 18 dwt copper).

4. See P. Spufford, *Money and its Use in Medieval Europe* (Cambridge: Cambridge University Press, 1988), pp. 226–7; F. C. Lane and R. Mueller, *Money and Banking in Medieval and Renaissance Venice*, vol. 1: *Coins and Moneys of Account* (Baltimore, MD, and London: The Johns Hopkins University Press, 1985), pp. 10–11, 114–15 (noting that the decision to issue *grossi* coins may date from 1194); Fournial, *Histoire monétaire*, pp. 78–9.

5. A. Blanchet and A. Dieudonné (eds), *Manuel de numismatique française*, 2 vols (Paris: Ricard, 1916), vol. 2, pp. 218-22.

6. Blanchet and Dieudonné, *Manuel de numismatique*, pp. 225–42. St Louis's *gros tournois* was struck at a full 12 deniers *argent-le-roy*, with 58 struck to the *marc de Troyes*; in 1303, he reduced the fineness to 9 *deniers*; with a partial monetary reform in 1306, he restored its former fineness, but with a face value of 13.125d *tournois*. In Flanders, the market value rose much further during these years (to 36d *parisis* = 28.8d *tournois*). Under Philip V (1316–22), the *gros tournois* retained its full fineness (12 *deniers*), but with a reduced weight (59.167 to the *marc*) and an increased face value of 15d *tournois*.

7. The medieval terms for bullion were: *billon, billoen, billio* – as defined above in the text. See J. H. Munro, 'Billon – Billoen – Billio: From Bullion to Base Coinage', *Revue belge de philologie et d'histoire/ Belgisch tijdschrift voor filologie en geschiedenis*, 52 (1974), pp. 293–305, which explains how the meaning of *billon* changed, over the centuries, so that the modern term 'billon' means a base or petty coin, one in which silver constitutes less than half of the metallic content.

8. See J. H. Munro, 'Bullionism and the Bill of Exchange in England, 1272–1663: A Study in Monetary Management and Popular Prejudice', in Center for Medieval and Renaissance Studies, UCLA (ed.), *The Dawn of Modern Banking* (New Haven, CT, and London: Yale University Press, 1979), appendices A–B, pp. 216–25, citing in particular statutes 38 Ed III, stat. 2, c. 14 (1364) and 15 Car.II, c. 7 (1663); and J. H. Munro, 'The Coinages and Monetary Policies of Henry VIII (r. 1509–47)', in *The Collected Works of*

Erasmus: The Correspondence of Erasmus, vol. 14: *Letters 1926 to 2081, A.D. 1528,* tr. C. Fantazzi and ed. J. Estes (Toronto: University of Toronto Press, 2011), pp. 423–76.

9. See accounts in Victor Gaillard (ed.), *Recherches sur les monnaies des comtes de Flandre,* 2 vols (Ghent: H. Hoste, 1856); J. H. Munro, *Wool, Cloth, and Gold: The Struggle for Bullion in Anglo-Burgundian Trade, 1340–1478* (Brussels and Toronto: Éditions de l'Université de Bruxelles, 1973).

10. See Rolnick et al., 'The Debasement Puzzle', pp. 789–808, in n. 1 above. More recently, the view that medieval coins did circulate by tale has been reluctantly accepted (by Velde) in T. Sargent and F. Velde, *The Big Problem of Small Change* (Princeton, NJ, and Oxford: Princeton University Press, 2002), pp. 16–19, 22, 75–322: 'that the market often valued coins partly by tale'.

11. See the evidence cited in Munro, *Wool, Cloth, and Gold*; and in studies in J. H. Munro, *Bullion Flows and Monetary Policies in England and the Low Countries, 1350–1500,* Variorum Collected Studies series, CS 355 (Aldershot and Brookfield, VT: Ashgate Publishing, 1992).

12. An examination of the official values or exchange rates for foreign gold coins circulating in the Low Countries (e.g. ducats, florins, English nobles, French *écus*), and in England in the 1520s, reveals that they also had such a premium: an *agio* lower than that on domestic Flemish gold coins but an amount still higher than the mint price for gold bullion. See exchange rates listed in J. H. Munro, 'Money, Wages, and Real Incomes in the Age of Erasmus: The Purchasing Power of Coins and of Building Craftsmen's Wages in England and the Southern Low Countries, 1500– 1540', in *The Collected Works of Erasmus: The Correspondence of Erasmus*, vol. 12: *Letters 1658–1801, January 1526–March 1527,* ed. A. Dalzell and C. G. Nauert, Jr. (Toronto: University of Toronto Press, 2003), appendix, pp. 551–699; and J. H. Munro, 'The Coinages and Monetary Policies of Henry VIII (r. 1509–47)', in *The Collected Works of Erasmus: The Correspondence*, vol. 14, pp. 423–76.

13. The mathematical formula for computing the *traite* is: $T = t.V/F$; or *traite* = *taille* per marc (number of coins cut from the marc) times the face value of the coin, divided by the percentage fineness (alloy) of the coin. For the *pied de la monnaie*, which is the *traite* multiplied by 5, see Fournial, *Histoire monétaire*, pp. 30–1.

14. Original text from *De origine, natura, jure et mutationibus monetarum,* published in C. Johnson (ed.), *The 'De Moneta' of Nicholas Oresme and English Mint Documents* (London: Thomas Nelson & Sons, 1956), ch. 15, p. 24. On Oresme's monetary philosophies, see Spufford, *Money and its Use,* pp. 295–304; and É. Bridrey, *La Théorie de la monnaie au XIVe siècle: Nicole Oresme. Étude d'histoire des doctrines et des faits économiques* (Paris: Girard & Brière, 1906).

15. The *mite* or *mijt* was a petty Flemish coin, largely copper, of which 24 mites = 1 d. groot. See also n. 46 below.

16. P. Grierson, *Numismatics* (Oxford: Oxford University Press, 1975), pp. 100–11, 150–5; P. Grierson, 'Medieval Numismatics', in J. Powell (ed.), *Medieval Studies: An Introduction* (Syracuse: Syracuse University Press, 1976), pp. 124–34; P. Grierson, 'Coin Wear and the Frequency Table', *Numismatic Chronicle,* 7th ser., 3 (1963), pp. i–xv; Philip Grierson, 'Weight and Coinage', *Numismatic Chronicle,* 7th ser., 4 (1964), pp. iii–xvii; Albert Girard, 'La Guerre des monnaies', *Revue de synthèse,* 19 (1940–5), pp. 83–101; Fournial, *Histoire monétaire*, pp. 9–38.

17. See J. H. Munro, 'Money, Prices, Wages, and "Profit Inflation" in Spain, the Southern Netherlands, and England during the Price Revolution era, ca. 1520–ca. 1650', *História e Economia: Revista Interdisciplinar,* 4:1 (2008), pp. 13–71.

18. See N. Gandal and N. Sussman, 'Asymmetric Information and Commodity Money: Tickling the Tolerance in Medieval France', *Journal of Money Credit and Banking*, 29:4 (November 1997), pp. 440–57.
19. See Peter Spufford's chapter in this volume.
20. For the Flemish Consumer Price Index, see also J. H. Munro, 'Wage-Stickiness, Monetary Changes, and Real Incomes in Late-Medieval England and the Low Countries, 1300–1500: Did Money Matter?', *Research in Economic History*, 21 (2003), pp. 185–297, table 1, p. 231.
21. They are discussed, in depth, in Peter Spufford's chapter in this volume.
22. See n. 22 above.
23. The English CPI statistics are taken from my revisions of E. H. Phelps Brown and S. V. Hopkins, 'Seven Centuries of the Prices of Consumables Compared with Builders' Wage-Rates', *Economica*, NS 23:92 (November 1956), pp. 296–314: reprinted in E.H. Phelps Brown and S. V. Hopkins, *A Perspective of Wages and Prices* (London: Methuen, 1981), pp. 13–59. My revised series is based on the price data contained in their working papers, in Box Ia:324, in the Archives of the British Library of Political and Economic Science (London School of Economics).
24. See Munro, 'Coinages of Henry VIII', pp. 423–76; J. H. Munro, 'The Monetary Origins of the "Price Revolution"', in Flynn et al. (eds), *Global Connections*, pp. 1–34.
25. Ibid. Edward IV's aggressive debasement of 1464, reducing the silver content by 20.0 per cent and raising the silver *traite* by 25.0 per cent, was followed by a 19.81 per cent rise in the CPI (1451–75=100), by 1466: to 105.51; but the CPI then began to fall over the ensuing decade, reaching a nadir of 84.62 in 1477, for a decline of 19.80 per cent, indicating the deflationary forces of the current 'bullion famine'.
26. For declining rates of interest, both nominal and real, in the sixteenth century, see S. Homer and R. Sylla, *A History of Interest Rates*, 3rd rev. edn (New Brunswick, NJ: Rutgers University Press, 1996), pp. 89–143, especially table 11 (pp. 137–8), and chart 2 (p. 140); and H. Van der Wee, *The Growth of the Antwerp Market and the European Economy (Fourteenth–Sixteenth Centuries)*, 3 vols (The Hague: Martinus Nijhoff, 1963), vol. 1: *Statistics*, appendix 45/2, pp. 525–7.
27. For evidence that increases in the money supply usually did lead to a fall in the income velocity of money, except during the sixteenth-century Price Revolution era, see N. J. Mayhew, 'Population, Money Supply, and the Velocity of Circulation in England, 1300–1700', *Economic History Review*, 48:2 (May 1995), pp. 238–57.
28. The fine silver content of the English penny from 1526 to 1542 was 0.639 g; by April 1551, during the worst phase of the Great Debasement (ending in June 1553), the penny contained only 0.169 g fine silver. The corresponding *traite* value of fine silver rose from £6.517 to £38.568 per kg over this period. See Munro, 'Coinages of Henry VIII', table 1, pp. 457–63.
29. Munro, *Wool, Cloth, and Gold*, pp. 100–3, 168–71, tables J–K, pp. 208–11; P. Spufford, *Monetary Problems and Policies in the Burgundian Netherlands, 1433–1496* (Leiden: Brill, 1970), ch. 3, 'Currency', pp. 55–73; ch. 4, 'La Guerre monétaire', pp. 74–129.
30. See Munro, *Wool, Cloth, and Gold*, pp. 157–71; see p. 31 and n. 39.
31. J. H. Munro, 'A Maze of Medieval Monetary Metrology: Determining Mint Weights in Flanders, France and England from the Economics of Counterfeiting, 1388–1469', *Journal of European Economic History*, 29:1 (Spring 2000), pp. 173–99; Munro, *Wool, Cloth, and Gold*, pp. 43–88, table F, pp. 202–3.

32. See many fifteenth-century examples in J. H. Munro, 'An Aspect of Medieval Public Finance: The Profits of Counterfeiting in the Fifteenth-Century Low Countries', *Revue belge de numismatique et de sigillographie*, 118 (1972), pp. 127–48.

33. Munro, *Wool, Cloth, and Gold*, pp. 70–84.

34. See J. H. Munro, 'Gresham's Law', in Joel Mokyr (ed.), *The Oxford Encyclopedia of Economic History*, 5 vols (Oxford and New York: Oxford University Press, 2003), vol. 2, pp. 480–1; Munro, *Wool, Cloth and Gold*, pp. 11–41. Sir Thomas Gresham was a merchant-banker and royal agent in Antwerp, and financial adviser to Queen Elizabeth I; he was also the founder of the Royal Exchange, in London (1565).

35. See Sargent and Velde, *Big Problem of Small Change*, pp. 45–68.

36. See C. Patterson, 'Silver Stocks and Losses in Ancient and Medieval Times', *Economic History Review*, 2nd ser., 25:2 (May 1972), pp. 205–35; N. J. Mayhew, 'Numismatic Evidence and Falling Prices in the Fourteenth Century', *Economic History Review*, 2nd ser. 27:1 (February 1974), pp. 1–15; A. Feavearyear, *The Pound Sterling: A History of English Money*, 2nd rev. edn. by E. Victor Morgan (Oxford: Clarendon Press, London, 1963), pp. 1–45.

37. For these and related problems with medieval Venetian coinages, see Lane and Mueller, *Money and Banking*, vol. 1, pp. 24–35, 380–415.

38. On this, see Feavearyear, *Pound Sterling*, pp. 1–45. For early-modern Europe, see very similar arguments in D. Glassman and A. Redish, 'Currency Depreciation in Early Modern England and France', *Explorations in Economic History*, 25:1 (1988), pp. 75–97. For the importance of both coinage 'wear and tear' and Gresham's law in Henry VIII's defensive debasement of 1526, see Munro, 'Coinages of Henry VIII', pp. 437–50.

39. Munro, *Wool, Cloth, and Gold*, table G, p. 204. An even more glaring contrast can be found with the coinages of Henry VIII. With his purely defensive debasement of November 1526, total mintage fees (seigniorage and brassage) amounted to 2.22 per cent of the silver *traite*; at the peak of the Great Debasement in April 1546, they amounted to 61.11 per cent of the *traite*; but in the reformed coinages of June 1557 and November 1560, they were only 2.50 per cent of the *traite*. See Munro, 'Coinages of Henry VIII', table 1, part 3, pp. 462–3.

40. Munro, *Wool, Cloth, and Gold*, pp. 100–3; table C, pp. 198–9; table G, p. 204. The consequent deflation, given the contraction of the coined money supply was far steeper: by 22.39 per cent with a fall in the CPI (1451–75=100) from 139.092 in 1433 to 108.046 in 1435 (98.777 in 1436).

41. Munro, *Wool, Cloth, and Gold*, pp. 43–63, table C, pp. 198–9; table G, p. 204; J. H. Munro, 'Mint Policies, Ratios, and Outputs in England and the Low Countries, 1335–1420: Some Reflections on New Data', *Numismatic Chronicle*, 141 (1981), pp. 71–116.

42. Feavearyear, *Pound Sterling*, appendix III:ii, p. 439; C. E. Challis, Appendix 2: 'Mint Contracts', in C. E. Challis (ed.), *A New History of the Royal Mint* (Cambridge and New York: Cambridge University Press, 1992), pp. 699–758.

43. See Spufford, *Money and its Use*, pp. 339–63.

44. Sargent and Velde, *Big Problem of Small Change*, pp. 5, 7–8, 10, 40, 152, 187, 261, 321, 32 4. See in particular, p. 261 (and n. 1): 'We interpret many of these debasements as having been designed to cure shortages of small change, not primarily to gather seigniorage'. They admit that fiscal motives did predominate in Henry VIII's Great Debasement.

45. The Habsburg Netherlands were the first to strike all-copper coins in 1543; France followed in 1577; Habsburg Spain in 1599; and England only in 1672. See H. E. Van Gelder and M. Hoc, *Les Monnaies des Pays-Bas bourguignons et espagnols, 1434–1713: Répertoire générale* (Amsterdam: J. Schulman, 1960); Van der Wee, *The Growth of the Antwerp*

Market, vol. 1, pp. 123–35; F. Spooner, *The International Economy and Monetary Movements in France, 1493–1725* (Paris, 1956; Cambridge, MA: Harvard University Press, 1972, for the English edn), appendix A, p. 332; E. J. Hamilton, *American Treasure and the Price Revolution in Spain, 1502–1650* (Cambridge, MA: Harvard University Press, 1934), pp. 49–64; C. E. Challis, 'Lord Hastings to the Great Silver Recoinage, 1464–1699', in Challis (ed.), *A New History of the Royal Mint,* pp. 365–78; and Appendix 1: 'Mint Output, 1220–1985', p. 689.

46. J. H. Munro, 'Deflation and the Petty Coinage Problem in the Late-Medieval Economy: The Case of Flanders, 1334–1484', *Explorations in Economic History,* 25:4 (October 1988), pp. 387–423: estimating that normally only about one per cent of the total amount of silver coined in the Burgundian Low Countries (1384–1482) was in petty coins known, as *mites* (= 1/24 of a penny): single and double.

47. One exception that Sargent and Velde do not note was the Burgundian-Flemish monetary ordinance of 31 August 1457, during an era of very low mint outputs. It required the mint to strike a greater number of billon coins known as *courtes* or double-mites (= ¹⁄₁₂th of a penny groot) from the alloyed *marc*: 240 *courtes* in place of the previously required 216 per marc. Nevertheless, in the quinquennium 1456–60, only 51.302 kg of fine silver were minted – compared to 112 times as much in 1426–30: 5,724.645 kg. See Munro, 'Petty Coinage', table 3, p. 396.

48. See n. 38 above; and other studies in this volume for such monetary phenomena, especially in seventeenth-century Spain.

2 Harl, 'From Aurelian to Diocletian'

1. See A. H. M. Jones, *The Later Roman Empire, 284–602: A Social, Economic and Administrative Survey* (Norman, OK: University of Oklahoma Press 1965), pp. 427–69; R. MacMullen, *Roman Government's Response to Crisis, A.D. 235–337* (New Haven, CT: Yale University Press, 1976), pp. 96–181, and cf. G. Depeyrot, *Crises et inflation entre antiquité et moyen age* (Paris: A Colin, 1991); C. Brenot, X. Loriot, and D. Nony. *Aspects d'histoire économique et monétaire de Marc Aurèle à Constantin 161–337 après J.-C.* (Paris: CDU Sedes, 1999) and L. Camilli and S. Sorda (eds), *L'inflazione nel quarto secolo d. C. Atti dell'incontro di studio Roma 1988* (Rome: Annali dell'Istituto Italiana di Numismatica, 1993).

2. See M. I. Finley, *The Ancient Economy,* rev. edn (Berkeley, CA: California University Press, 1999), pp. 165–7, and S. von Reden, *Money in Classical Antiquity* (Cambridge: Cambridge University Press, 2010), pp. 54–5.

3. See P. Temin, 'Estimating the GPD of the Early Roman Empire', in E. Lo Cascio (ed.), *Innovazione tercnica e progresso economico nel mondo romano* (Bari: Edipuglia, 2006), pp. 31–54, arguing for a GDP of 10–12 billion HS (= 2.3–3 billion *denarii* for a population of 60 million. See R. W. Goldsmith, 'An Estimate of the Size and Structure of the National Product of the Early Roman Empire', *Review of Income and Wealth,* 10 (1984), pp. 263–88, for calculation of wealth based on wheat prices, but see reservations by A. Bowman, 'Quantifying Egyptian Agriculture', in A. Bowman and A. Wilson (eds) *Quantifying the Roman Economy: Methods and Problems* (Oxford: Oxford University Press, 2009), pp. 194–5, and W. Scheidel, 'A Model of Real Income Growth in the Roman Age', *Historia,* 56 (2007), pp. 322–46. See R. P. Duncan-Jones, *Money and Government in the Roman Empire* (Cambridge: Cambridge University Press, 1996), pp, 163–8 and

table 11. 1–2, who argues for an annual production of 22 million *denarii* in 64–235. He estimates a total output of 443 million *denarii* under Antoninus Pius and 532 million *denarii*, under Septimius Severus. The method is controversial. Gold and silver coins were subject to recall and recoinage whenever the standard was lowered; see K. W. Harl, *Coinage in the Roman Economy 300 B.C. to A.D. 700*, (Baltimore, MD: Johns Hopkins University Press, 1996), pp. 11–16 and 125–36.

4. See W. Scheidel, 'The Monetary Systems of the Han and Roman Empires', in W. Scheidel (ed.), *Rome and China: Comparative Perspectives on Ancient World Empires* (Oxford: Oxford University Press 2009), pp. 137–206, who concludes the Roman economy was vastly more monetized. See P. F. Bang, *The Roman Bazaar: A Comparative Study of Trade and Markets in a Tributary Empire* (Cambridge: Cambridge University Press, 2008), pp. 17–57, for comparisons to Mughal India and the Ottoman Empire but without discussion of coinage or monetization.

5. See Finley, *Ancient Economy*, pp. 166–8, and cf. von Reden, *Money in Classical Antiquity*, pp. 89–91.

6. See B. Borg and C. Witschel, 'Veranderung im Repräsentationsverhalten der römischen Eliten während des 3. Jhr. N. Chr.', in *Inschriftliche Denkmäler als Medien de Selbstdarstellung in der römischen Welt*, ed. G. Alföldy and S. Panciera (Stuttgart: Franz Steiner, 2001), pp. 47–120. See discussion of histriography by C. F. Noreña, *Imperial Ideals in the Roman West. Representation, Circulation, Power* (Cambridge: Cambridge University Press, 2011), pp. 294–7.

7. See Harl, *Coinage in the Roman Economy*, p. 142, table 6.4; based on D. R. Walker; *The Metrology of Roman Silver Coinage* (Oxford: British Archaeological Reports, 1976–7), Part I, pp. 149–57 and Part II, pp. 114–16. Although this table does not account for the process of surface enrichment, it does convey the relative rate of debasement of imperial silver currency.

8. For surface enrichment of coins with silver, see K. Butcher and M. Ponting, 'The Roman Denarius under the Julio-Claudian Emperors: Mints, Metallurgy and Technology', *Oxford Journal of Archaeology*, 24:2 (2005), 163–97, and 'Rome and the East: Production of Roman Provincial Silver Coinage for Caesarea in Cappadocia under Vespasian A.D. 69–79', *Oxford Journal of Archaeology*, 14:1 (1995), 63–77. See also H. Gitler and M. Ponting, The *Silver Coinages of Septimius Severus and his Family (A.D 193–211)* (Milan: Ennerre, Glaux 16, 2003). For the strict regulation of standards of fineness, see M. Potting, 'Roman Silver Coinage: Mints, Metallurgy, and Production', in Bowman and Wilson (eds), *Quantifying the Roman Economy*, pp. 269–79.

9. See Harl, *Coinage in the Roman Economy*, pp. 126–36 and cf. 216–20. The tables of debasement are based on Walker's metrological analysis.

10. See R. S. Bagnall, *Currency and Inflation in Fourth Century Egypt* (Chico, CA: BASP Supplement 5, 1986), pp. 9–19.

11. See R. MacMullen, 'Some Tax Statistics from Roman Egypt', *Aegyptus*, 42 (1964), pp. 159–84, for increased survival of documentary papyri under the Tetrarchy.

12. See D. Rathbone, 'Earnings and Costs: Living Standards and the Economy of the Roman Empire', in Bowman and Wilson (eds) *Quantifying the Roman Economy*, pp. 299–326, and cf. R P. Duncan-Jones, 'The Price of Wheat in Roman Egypt under the Principate', *Chiron*, 6 (1976), pp. 241–62. For estimates of spending per capita and purchasing power of wages, see R. C. Allen, 'How Prosperous were the Romans?: Evidence from Diocletian's Price Edict', in Bowman and Wilson (eds), *Quantifying the Roman Economy*, pp. 327–43.

13. For long-term stability of wheat prices, see D. Rathbone, 'Monetization Not Price Inflation', in C. E. King and D. G. Wigg (eds), *Coin Finds and Coin Use in the Roman Empire*, SFMA 10 (Frankfurt, 1996), pp. 321–9, and 'Prices and Price Formation in Roman Egypt', in J. Andreau, P. Briant, and R. Descat (eds), *Économique antique: Prix et formation des prix dans les économies antiques*, Entretiens d'archéologie et d'histoire, 3 (Saint-Bertrand-de-Comminges, 1997), pp. 183–244. See Bang, *The Roman Bazaar*, pp. 153–73, for an unconvincing critique of Rathone's methods and conclusions.

14. See W. Scheidel, 'A Model of Demographic and Economic Change in Egypt after the Antonine Plague', *Journal of Roman Archaeology*, 15 (2002), pp. 97–114.

15. See J. E. Lendon, 'The Face on the Coin and Inflation in Roman Egypt', *Klio*, 72 (1990), pp. 110–11, for fourfold inflation of wheat prices after 275, but the thesis is difficult to sustain. Lendon fails to account for the fiduciary nature of the Egyptian *tetradrachma*, and the recoinage necessitated by the reform of the coinage in Egyptian regnal year AD 274/5; see Harl, *Coinage in the Roman Economy*, pp. 118–24.

16. See G. Mickwitz, *Geld und Wirtschaft in römischen Reich des vierten Jahrhunderts n. Chr.* (Helsinki: Societas Scientiarum Fennica, 1932), pp. 80–178. See J. Banaji, *Agrarian Change in Late Antiquity: Gold, Labour, and Aristocratic Dominance* (Oxford: Oxford University Press, 2000), pp. 23–38, for critique of how Mickwitz and Weber shaped all subsequent views of the later Roman economy

17. For revision of this established view, see now Banaji, *Agrarian Change*, pp. 39–79, and cf. M. Corbier, 'Coinage and Taxation: The State's Point of View, A.D. 193–337', in A. Bowman, P. Garnsey and A. Cameron (eds), *The Cambridge Ancient History*, vol. 12, 2nd edn (Cambridge: Cambridge University Press, 2005), pp. 381–6, for summary of the traditional opinion.

18. See e.g. D. Potter, *The Roman Empire at Bay A.D. 180–395* (New York: Routledge, 2004), pp. 294–6 and 334–6. See S. Williams, *Diocletian and the Roman Recovery* (London: Methuen Inc., 1985), pp. 115–39, who sums up the preceding scholarship as indicative of a 'command economy'.

19. See J. P. C. Kent, 'Gold Coinage in the Later Roman Empire', in R. A. G. Carson and C. H. V. Sutherland (eds), *Essays in Roman Coinage Presented to Harold Mattingly* (Oxford: Oxford University Press, 1965), pp. 190–204.

20. C.Th. 12. 6. 12 (366), cf. C.Th. 12. 6. 13 (367); see Kent, *Essays in Roman Coinage*, pp 191–3, and cf. Harl, *Coinage in Roman Economy*, pp. 159–60.

21. See C. Howgego, *Ancient History from Coins* (London: Routledge, 1995), pp. 118–19, and Banaji, *Agrarian Change in Late Antiquity*, pp. 66–70, for recent restatements of the thesis of two distinct currencies – the first of precious metal coins (gold and silver) floating according to bullion value and the second of base metal or billon fractions. For a sensible critique of this thesis, see J.-J. Aubert, 'Monetary Policy and Gresham's Law in the Late Third Century', in E. Lo Cascio (ed.), *Credito e moneta nel mondo romano: Atti degli incontri capresi di storia dell'economia antica (Capri 12–14 ottobre 2000)* (Bari: Epdipulgia, 2003), pp. 250–63.

22. See Jones, *The Later Roman Empire, 284–602*, pp. 462–629, and MacMullen, *Roman Government's Response to Crisis*, pp. 96–128.

23. See Rathbone, in Bowman and Wilson (eds) *Quantifying the Roman Economy*, pp. 301–3, for methods for constructing a series of wheat prices. Ibid., pp. 303–21, for calculating prices and wages in silver bullion, and cf. Bagnall, *Currency and Inflation*, pp. 37–48. For calculating prices and wages in gold bullion, see S. Mrozek, *Prix et rémuneration dans l'Occident romain (31 av. n.è–250 de n.è)* (Gdansk: Societas Scientiearum Gedanensis,

1975) and cf. E. Lo Cascio, 'Prezzi in oro e prezzi in unità di conto tra il III e il IV sec. d. C.', in Andreau et al. (eds), *Économique antique,* pp. 183–244. See M. Corbier, 'Dévaluations et évolution des prix (I–IIIe siècles)', *Revue Numismatique,* 6:27 (1985), pp. 69–106, for reckoning prices in silver *denarii* and adjusting for the lower purity of later *denarii* by adjusting according to the gold:silver bullion ratios. For constructing price series based on equating different coins, see F. Heichelheim, 'On Ancient Price Trends from the End of Early First Millennium B.C. to Heraclius', *Finanzarchiv,* 15 (1954–5), pp. 498–511.

24. See Bagnall, *Currency and Inflation,* pp. 37–48, who converts accounting units into equivalents of silver bullion, and cf. Bang, *The Roman Bazaar,* pp. 153–73, reckoning by the units of account so that the reconstructed series reflects only relative fluctuations in prices.

25. *Contra* Scheidel, in *Rome and China,* pp. 176–78, arguing for the absolute primacy of gold as currency in the fourth and fifth centuries. The comparison of the *solidus* and gold ingots of the Dominate to the gold biscuits of Han China is misleading, and unconvincing. See Banaji, *Agrarian Conditions,* pp. 38–57, emphasizing gold as the only significant money. Such a position fails to account for the imperial government's repeated efforts to reform fiduciary or token coins used in daily transactions; see Harl, *Coinage in the Roman Economy,* pp. 158–80.

26. See R. A. G. Carson, 'The Reform of Aurelian', *Revue Numismatique,* 6:7 (1965), p. 232. This initial reform in 271 followed the revolt of the moneyers at Rome, see V. Cubelli, *Aureliano imperatore: La rivolta dei monetieri e la cosiddetta riforma monetaria* (Florence: La Nuova Italia Editrice, 1992), pp. 17–18 and 51–4.

27. See Zon. 1. 61.3, and see discussion by Carson, 'The Reform of Aurelian', pp. 232–5. For the value of the aurelianianus at 5 d.c, see K. W. Harl, 'Marks of Value on Tetrarchic Nummi and Diocletian's Monetary Policy', *Phoenix,* 39 (1985), p. 268; the value of 20 *asses* and so a value is implausible; *contra* M. H. Crawford, 'Finance, Coinage, and Money from the Severans to Constantine', in H. Temporini (ed.), *Aufstieg und Niedergang der römischen Welt,* 2/2 (Berlin: Walter de Gruyter, 1975), pp. 575–6. For fineness of 5 per cent, see J.-P. Callu, C. Brenot, and J.-N. Barrandon, 'Analyses de séries atypiques (Aurélien, Tacite, Carus, et Licinius', *Numismatica e Antichità Classiche. Quaderni Ticinesi,* 8 (1979), pp. 241–54.

28. For the initial publication of the Venerà hoard, see L. A. Milani, *Il Ripostiglio della Venerà: Monete romane della seconda meta dei terzo secolo* (Rome: Reald Accademia dei Lincei, 1880). The hoard has been republished (with the catalogue of the coins of Probus forthcoming). See J.-B. Giard, *Ripostiglio della Venerà: Nuovo Catalogo Illustrato,* vol. 1: *Gordiano-Quintillo* (Rome: L'herma di Bretschneider, 1995); S. Estiot, *Ripostiglio della Venerà: Nuovo Catalogo Illustrato,* vol. 2/1: *Aureliano* (Rome: L'herma di Bretschneider, 1995); S. Estiot, *Ripostiglio della Venerà: Nuovo Catalogo Illustrato,* vol. 2/2: *Tacito e Floriano* (Rome: L'herma di Bretschneider, 1987); and D. Gricourt, *Ripostiglio della Venerà: Nuovo Catalogo Illustrato,* vol. 4: *Caro-Diocletizano* (Rome: L'herma di Bretschneider, 2000).

29. The total number of earlier coins prior to the reign of Aurelian is 10,459; the total number of pre-reform coins of Aurelian is 8,419; the total number of *aurelianiani* is 26,984 with 2 *denarii communes.*

30. The total number of coins of Aurelian is 11,461: 618 coins of *divus* Claudius II, minted in 270–1 (5 per cent), 240 pre-reform *antoniniani* of 270–1 (2 per cent), and 7,561 coins minted after the first reform, in 271–4 (66 per cent), and 3,042 *aurelianiani* of

274–5 (27 per cent). In the last group is included two *denarii communes* (Venerà 1521 and 10,847).

31. See Harl, *Coinage in the Roman Economy*, pp. 148–9, and see analysis of hoards by C. E. King, 'The Circulation of Coins in the Western Provinces, A.D. 260–295', in A. King and M. Henig (eds), *The Roman West in the Third Century: Contributions from Archaeology and History* (Oxford: Bristish Archaeological Reports, International Series 109, 1981), pp. 92–7.

32. See W. E. Metcalf, 'Aurelian's Reform at Alexandria', in R. Ashton and S. Hurter (eds), *Studies in Greek Numismatics in Memory of Martin Jessop Price* (London: Spink and Son Ltd., 1998), pp. 269–76.

33. See E. Christensen, *Coinage in Roman Egypt: The Hoard Evidence* (Aarhus: University of Aarhus Press, 2003), pp. 126–8; this recoinage and the survival of hoards are not indices of price surges, as argued by Lendon, 'The Face on the Coin', pp. 111–12 and 121–3, and followed by Harl, *Coinage in the Roman Economy*, p. 147.

34. See W. E. Metcalf, 'From Greek to Latin Currency in Third Century Egypt', in H. Huvelin, M. Christol and G. Gautier (eds), *Mélanges de numismatique offerts à Pierre Bastien à l'occasion de son 75e anniversaire* (Wetteren: University of Louvain Press, Acta Archaeologica Lovaniensia 25, 1986), pp. 157–68. The last *tetradrachmae* of Diocletian dated to his Egyptian regnal year 12 (295/6) were struck just prior to the rebellion of L. Domitius Domitianus. See also C. H. V. Sutherland, 'Diocletian's Extension of the "Latin" Follis to Egypt: The Date and Sequence of Issues', in *Congresso internazionale di numismatica II. Atti, Roma, 1961* (Rome: Istituto italiano di numismatica, 1965), pp. 341–6, and J. Schwartz, 'La Monnaie d'Alexandrie et la réforme de Dioclétien', *Schweizer Münzblätter*, 14 (1964), pp. 98–102.

35. See C. H. V. Sutherland, *The Roman Imperial Coinage* (London: Spink and Son Ltd., 1973), vol. 6, pp. 662–3, nos. 14a–17a, for an initial series of *nummi*, in *c.* 295–6, struck for all four Tetrarchs. The next series comprised *nummi* of the Tetrarchs (p. 663, nos. 18a–b and 21a–b) and for Domitus Domitianus (p. 663, nos. 19–20). The next series of *nummi* were struck only for the Tetrarchs (pp. 663–4, nos. 22–3). The series carry the same mint and officina marks.

36. See J.-P. Callu, *Genio Populi Romani (295–316): Ccontribution à une histoire numismatique de la Tétrarchie* (Paris: Champion, Bibliothèque l'École des hautes études, 1960), p. 27, and M. Thirion, 'Folles d'Alexandrie (295–304)', *Revue belge de numismatique*, 107 (1961), pp. 192–209, for the *nummi* of Domitius Domitianus. See also J. Schwartz, *Domitius Domitianus* (Brussels: Papyrolpgoca Brixellensis 12, 1974), pp. 141–4; noting that the *tetradrachma* and new imperial *nummus* (*noummion Italikon*) briefly circulated together. If so, the *tetradrachma* too (just like the *aurelianianus*) might have been lowered to a tariffing of 2 *d.c.*

37. See D. O. A. Klose, *Die Münzprägung von Smyrna in der römischen Kaiserzeit* (Berlin: Walter de Gruyter, 1987), pp. 110–12, and cf. C. Howgego, *Greek Imperial Countermarks: Studies in the Provincial Coinage of the Roman Empire* (London: Royal Numismatic Society, Special Publication 17, 1970), nos 559–61 and 802–5, who fails to distinguish the two periods of countermarking. See A. Johnston, 'Questions of Survival', in Ashton and Hurter (eds), *Studies in Greek Numismatics*, pp. 155–62, who cautions against drawing conclusions of massive inflation based on the die counts for the bronze coins of Perge and Side struck during the period of countermarking. Hence, the dismal state of circulating currency in eastern cities is likely overstated by D. M. MacDonald, 'Aphrodisias and the Currency of the East, A.D. 259–305', *American Journal of Archaeol-*

ogy, 78 (1974), 279–86, and cf. C. Katsari, 'The Monetization of Roman Asia Minor in the Third Century A.D', in S. Mitchell and C. Katsari (eds), *Patterns of the Economy of Roman Asia Minor* (Swansea: University of Swansea Press, 2005), pp. 261–88.

38. Harl, *Coinage in the Roman Economy,* p. 147, and pp. 424–5, n. 49. See W. W. Esty, N. Equall and R. J. Smith, 'The Alloy of the "XI" Coins of Tacitus', *Numismatic Chronicle,* 153 (1993), pp. 201–4.

39. See *P. Merton* 88. See also *P. Rylands.* IV. 604; *PSI* 969 and *P. Oslo* III. 88, for comparable panic when Licinius halved the tariffing of the *nummus* from 25 *d.c.* to 12½ *d.c.* For tariffing of the denominations in 293–305, see Harl, 'Marks of Value on Tetrarchic Nummi', pp. 265–7 and M. Hendy, *Studies in the Byzantine Monetary Economy c. 300–1450* (Cambridge: Cambridge University Press , 1985), pp. 459–60. The continued circulation of *aureliani* is borne out by the Ankara hoard, concealed in *c.* 310. The hoard comprised 883 coins: 576 *aureliani* or post-reform radiates struck after 293 (65 per cent) and 304 nuumi (35 per cent). The 576 *aureliani* or post-reform radiates struck after 293 are as follows: 3 coins of Aurelian (0.5 per cent), 1 of Tacitus (0.1 per cent), 46 of Probus (8.0 per cent), 32 of Carus and Carinus (5.6 per cent), and 494 *aureliani* and post-reform radiates struck after 293. See D. Kienast, 'Der Münzfund von Ankara (270–310 n. Chr.)', *Jahrbuch für Numismatik und Geldgeschichte,* 12 (1962), pp. 65–112.

40. See Harl, *Coinage in Roman Economy,* pp. 152–7. The problem might have arisen over the exchange rates between silver-coated *nummus* and pure silver argenteus. See Aubert, 'Monetary Policy', in Lo Cascio (ed.), *Credito e moneta,* pp. 254–60.

41. For the Monetary Edict of 1 September 301, see K. T. Erim, J. M Reynolds and M. H. Crawford, 'Diocletian's Currency Reform: A New Inscription', *Journal of Roman Studies,* 61 (1971), pp. 175–6. But the value of the *nummus* should be restored as 25 (and not 20); see Harl, 'Marks of Value on Tetrarchic Nummi', pp. 263–70.

42. Harl, *Coinage in the Roman Economy,* pp. 163–7.

43. *Edictum de Pretiis Maximis,* pref. 14, and cf. 6, for general complaints.

44. For the date of the Price Edict, see T. B. Barnes, *The New Empire of Diocletian and Constantine* (Cambridge, MA: Harvard University Press, 1982), pp. 19-25, who notes Diocletian's title of *tribunica potestas* XVIII and Imperator XVIII can only date to this period. But the titles are given in an inscription from Egypt so the titles might reflect the date of the cutting of the stone rather than the issuing of the edict. See S. Corcoran, *The Empire of the Tetrarchs: Imperial Pronouncements, and Government AD 284–324* (Oxford: Oxford University Press, 1996), p. 206, n. 3. See Crawford, 'Finance, Coinage, and Money from the Severans to Constantine', in Temporini (ed.), *Aufsteig und Niedergang der römischen Welt,* 2/2, p. 579, n. 77, who rejects this date and argues for issuing of the Price Edict before the Monetary Edict of 1 September 301. The same sequence was adopted by Harl, *Coinage in the Roman Economy,* pp. 152–5.

45. See R. MacMullen, *Soldier and Civilian in the Later Roman Empire* (Cambridge, MA: Harvard University Press, 1966), pp. 176–7.

46. See foremost *OGIS* 484 (Provisions of Pergamum), issued by Hadrian, and cf. Corcoran, *The Empire of Tetrarchs,* pp. 213–15, for precedents.

47. See Allen, 'How Prosperous were the Romans?', in Bowman and Wilson (eds) *Quantifying the Roman Economy,* pp. 330–6, for the possible purchasing power of this daily wage.

48. See Lac., *De mort. persc.* 7.7, implying an immediate failure of the edict, but the date of its withdrawal is uncertain; see Corcoran, *The Empire of Tetrarchs,* pp. 232–3.

49. *CJ* 11.11.2; see translation and discussion in Hendy, *Studies in Byzantine Monetary Economy*, p. 473; the law was likely issued in tandem with *C.Th.* 11.21.1 (371) that ended the striking of silver-clad coins.
50. See *C.Th.* 11.21.1.
51. See J. P. C. Kent, *The Roman Imperial Coinage,* vol. 8 (London: Spink and Son Ltd., 1981), pp. 46–7; the total number of officinae was reduced from 73 to 35 officinae, a reduction of 52 per cent.
52. See e.g. A. J. Dowling, 'Calculating Britain's Requirements for Decimal Coinage', *British Numismatic Journal,* 41 (1972), pp. 168–72.
53. See C. E. King and D. R. Walker, 'The Earliest Tiberian Tetradrachms and Roman Monetary Policy towards Egypt', *Zeitschrift für Papyrologie und Epigraphik,* 21 (1976), pp. 256–69, and A. Burnett, 'The Imperial Coinage of Egypt in the First Century A.D', in F. Duyat and O. Picard (eds), *L'Exception égyptienne? Production et échanges monétaires d'Égypte héllenistiques et romaine. Actes du colloque d'Alexandrie, 13–15 avril 2002* (Cairo: Institute Français d'Archéologie Orientale, Études alexandrienes 10, 2005), pp. 261–77. For new analysis of the fineness of the *tetradrachma* with silver enriched surface, see K. Butcher and M. Ponting, 'The Egyptian Billon Tetradrachma under the Julio-Claudian Emperors: Fiduciary or Intrinsic', *Schweizer Münzblätter,* 84 (2005), pp. 93–124.
54. See Banaji, *Agrarian Change,* pp. 39–88, for critique, and case for a monetary economy.
55. See S. Bolin, *State and Currency in the Roman Empire to 300 A.D.* (Uppsala: Almqvist & Wiksells Boktyckeri AB, 1960), pp. 300–2.
56. *CPR* V.26.604–5; see discussion by Harl, *Coinage in Roman Economy*, pp. 177–8.
57. See Harl, *Coinage in Roman Economy*, pp. 235–8 and table 9. 4, based on *P. Mich.* 223–5.
58. See von Reden, *Money in Classical Antiquity*, pp. 148–155 and pp. 199–205, appendix of wheat prices.
59. The gold dollar was thus reckoned at 23.22 grains or 1.5046 grs. of pure gold. The production of silver certificate one dollar bills (redeemable in silver) was ended in 1963. In 1964, dollar bills were not longer redeemable in silver coin; in 1968 they were no longer redeemable in silver bullion.

3 Stahl, 'The Making of a Gold Standard'

1. P. de Mézières, *Le Songe du vieil pélérin,* ed. G. W. Coopland. 2 vols (London: Cambridge University Press, 1969), vol. 1, p. 371, 'comme il appert part la monnoye de la seigneurie de Venise, qui ix^c ans a dure sans faire mutacion ; c'est assavoir de fins ducaz d'or de XX et quatre quarraz'.
2. The classic account is R. Lopez, 'Settecento anni fa: Il ritorno all'oro nell'occidente duecentesco', *Rivista Storica Italiana,* 65 (1963), pp. 19–55, 161–98. See also P. Spufford, *Money and its Use in Medieval Europe* (Cambridge: Cambridge University Press, 1988), pp. 176–8.
3. M. Bernocchi, *Le monete della repubblica fiorentina,* 5 vols (Florence, 1974–85), vols 2 and 5.
4. A. M. Stahl, *Zecca: The Mint of Venice in the Middle Ages* (Baltimore, MD: Johns Hopkins University Press, 2000), pp. 30–3. The act authorizing its introduction was passed on 31 October 1284; actual minting of the coin began in March 1285.
5. Stahl, *Zecca,* pp. 47–50.
6. Ibid., pp. 26, 199–200.
7. Ibid., pp. 32–3, 86–91, 193–8.

8. N. Papadopoli [Aldobrandini], *Le monete di Venezia*, vol. 2 (Venice, 1907), pp. 62, 72, 101, 130, 146, 182, 218.
9. Ibid., vol. 2, pp. 211–13. There was in this period also another Venetian coin of less fine gold and lighter weight called the 'scudo'.
10. Ibid., vol. 2, p. 270.
11. Ibid., vol. 3 (Venice, 1919), pp. 8–9.
12. A. M. Stahl and C. Tonini, 'Venezia (Veneto)', in L. Travaini (ed.), *Le Zecche Italiane fino all'Unità*, 2 vols (Rome, 2011), vol. 1, pp. 1217–24.
13. F. Muntoni, *Le monete dei papi e degli stati pontifici*, 4 vols (Rome, 1972–3), vol. 1, pp. 68–70; and vol. 4, pp. 194–9.
14. G. Schlumberger, *Numismatique de l'Orient Latin* (Paris, 1878), pp. 255-69; A. L. Friedberg et al., *Gold Coins of the World*, 7th edn (Clifton. NJ, 2003), pp. 490–2; C. R. Bruce et al., *Standard Catalogue of World Coins 1701–1800*, 4th edn (Iola, WI, 2007), p. 1011.
15. Schlumberger, *Numismatique*, pp. 420-2, 439–42.
16. H. Ives and P. Grierson, *The Venetian Gold Ducat and its Imitations*, Numismatic Notes and Monographs, 128 (New York, 1954).
17. Friedberg, *Gold Coins*, pp. 471, 210–11, 179.
18. L. Bellocchi, *Le monete di Bologna* (Bologna, 1987), pp. 111–57.
19. Friedberg, *Gold Coins*, pp. 442, 450–1, 456–7, 462–3.
20. A. Heiss, *Descripción general de las monedas hispano-cristianas*, 3 vols (1865–9; repr. Saragosa, 1962), vol. 1, pp. 134–5; vol. 2, pp. 37–8 and 245–6.
21. Spufford, *Money and its Use*, p. 321.
22. *El Tesoro de Sant Pere de Rodes* (Barcelona, 1999).
23. P. Spufford, *Handbook of Medieval Exchange* (London: Royal Historical Society, 1986), p. 240.
24. G. Probszt, *Österreichische Münz- und Geldgeschichte* (Vienna, 1973), p. 290.
25. Ibid., p. 352.
26. Ibid., pp. 373–4.
27. A. Feaveayear, *The Pound Sterling: A History of English Money*, 2nd rev. edn, E. Victor Morgan (Oxford: Clarendon Press, 1963), appendix III.ii, p. 439; C. E. Challis, Appendix 2: 'Mint Contracts, 1279–1817', in C. E. Challis (ed.), *A New History of the Royal Mint* (Cambridge and New York: Cambridge University Press, 1992), pp. 717–21.

4 Spufford, 'Debasement of the Coinage and its Effects on Exchange Rates and the Economy'

1. P. Spufford, *Handbook of Medieval Exchange* (London: Royal Historical Society, 1986) p.xix.
2. D. W. Sorenson, 'Silver and Billon Coinage in France under Charles VI', (unpublished PhD thesis, University of Cambridge, 1988); Nathan Sussman, 'Mints and Debasements: Monetary Policy in France during the Second Phase of the Hundred Years War, 1400–1425' (unpublished PhD thesis, University of California, Berkeley, 1990).
3. Note that such debasements deliberately made in emergencies, with the intention of making a profit, were different from the necessary reductions in the weight of coinage at intervals to cope with the wear and tear of the currency in circulation. In England such reductions took place in 1351, 1412 and 1526. The crown made some profit on such occasions, but such mild weight reductions were not the consequence of fiscal pressures.

Edward IV's debasement of 1464, though seemingly defensive, since the coinage had not been altered in over 50 years, was also aggressive, as indicated by its high seigniorage rate. See J. H. Munro, 'The Coinages and Monetary Policies of Henry VIII (r. 1509–47)', in *The Collected Works of Erasmus: The Correspondence of Erasmus*, vol. 14: *Letters 1926 to 2081, A.D. 1528*, tr. Charles Fantazzi and ed. James Estes (Toronto: University of Toronto Press, 2011), pp. 423–76.

4. P. Spufford, 'Münzverschlechterung und Inflation im spätmittelalterlichen und frühneuzeitlichen Europa', in M. North (ed.), *Geldumlauf, Währungssysteme und Zahlungsverkehr in Nordwesteuropa 1300–1800*, Quellen und Darstellungen zur Hansischen Geschichte, NS 35 (Cologne, 1989). Much of the evidence that I then used came from C. E. Challis, *The Tudor Coinage* (Manchester: Manchester University Press, 1978).

5. J. D. Gould, *The Great Debasement: Currency and the Economy in Mid-Tudor England* (Oxford: Clarendon Press, 1970). The actual number of rolls of cloth involved was far greater, since other cloths were also reckoned for customs purposes in terms of these standard broadcloths, known as cloths of assize. Many of the actual broadcloths exported were half-broadcloths, while three of the increasingly popular kerseys were reckoned for customs purposes as one standard broadcloth, and between five and eight straits or narrows were reckoned as one broadcloth.

6. The debasement years were part of a general trend for the improved quality and price of English cloth exports. J. Oldland, 'The Variety and Quality of English Woollen Cloth Exported in the Late Middle Ages', *Journal of European Economic History*, 39:2 (Fall 2010), pp. 211–51.

7. P. Spufford, 'Merchants and Trade in England at the End of the Middle Ages, 1469–1504', in H. Casado Alonso and A. Garcia-Baquero (eds), *Comercio y hombres de negocios en Castilla y Europa en tiempos de Isabel la Católica* (Madrid: Sociedad Estatal de Conmemoraciones Culturales, 2007), pp. 65–89.

8. *Discourse of the Common Weal of this Realm of England*, written 1549, revised 1576, printed 1581, fo. 6, ed. E. Lamond (Cambridge: Cambridge University Press, 1893), pp. 16–17. The contention that the authorship was by Sir Thomas Smith may be found in M. Dewar, 'The Authorship of the "Discourse of the Common Weal"', *Economic History Review*, 2nd ser., 19:2 (1966), pp. 388–400.

9. J. Thirsk, 'The Constructive Phase of Projects 1540–1580', *Economic Policy and Projects* (Oxford: Clarendon Press, 1978), pp. 24–50.

10. A. F. Sutton, *The Mercery of London: Trade, Goods and People, 1130–1578* (Aldershot: Ashgate, 2005), p. 470.

11. Ibid.

12. Oldland, 'Variety', p. 227.

13. Sutton, *The Mercery*, p. 420. O. de Smedt, *De Engelse Natie te Antwerpen in de 16e eeuw, 1496–1582*, vol. 2 (Antwerp: De Sikkel 1954), pp. 416–24, lists the enormous quantities and varieties of goods shipped out of Antwerp to England by Merchants Adventurers between 2 November 1551 and 5 January 1552. All the commodities listed by Sir Thomas Smith two years earlier are there, and many more.

14. A. Crawford, *A History of the Vintners' Company* (London : Constable, 1977), p. 55.

15. Details are printed in appendix II to Thirsk, *Economic Policy and Projects*, pp. 181–5. I have rounded my figures to the nearest thousand pounds.

16. C. J. Harrison, 'Grain Price Analysis and Harvest Qualities, 1465–1634', *Agricultutral History Review*, 19 (1971), pp. 135–55, which drew heavily on the earlier work of W. G. Hoskins and P. Bowden.

17. J.-M. Cauchies, *Philippe le Beau: Le Dernier Duc de Bourgogne* (Turnhout: Brepols, 2003), pp. 8–9.

18. The unchanged Hungarian ducat and the Florentine florin were exchanged for 6 Viennese schillings of 30 pfennigs up to 1441, but for 11 schillings and 15 pfennigs in 1475, before the currency was restabilized. This 35-year deterioration in the value of the Austrian coinage was mostly a long slow decline. It fell within the intermittent and ineffectual rule of Maximilian's father, the impecunious Emperor Frederick III, as duke and then archduke of Austria (1439–93). Only once was there a major debasement. In 1459 Frederick, under attack from his brother Albert and his assembled Estates, cut the silver content of his coinage violently in order to pay his troops. All in vain. Frederick was driven ignominiously from Vienna, and his brother Albert restored the coinage, not to what it had been immediately beforehand, but to what it had been two decades earlier, before Frederick's accession in 1439, at the end of their father Albert II's reign. (Each Hungarian ducat was exchanged for around 6 Austrian schillings of 30 pfennigs in 1437–41, for 7 schillings and 12 pfennigs in 1458, for 34 schillings in 1459, and 6 schillings again in 1460.) Frequent minor debasements followed over the next fifteen years. Maximilian himself was born in 1459 and grew up with debasement as a normal means of funding emergencies, particularly civil war within and between the Habsburg principalities. The figures for the exchanges used here are derived from figures collected by Oliver Volckart.

19. In this first part of his reign, from 1419 to 1433, Philip the Good had, however, engaged in very extensive and fiscally motivated debasements, though more so in his adjacent and newly acquired realms in Namur, Holland-Zeeland, and Brabant, than in Flanders. During this fourteen-year period, his mints earned the very large sum of £30,013 groot Flemish (£20,886 from gold and £9,127 from silver), for an annual average sum of £2,143.786 . The peak years were from 1426 to 1433, with the highest total seigniorage, of £5,473 , in Michaelmas 1432–3, the final year before the Burgundian monetary reform. See J. H. Munro, *Wool, Cloth, and Gold: The Struggle for Bullion in Anglo-Burgundian Trade, 1340–1478* (Brussels: Éditions de l'Université de Bruxelles, 1973), table III, p. 83; and appendix: tables H and I, pp. 205–8.

20. Although Malines (Mechelen) lay within the duchy of Brabant, it was a separate lordship, nominally dependent on the bishops of Liège, but effectively run since the mid-fourteenth century by the counts of Flanders. It was therefore a convenient place for a mint for both Flanders and Brabant.

21. Account of Louis Quarre, Arch.Nord, B.2136. Mint receipts of 113,000 livres of 40 gros out of total receipts of 469,000 livres of 40 gros. Of this sum, 69,693 livres came from the mint at Malines, 26,620 livres from that at Zaltbommel, 15,514 livres from that at Dordrecht, 750 livres from the mint at Luxemburg, and, rather bizarrely, a further 330 livres from the Hainault mint at Valenciennes, from which there are neither surviving coins nor mint accounts later than the 1460s.

22. P. Spufford, *Monetary Problems and Policies in the Burgundian Netherlands, 1433–1496* (Leiden: Brill, 1970), pp. 133–46.

23. Spufford, *Handbook of Medieval Exchange*, pp. 222–3. Similarly, when the Breton mint price went up sixfold, from £9 per marc before March 1487, to £54 per marc from March 1489 to February 1490, and returned to £9, the exchange rate with French currency followed, with a time lag of six weeks.

24. Spufford, *Monetary Problems*, pp. 58–9, 65–8, 209–10.

25. P. Grierson et al., *Medieval European Coinage*, vol. 7B: *The Northern Netherlands* (Cambridge: Cambridge University Press, forthcoming).

26. *Bronnen tot de bouwgeschiedenis van den Dom te Utrecht*, part 2, vol 2, *Accounts, 1480/81–1506/07*, ed. W. Jappe Alberts, Rijks geschiedkundige publicatiën. Large Series, 129 (Utrecht, 1946).

27. J. Craeybeckx, *Un grand commerce d'importation: Les Vins de France aux anciens Pays Bas* (Paris, 1958). Prices in H. Van der Wee, *The Growth of the Antwerp Market and the European Economy (Fourteenth-Sixteenth Centuries)*, 3 vols (The Hague: Martinus Nijhoff, 1963), vol. 1: *Statistics*, p. 298. A gelte was 2.84 litres, approximately 5 pints or nearly 4 modern 75 cl bottles. Note that from the Burgundian monetary reforms and unification of 1433–5, 1d groot Flemish = 1.5d groot Brabant (from then until the French Revolution), in money of account.

28. Van der Wee, *The Growth of the Antwerp Market*, vol. 1, p. 302

29. A standard English broadcloth of assize, when fully finished, measured 24 yds (22.946 m) by 1.75 yd (1.600 m), and weighed about 60 lb (27.191 kg). See the next note.

30. E. M. Carus Wilson and O. Coleman, *England's Export Trade 1275–1547* (Oxford, 1963), pp. 109–10.

31. Van der Wee, *The Growth of the Antwerp Market*, vol. 1, p. 292.

32. M. Van Tielhof, *De Hollandse graanhandel 1470–1570: Koren op de Amsterdamse molen*, Hollandse Historische Reeks, 23 (The Hague: Stichting Hollandse Historische Reeks, 1995).

33. Archives de l'Assistance Public, quoted by M.-L. Tits-Dieuaide, *La Formation des prix céréaliers en Brabant et en Flandre au XVe siècle* (Brussels: Éditions de l'Université de Bruxelles, 1975), appendix IV, pp. 282–4, and graph 6. Van der Wee constructed quarterly figures from the same source, *The Growth of the Antwerp Market*, vol. 1, p. 185.

34. C. Verlinden (ed), *Dokumenten voor de geschiedenis van prijzen*, (Bruges: de Temple, 1959), vol. 1.

35. Those for Diksmude survive from 1482 to 1615, and were copied for Verlinden's *Dokumenten voor de geschiedenis van prijzen*.

36. E. Thoen, *Landbouwekonomieen bevolking in Vlaanderen gedurende de late Middeleeuwen en het begin van de Moderne Tijden* (Ghent, 1988).

37. Leendert Noordegraaf, *Hollands Welvaren? Levenstandaard in Holland 1450–1650* (Bergen: North Holland, 1985), pp. 116–23.

38. See J. H. Munro, 'Wage-Stickiness, Monetary Changes, and Real Incomes in Late-Medieval England and the Low Countries, 1300–1500: Did Money Matter?', *Research in Economic History*, 21 (2003), pp. 185–297; and J. H. Munro, 'Builders' Wages in Southern England and the Southern Low Countries, 1346–1500: A Comparative Study of Trends in and Levels of Real Incomes', in S. Cavaciocchi (ed.), *L'Edilizia prima della rivoluzione industriale, secoli XIII–XVIII*, Atti delle 'Settimana di Studi' e altri convegni, 36, Istituto Internazionale di Storia Economica 'Francesco Datini' (Florence: Le Monnier, 2005), pp. 1013–76.

39. Van der Wee, *The Growth of the Antwerp Market*, vol. 1, p. 260. Similarly the cheap heavy woollen cloth of Weert in Limburg bought for clothing the poor of Lier at the St Bavo Fair in Antwerp went down from 21½ Brabant groten per ell in October 1487 to 18 groten in October 1489, ibid., p. 271.

40. M. Boone, 'Plus dueil que joie: Les Ventes de rentes par la ville de Gand pendant la période bourguignonne. Entre intérêts privés et finances publiques', *Bulletin Trimestriel du Crédit Communal de Belgique*, 176 (1991/2), p. 12.

41. Verlinden (ed.), *Dokumenten voor de geschiedenis van prijzen*, I, pp. 369–71.

42. Cited in *Chroniques de Jean Molinet*, ed. G. Doutrepont and O. Jodogne (Brussels: Académie Royale de Belgique, 1937), vol. 2, pp. 24–31.

43. Ibid., ch. 211, vol. 3, p. 173.

44. Very reminiscent of the reform in Austria in 1460, which took the currency as it had been at the end of the previous reign in 1439 as a base – see above n. 15.

45. Rare copies survive of these regulations as printed in 1489, in both French and Flemish. The French text was reprinted in L. Deschamps de Pas, 'Essai sur l'histoire monétaire des comtes de Flandre de la maison de Bourgogne', *Revue Numismatique*, NS 14 (1869), pp. 45–55.

> Before St John 1487 Andries Gulden to be reckoned at 3s 4d gr fl
> St John 1487 – Christmas 1487 Andries Gulden reckoned at 6s gr fl
> Christmas 1487 – St John 1488 Andries Gulden reckoned at 7s gr fl
> St John 1488 – Christmas 1488 Andries Gulden reckoned at 8s gr fl
> Christmas 1488 – St John 1489 Andries Gulden reckoned at 9s gr fl
> St John 1489 – December 1489 Andries Gulden reckoned at 10s gr fl
> From December 1489 Andries Gulden reckoned at 3s 4d gr fl

The effect of this was that an annuity of £10. gr. Fl., which could have been met by payments of 40 Andrew's gulden early in 1487 (when the gulden was actually passing for 5s), and by a payments of only 20 gulden in the second half of 1489, was now reckoned to require payments of 60 gulden.

46. Consilium 105, quoted by Alain Wijffels at a conference on Money and Law in 2011. Proceedings to be published.

47. Authorized by him on 17 January 1488.

48. Erik Thoen similarly found that most of his sources for the castellanies of Aalst and Oudenaarde broke down in these years. E. Thoen, *Landbouwekonomie en bevolking in Vlaanderen gedurende de late Middeleeuwen en het begin van de Moderne Tijden. Testregio: de kasselrijen van Oudenaarde en Aalst*, Belgisch Centrum voor Landelijke Geschiedenis, nr. 90, (Gent: Universiteit Gent, 1988)

49. A. Verhulst in C. Verlinden (ed.), *Dokumenten voor de geschiedenis van prijzen*, vol. 2A (Bruges: de Temple 1965), p. 33. The hoet or heud at Bruges was between 166 and 172 litres.

50. Ibid., vol. 1. The *stoop* contained 2.26 litres, and the *steen* weighed 8 lb.

5 Van der Wee, 'The Amsterdam Wisselbank's Innovations in the Monetary Sphere'

1. This study is based upon a lifetime of research in the archives, other primary sources and a very wide range of secondary sources. The principal sources are listed here, in alphabetical order (by author or editor): P. W. N. M. Dehing, 'De Amsterdamse Wisselbank en Venetië in de zeventiende eeuw', in M. De Roever (ed.), *Amsterdam: Venetië van het Noorden* (The Hague: Martinus Nijhoff, 1991), pp. 120–36; J. De Vries and A. Van der Woude, *The First Modern Economy: Success, Failure, and Perseverance of the Dutch Economy, 1500–1815* (Cambridge: Cambridge University Press, 1997); L. Gillard, *La Banque d'Amsterdam et le florin européen au temps de la République néerlandaise (1610–1820)* (Paris: Ecole des Hautes Etudes en Sciences Socials, 2004); R. W. Goldsmith, *Premodern Financial Systems: A Historical Comparative Study* (Cambridge: Cambridge University Press, 1987); V. Janssens, 'Het ontstaan van de dubbele koers courantgeld-wisselgeld in het geldwezen van de Zuidelijke Nederlanden', *Bijdragen voor de geschiedenis der Nederlanden*, 9 (1955), pp. 1–18; C. Kindleberger, *A Financial History of Western Europe*, 2nd edn (New York: Oxford University Press, 1993); W. Korthals Altes, *Van pond Hollands tot Nederlandse florijn* (Amsterdam: Nederlands Economisch-Historisch Archief, 1996); R. Mees, *Proeve eener geschiedenis van het bankwezen in Nederland gedurende den tijd der Republiek* (Rotterdam: W. Messchert, 1838); L. Neal, *The Rise of Financial Capitalism: International Capital Markets in the Age of Reason* (Cambridge: Cambridge University Press, 1990); G. Parker, 'The Emergence of Modern Finance in Europe', in C. Cipolla (ed.), *The Fontana Economic History of Europe*, vol. 2 (London: Collins/Fontana, 1977), pp. 527–94; J. Phoonsen, *Wissel-styl tot Amsterdam* (Amsterdam: Andries van Damme & Joannes Ratel-

band, 1711); J. F. Richards (ed.), *Precious Metals in the Later Medieval and Early Modern Worlds* (Durham, NC: Carolina Academic Press, 1983); J. Riley, *International Government Finance and the Amsterdam Capital Market, 1740–1815* (Cambridge: Cambridge University Press, 1980; M. 't Hart, J. Jonker and J. L. Van Zanden (eds), *A Financial History of the Netherlands* (Cambridge: Cambridge University Press, 1997); H. Van der Wee, *The Growth of the Antwerp Market and the European Economy (Fourteenth-Sixteenth Centuries)*, 3 vols (The Hague: Martinus Nijhoff, 1963); H. Van der Wee, 'Monetary, Credit and Banking Systems', in E. E. Rich and C. H. Wilson (eds), *The Cambridge Economic History of Europe*, vol. 5 (Cambridge: Cambridge University Press, 1977), pp. 290–393; H. Van der Wee, *The Low Countries in the Early Modern World*, tr. L. Fackelman (Aldershot: Variorum, 1993); H. Van der Wee, 'European Banking in the Middle Ages and Early Modern Times, 476–1789', in H. Van der Wee and G. Van Hentenryk (eds), *A History of European Banking, 476–1789,* 2nd edn (Antwerp: Mercator Fonds, 2000), pp. 71–264; J. G. Van Dillen, 'Amsterdam: marché mondial des métaux précieux', *Revue historique*, 2:2 (1926), pp. 194–201; J. G. Van Dillen (ed.), *History of the Principal Public Banks* (The Hague: Martinus Nijhoff, 1934); J. G. Van Dillen, 'La Banque de change et les banquiers privés à Amsterdam aux XVIIe et XVIIIe siècles', in *Troisième conférence internationale d'histoire économique, Munich, 1965 (Actes)* (Paris: Mouton & Co., 1974), pp. 177–85.

2. Cited in Dehing, 'De Amsterdamse Wisselbank', pp. 120–36.

3. Van der Wee, 'European Banking in the Middle Ages', pp. 71–264.

4. E.g. the fine silver content of the Brabant *stuiver* (worth 2d groot*)* was reduced by half: from 0.64 g in 1551 to just 0.32 g in 1644, Van der Wee, *The Growth of the Antwerp Market*, vol. 1: *Statistics*, table XV, pp. 128–9.

6 Mayhew, 'Silver in England, 1600–1800'

1. For a discussion of this shift of opinion see A. Feavearyear, *The Pound Sterling: A History of English Money* (Oxford: Oxford University Press, 1963), pp. 132–49.

2. See e.g. K. N. Chaudhuri, *The Trading World of Asia and the English East India Company, 1660–1760* (Cambridge: Cambridge University Press, 1978), and *The English East India Company: The Study of an Early Joint-Stock Company 1600–1640* (London: Routledge, 1999).

3. J. H. Munro, '*South German Silver, European Textiles, and Venetian Trade with the Levant and Ottoman Empire, c. 1370 to c. 1720: A Non-Mercantilist Approach to the Balance of Payments Problem*', in Cavaciocchi (ed.), *Relazione economiche tra Europa e mondo islamico*, pp. 907–62. Available online at http://mpra.ub.uni-muenchen.de/11013.

4. See especially D. O. Flynn and A. Giraldez, 'Global Economic Unity through the Mid-Eighteenth Century', *Journal of World History*, 13:2 (2002), pp. 391–427, and also the earlier J. F. Richards (ed.), *Precious Metals in the Medieval and Early Modern Worlds* (Durham, NC: Carolina Academic Press, 1983).

5. S. Quinn, 'Gold, Silver, and the Glorious Revolution: Arbitrage between Bills of Exchange and Bullion', *Economic History Review*, 49 (1996), pp. 473–90.

6. Goldsmiths of course also worked with silver.

7. Chaudhuri, *Trading World*, table A.6., p. 166.

8. J. S. Forbes, *Hallmark: A History of the London Assay Office* (London: Unicorn, 1999). D. Mitchell, 'Innovation and the Transfer of Skill in the Goldsmiths' Trade in Restoration London', in D. Mitchell (ed.), *Goldsmiths, Silversmiths and Bankers*, Centre for Metropolitan History Working Paper Series, 2 (1995).

9. Silver and gold thread escaped the requirement, being too small to bear the mark.

10. The Troy pound weight of silver was struck into 62 shillings face value.

11. N. J. Mayhew, 'Currency and Plate: Some Thoughts Based on Oxford Coinage and the Civil War', *Silver Society Journal,* 11 (1999), pp. 236–9; E. Besly, *Coins and Medals of the English Civil War* (London: Seaby, 1990).

12. C. E. Challis (ed.), *A New History of the Royal Mint* (Cambridge and New York: Cambridge University Press), pp. 320–1.

13. T. Violet, *A Humble Declaration ... touching the transportation of gold and silver* (1643).

14. 1669. Goldsmiths' Court Book 6, p. 39v.

15. Goldsmiths' Court Book 10, p. 143r.

16. Forbes, *Hallmark,* pp. 161, 185.

17. Ibid., p. 166.

18. Small denomination notes of under a pound were common in the eighteenth century until banned in 1765 (Scotland) and 1775 (England). Feavearyear, *Pound Sterling,* p. 174.

19. See the chapter by Renate Pieper in this volume.

20. Dyer estimates that 'The copper coinage was virtually doubled by counterfeits', while Irish halfpennies after 1737 perhaps added as much as a further 50 per cent to the English issue. The widespread acceptance of counterfeit copper coins argues that for most of the eighteenth century copper of any description served a genuine need. Though copper was technically only legal tender up to a limit of 6d, the shortage of silver coin ensured that halfpennies in fact passed in sums above 6d, and the poor were said to have been paid largely in copper. G. P. Dyer and P. P. Gaspar, 'Reform, the New Technology and Tower Hill, 1700–1966', in Challis (ed.) *A New History of the Royal Mint,* pp. 435–7.

21. The exact division between halfpence and farthings is not known, though in the eighteenth century halfpennies certainly predominated.

22. Ibid., p. 431.

23. Ibid., pp. 440–1.

24. See, however, Alice Dolan's forthcoming study of the actual money reported in men's and women's pockets in Old Bailey pickpocketing cases from 1730 to 1750, 1765 to 1780 and 1795 to 1810.

25. Forbes, *Hallmark,* p. 235.

26. The Goldsmiths' Court Books indicate that while small wares account for up to around 10 per cent of the totals hallmarked in the period 1718 to 1727, from 1773 to 1799 they are always over 30 per cent and pass 50 per cent between 1778 and 1784.

7 Mateos Royo, 'The Burdens of Tradition'

1. D. Glassmann and A. Redish, 'Currency Depreciation in Early Modern England and France', *Explorations in Economic History,* 25 (1988), pp. 75–97.

2. T. Sargent and F. Velde, *The Big Problem of Small Change* (Princeton, NJ, and Oxford: Princeton University Press, 2002).

3. F. Zulaica, 'Economía monetaria y política monetaria en el reino de Aragón en la Edad Media', in *XVII Congreso de Historia de la Corona de Aragón* (Barcelona: University, 2003), vol. 1, pp. 607–32.

4. The denomination *'jaquesa'* for local billon currency refers to the town of Jaca, the original capital of the kingdom of Aragon, where these coins were first minted during the medieval period.

5. F. Mateu, 'El sistema monetario en Aragón: Síntesis histórica', in *La moneda aragonesa* (Saragossa: Institución Fernando el Católico, 1983), pp. 93–134, on pp. 113–15.

6. P. Savall and S. Penen, *Fueros, observancias y actos de corte del reino de Aragón* (Saragossa: Imprenta de Francisco Castro y Bosque, 1866), vol. 1, pp. 335–6, and vol. 2, p. 342. All

of the official documentation alludes to this legislation to determine the intrinsic value of the silver coins issued in Aragon in the early modern period. However, if the fineness of the Castilian *real* was 22.16 carats, or 11 *dineros* and 4 grains, that of the silver coins of Aragon was set at only 22 carats, or 11 *dineros*, in 1484, and it thereafter remained unchanged throughout the sixteenth and seventeenth centuries.

7. In 1593 the viceroy of Aragon was still arguing in reports to the Council of Aragon that market demand for billon could be met through modest issues of local coins. See Archive of the Crown of Aragon, Council of Aragon, file 35.

8. G. Redondo, 'Numismática aragonesa en la Edad Moderna', in *La moneda aragonesa*, pp. 197–214, on pp. 209–10.

9. Municipal Archive of Saragossa, manuscript 10.

10. J. Santiago, *Política monetaria en Castilla durante el siglo XVII* (Valladolid: Junta de Castilla y León, 2000), pp. 51–5, 153–74.

11. Ibid.

12. J. I. Gómez Zorraquino, *La burguesía mercantil en el Aragón de los siglos XVI y XVII* (Saragossa: Diputación General, 1987) and *Zaragoza y el capital comercial* (Saragossa: City Council, 1987).

13. G. Redondo, *Las corporaciones de artesanos en Zaragoza en el siglo XVII* (Saragossa: Institución Fernando el Católico, 1982).

14. G. Redondo, 'Las relaciones comerciales Aragón-Francia en la Edad moderna: Datos para su estudio en el siglo XVII', *Estudios*, 85–6 (1985), pp. 123–54.

15. Redondo, 'Numismática aragonesa', pp. 210–11.

16. A. C. Floriano, 'Teruel en el siglo XV', *Boletín de la Real Academia de Historia*, 88 (1926), pp. 785–825, on pp. 807–20.

17. Archive of the Crown of Aragon, Council of Aragon, files 59, 91, and 1,369.

18. Redondo, 'Numismática aragonesa', p. 211; J. A. Mateos Royo, *Auge y decadencia de un municipio aragonés* (Daroca: Institución Fernando el Católico, 1997), p. 262.

19. Archive of the Crown of Aragon, Council of Aragon, files 48, 76.

20. Mateos Royo, *Auge*, pp. 262–3; Municipal Archive of Saragossa, boxes 8117, 8118.

21. E. J. Hamilton, *El tesoro americano y la revolución de los precios en España, 1501–1650* (Barcelona: Ariel, 1975); Santiago, *Política monetaria*.

22. J. Carrera, *Historia de la economía española* (Barcelona: Bosch, 1944–7), vol. 2, p. 416.

23. Archive of the Crown of Aragon, Council of Aragon, file 91. This small silver premium is also found in Valencia. See Hamilton, *El tesoro*, p. 144.

24. J. M. Sánchez Molledo, *El pensamiento arbitrista en el reino de Aragón en los siglos XVI y XVII* (Madrid: Complutense University, 1997; CD-rom), p. 1345.

25. Archive of the Crown of Aragon, Council of Aragon, files 36, 59 and 92. This high intrinsic value of Aragonese billon coins led to enthusiastic take-up in Valencia from the end of the sixteenth century onwards.

26. This matter was a source of frequent arguments between the council and guilds of Saragossa during the seventeenth century. See Redondo, *Las corporaciones*.

27. The obligation to maintain the weight and purity of *jaquesa* coins was reflected in Acts of Parliament, especially under James I (1247) and James II (1307), although these strictures were not always respected by the kings of Aragon. After Peter IV depreciated the local currency and proceeded to produce counterfeits of Castilian coins in the mid-fourteenth century, the Parliament of 1372 legislated a ban on minting of coins or altering their intrinsic value without its express approval. See Savall and Penen, *Fueros*, vol. 1, pp. 328–35.

28. D. J. Dormer, *Discursos históricos políticos* (Saragossa: l'Astral, 1989), p. 32.

29. Savall and Penen, *Fueros*, vol. 1, pp. 328–35; C. Orcastegui, 'La reglamentación del impuesto del monedaje en Aragón en los siglos XIII–XIV', *Aragón en la Edad Media*, 5 (1983), pp. 113–21. That had also been the case with the *jaquesa* petty coinage in the medieval period.

30. Archive of the Crown of Aragon, Council of Aragon, file 91; G. Borras, *La guerra de sucesión en Zaragoza* (Saragossa: Institución Fernando el Católico, 1972), pp. 119–20.

31. In 1519 this committee was formed by royal officials and members of the *Diputación*, and in 1528 by delegates of the king and the four estates of the Aragonese Parliament. See Savall and Penen, *Fueros,* vol. 1, pp. 335–6 and vol. 2, p. 342.

32. Archive of the Crown of Aragon, Council of Aragon, file 91, *Provisiones de tránsito de moneda de plata en el reino de Aragón*. This document alludes to the examination of different petty coins minted over the past 160 years in Aragon carried out in 1609. These coins were two or three grains less fine than was established by tradition.

33. Archive of the Crown of Aragon, Council of Aragon, files 36, 92.

34. Archive of the Crown of Aragon, Council of Aragon, file 91.

35. Orcastegui, ʻLa reglamentación ʼ. This right was granted to the medieval and early modern monarchs of Aragon against the obligation to preserve the intrinsic value of the *jaquesa* coinage. See above, n. 27, for Aragon's parliamentary ban of 1372 on minting any coins without legislative assent. In 1474, Henry IV of Castile issued an ordinance known as the *Pragmatica*, renouncing any further seigniorage on the gold and silver coinages in return for assent to the crown's monetary reforms in suppressing about 150 baronial mints; and this *Pragmatica* was confirmed by Ferdinand of Aragon and Isabella of Castile in 1474 and again in 1497 (for Castile). See M.-T. Boyer-Xambeu, G. Deleplace and L. Gillard, *Private Money and Public Currencies: The 16th Century Challenge* (London: M. E. Sharpe, 1994), pp. 109–11; tr. A. Azodi: from *Monnaie privée et pouvoir des princes: L'Économie des relations monétaires à la Renaissance* (Paris: Éditions de CNRS, 1986).

36. Archive of the Crown of Aragon, Council of Aragon, files 36, 91.

37. The Aragonese Parliament of 1519 abolished customs duties on silver exported in ingots, but not on silver coins. See Savall and Penen, *Fueros*, vol. 2, p. 342.

38. Archive of the Crown of Aragon, Council of Aragon, files 36, 116.

39. Ibid. The privileges granted to Barcelona, which included the exclusive right to mint silver coins, and other towns to issue petty coins in Catalonia provided the council of Saragossa with a precedent for its petitions to kings Philip IV and Charles II. See Carrera, *Historia*, vol. 2, pp. 478–9.

40. Archive of the Crown of Aragon, Council of Aragon, file 106.

41. Archive of the Crown of Aragon, Council of Aragon, files 91, 92, 198.

42. Mateos Royo, *Auge*, p. 263.

43. A. C. J. Cayón, *Las monedas españolas* (Madrid: Jano, 1998), pp. 768, 782.

44. Archive of the Crown of Aragon, Council of Aragon, file 91.

45. J. M. Sánchez Molledo, 'Pensamiento aragonés sobre el comercio exterior en el siglo XVII: los arbitristas', *Cuadernos aragoneses de economía*, 8:1 (1998), pp. 59–72.

46. See n. 41 above, n. 65 below and Hamilton, *El tesoro*, p. 126.

47. Ibid., pp. 126–36; F. Mateu, *La ceca de Valencia y las acuñaciones valencianas de los siglos XIII al XVIII* (Valencia: City Council, 1929), pp. 129–49.

48. Ibid., p. 135; Archive of the Crown of Aragon, Council of Aragon, files 36, 92.

49. This paucity of references to other thinkers, even where borrowing sometimes from their writings, is a common feature of mercantilism in early modern Europe.

50. Sánchez Molledo, *El pensamiento*, pp. 1345–6, 1419–20, 1587.

51. P. Vilar, *Cataluña en la España Moderna* (Barcelona: Crítica, 1978), vol. 1, pp. 391–427; Carrera, *Historia*, vol. 2, pp. 364–7.
52. Santiago, *Política monetaria*, pp. 201–48.
53. Sánchez Molledo, *El pensamiento*, pp. 1076–96.
54. Santiago, *Política monetaria*, pp. 67–9, 112–14; E. M. García Guerra, *Moneda y arbitrios* (Madrid: Consejo Superior de Investigaciones Científicas, 2003), pp. 131–74.
55. Sánchez Molledo, 'Pensamiento', pp. 68–72.
56. Sánchez Molledo, *El pensamiento*, pp. 1082–98.
57. García Guerra, *Moneda*.
58. Sánchez Molledo, *El pensamiento*, pp. 1076–81; Archive of the Crown of Aragon, Council of Aragon, file 91; National Historical Archive, files 51, 361.
59. Sánchez Molledo, *El pensamiento*, pp. 272–3, 1070–5; Carrera, *Historia*, vol. 2, pp. 476–8; Archive of the Crown of Aragon, Council of Aragon, file 91.
60. E. Jarque and J. A. Salas, 'La Diputación aragonesa en el siglo XVI', *Ius Fugit*, 10–11 (2001–2), pp. 291–351, on pp. 296–7.
61. Julaica, 'Economía', p. 612. This can clearly be seen in the arrangements under which the nobility and the Church leased tax farming rights (ecclesiastical tithes and seigniorial tributes) to the leading merchants of Saragossa in the sixteenth and seventeenth centuries. These contracts generally set the sums payable to the lords for the taxes assigned in *libras* and *sueldos*, two of the units used in the official Aragonese accounting system. The *libra* was equal to 10 silver *reales* and the *sueldo* to half a *real*. Occasionally, however, the sum would be fixed directly in silver. See A. Abadía *La enajenación de rentas señoriales en el reino de Aragón* (Saragossa: Institución Fernando el Católico, 1998), pp. 34–70; Gómez Zorraquino, *La burguesía*, pp. 66–72, and *Zaragoza*, pp. 79–81.
62. Archive of the Crown of Aragon, Council of Aragon, file 91.
63. Ibid.
64. Carrera, *Historia*, vol. 2, pp. 259–72, 353–67. The consensus between the *Generalitat* and the city of Barcelona concerning economic matters in the seventeenth century was facilitated by the inclusion of the petty nobility in the city council and the parallel ennoblement of the burghers, which resulted in the convergence of the interests of these two social groups. See J. Amelang, *La formación de una clase dirigente: Barcelona, 1490–1714* (Barcelona: Ariel, 1986).
65. Mateu, *La ceca*, pp. 144–9. The seigniorage generated in Valencia at the end of the seventeenth century was 8 *dineros* per marc of silver and 2 *sueldos* and 6 *dineros* per marc of billon, representing 14.3 per cent of the face value of issues.
66. Borras, *La guerra*, pp. 117–21. Though the report argued for a metallic debasement of the Aragonese *real* in line with its Valencian counterpart, the 50 per cent reduction sought in the fineness of the *dinero* would have preserved an intrinsic value higher than that of Catalan and Valencian petty coins.
67. J. A. Mateos Royo, 'Política estatal y circulación monetaria: el vellón en Aragón durante el siglo XVIII', *Estudis*, 35 (2009), pp. 165–96.
68. See nn. 27 and 35 above.

8 Pieper, 'Money or Export Commodity for Asia?'

1. I would like to thank R. Dobado for a long conversation about the current issues and his support with his Excel-data file on Spanish quicksilver (mercury) deliveries. M. Denzel, *'La Practica della Cambiatura': Europäischer Zahlungsverkehr vom 14. bis zum 17. Jahrhundert* (Stuttgart: Franz Steiner Verlag, 1994).

2. J. E. Covarrubias, *La moneda de cobre en México, 1760–1842: Un problema administrativo* (Mexico: Universidad Nacional Autónoma de México and Instituto de Investigaciones Doctor José María Luis Mora, 2000).

3. P. Pérez Herrero, *Plata y Libranzas: La articulación comercial del México Borbónico* (Mexico: El Colegio de México, 1988).

4. E. J. Hamilton, *American Treasure and the Price Revolution in Spain, 1501–1650* (Cambridge, MA: Harvard University Press, 1934).

5. E. J. Hamilton, *War and Prices in Spain, 1651–1800* (Cambridge, MA: Harvard University Press, 1947).

6. The Wisselbank's florin or guilder of account consisted of 20 stuivers. From 1619 to 1681, the fine silver content of the *stuiver* (0.333 fine) was 0.4367 (= 8.734 g in the guilder or gulden of account; from 1681 to 1791, the fine silver content of the *stuiver* was somewhat higher: 0.4725 g (= 9.450 g for the guilder). From 1681 to 1806, the fine silver content of the actual silver gulden or guilder coin was 0.911 g. See H. E. Van Gelder and M. Hoc, *Les Monnaies des Pays Bas bourguignons et espagnols, 1434–1713: Répertoire générale* (Amsterdam: Schulman, 1960). But see also N. W. Posthumus, *Nederlandsche Prijsgeschiedenis*, vol. 1 (Leiden: E. J. Brill, 1943), p. cxiii: stating that the silver contents of the guilder in 1620–1659 was 10.28g; in 1660–81: 9.74g; 1682–1800: 9.61g. The weight of the peso was about 24.85g–24.43g of fine silver R.Vornefeld, *Spanische Geldpolitik in Hispanoamerika 1750–1808: Konzepte und Massnahmen im Rahmen der bourbonischen Reformpolitik* (Stuttgart: Franz Steiner Verlag, 1992), pp. 127–40.

7. J. I. Israel, *Dutch Primacy in World Trade, 1585–1740* (Oxford: Clarendon Press, 1990).

8. M. Grice-Hutchinson, *The School of Salamanca, Readings in Spanish Monetary Theory 1544–1605* (Oxford: Clarendon Press 1952).

9. J. J. TePaske and H. S. Klein, *The Royal Treasuries of the Spanish Empire in America*, 4 vols (Durham, NC: Duke University Press, 1982, 1990); R. L. Garner, 'Long-Term Silver Mining Trends in Spanish America: A Comparative Analysis of Peru and Mexico', *American Historical Review*, 93 (1988), pp. 898–935; H. S. Klein, *The American Finances of the Spanish Empire: Royal Income and Expenditures in Colonial Mexico, Peru, and Bolivia, 1680–1809* (Albuquerque, NM: University of New Mexico Press, 1998).

10. P. J. Bakewell, 'Registered Silver Production in the Potosí District, 1550–1735', *Jahrbuch für Geschichte von Staat, Wirtschaft und Gesellschaft Lateinamerikas*, 11 (1975), pp. 68–103; R. Dobado, 'Las Minas de Almadén, El Monopolio del Azogue y la Producción de Plata en Nueva España en el siglo XVIII', in J. Sánchez Gómez and G. C. Mira Delli-Zotti and R. Dobado, *La savia del imperio: Tres estudios de economía colonial* (Salamanca: Ediciones Universidad Salamanca, 1997), pp. 403–97, on pp. 480–1; R. Dobado and G. A. Marrero, 'The Role of the Spanish Imperial State in the Mining-Led Growth of Bourbon Mexico's economy', *Economic History Review*, 64:3 (2011), pp. 855–84.

11. B. Hausberger, *La Nueva España y sus metales preciosos: La industria minera colonial a través de los 'libros de cargo y data' de la Real Hacienda, 1761–1767* (Frankfurt a. M.: Peter Lang, 1997).

12. Pérez Herrero, *Plata y libranzas*; Covarrubias, *Moneda de cobre;* M. A. Irigoin, 'Gresham on Horseback: The Monetary Roots of Spanish American Political Fragmentation in the Nineteenth Century', *Economic History Review*, 62:3 (2009), pp. 551–75.

13. R. Garner, Economic History Data Desk, Economic History of Latin America, United States and New World, 1500–1900, TePaske Page, two files: Mexico Silver and Peru Silver https://home.comcast.net/~richardgarner05/tepaske.html [12 October 2011].

14. See Hamilton, *American Treasure*, pp. 73–103; and Hamilton, *War and Prices in Spain*, pp. 9–35. In 1599, the *vellón* coinage was minted at 140 per copper *marc* of 230.047g.

Iin 1602, that issue was changed to 280 per *marc*, thus reducing the weight of the copper coin by one half, from 1.653 g to 0.8216 g. A *marc* of copper was worth 34 marevedís. Hamilton erred, however (*American Treasure*, p. 52), in stating that 'the Crown exacted no seigniorage' on gold and silver coinages, but only brassage fees. In fact a traditional seigniorage was exacted on gold at the rate of 1 *escudo* per marc (230.0465 g); and on silver, at a rate of 50 *maravedís* per *marc* = 2.195 per cent (of the value of 2278 *maravedís* for the 67 silver *reals* struck per marc)

15. E. J. Hamilton, *Money, Prices and Wages in Valencia, Aragon and Navarre, 1351–1500* (Cambridge, MA: Harvard University Press, 1936); Hamilton, *American Treasure*; Hamilton, *War and Prices*.

16. A. J. Pearce, *British Trade with Spanish America, 1763–1808* (Liverpool: Liverpool University Press, 2007).

17. E. Pijning, 'A New Interpretation of Contraband Trade', *Hispanic American Historical Review*, 81:3–4 (2001), pp. 733–8.

18. Israel, *Dutch Primacy*; P. Bernardini and N. Fiering (eds), *The Jews and the Expansion of Europe to the West, 1450–1800* (New York: Berghahn, 2001); J. Postma and V. Enthoven (eds), *Riches from Atlantic Commerce: Dutch Transatlantic Trade and Shipping, 1585–1817* (Leiden: Brill, 2003); Pearce, *British Trade*, ch. 1; A. M. Crespo Solana, *Mercaderes Atlánticos: Redes del comercio flamenco y holandés entre Europa y el Caribe* (Córdoba: Universidad de Córdoba, 2009).

19. Posthumus, *Prijsgeschiedenis;* cf. R. C. Allen, *Consumer Price Indices, Nominal/Real Wages and Welfare Ratios of Building Craftsmen and Labourers, 1260–1913, datafile: Amsterdam,* http://www.iisg.nl/hpw/data.php, 12 October 2011. The data series of Posthumus are more homogeneous, so these data will be used.

20. Relations between specie and prices depended on a large set of variables. See articles in: D. O'Flynn, A. Giráldez and R. von Glahn, *Global Connections and Monetary History, 1470–1800* (Aldershot: Ashgate, 2003).

21. E. Flores Clair, *El Banco de Avío Minero novohispano: Crédito, finanzas y deudores* (Mexico: Instituto Nacional de Antropología e Historia, 2001).

22. D. Dehouve, *Quand les banquiers étaient des saints: 450 ans de l'histoire économique et sociale d'une province indienne du Mexique* (Paris: Éditions du Centre National de la Recherche Scientifique, 1990); M. P. Martínez López-Cano and G. del Valle Pavón (eds), *El crédito en Nueva España* (Mexico: El Colegio de México, 1998); G. von Wobeser, *El crédito eclesiástico en la Nueva España: Siglo XVIII*, 2nd edn (Mexico: Universidad Nacional Autónoma de México and Instituto de Investigaciones Históricas and Fondo de Cultura Económica, 2010).

23. J. P. Priotti, 'Metales preciosos, competencia comercial y transformación económica en el Atlántico franco-español (1550–1570)', *Jahrbuch für Geschichte Lateinamerikas*, 43 (2006), pp. 25–40.

24. Hamilton, *War and Prices*.

25. See Herman Van der Wee's chapter in this volume; and n. 6 above.

26. The importance of Amsterdam for Northern Europe is shown by: M. North, *From the North Sea to the Baltic: Essays in Commercial, Monetary and Agrarian History, 1500–1800* (Aldershot: Ashgate, 1996).

27. Hausberger, *Nueva España*, shows that this was due to the scattered mining fields in Mexico, whereas in Alto Peru and Peru there were a few big centres.

28. The average index numbers are: 1577–98: 60; 1600–7: 150; 1668–1783: 82; 1784–1805: 145.

29. H. Pietschmann, 'Anmerkungen zum Problem einer Geld- und Finanzgeschichte des kolonialen Hispanoamerika', in J. Schneider (ed.), *Wirtschaftskräfte und Wirtschaftswege:*

Festschrift für Hermann Kellenbenz, vol. 4 (Stuttgart: Franz Steiner Verlag, 1978), pp. 103–15; R. Romano, *Moneda, seudomonedas y circulación monetaria en la economía de México* (Mexico: Fondo de Cultura Económica and El Colegio de México, 1998).

30. J. A. Bátiz Vázquez and J. E. Covarrubias (eds), *La moneda en México, 1750–1920* (Mexico: Instituto de Investigaciones Doctor José María Luis Mora and El Colegio de Michoacán and El Colegio de México and Universidad Nacional Autónoma de México, 1998).

31. Martínez López-Cano and del Valle Pavón, *El crédito*.

32. For the direct connection to Asia see D. O'Flynn and A. Giráldez (eds), *European Entry into the Pacific: Spain and the Acapulco-Manila Galleons* (Aldershot: Ashgate Publishing, 2001); C. Martínez Shaw and M. Alfonso Mola (eds), *La ruta española a China* (Madrid: Ediciones El Viso, 2007). For the Atlantic and Caribbean connection see S. Kuntz Ficker and H. Pietschmann (eds), *México y la economía atlántica (siglos XVIII–XX)* (México: El Colegio de México, 2006).

33. A. M. Bernal, *La financiación de la Carrera de Indias* (Seville: Fundación Cajasol, 1992); C. Álvarez Nogal, *Sevilla y el imperio español en el siglo XVII: Dinero, crédito y privilegios* (Seville: Ayuntamiento de Sevilla, 2000).

34. Priotti, 'Metales preciosos'.

35. M. Khull-Kholwald, 'Expandieren in schweren Zeiten: Der Schuldschein als zentrales Finanzinstrument in der Steiermark (1515–1635)', (PhD dissertation, Karl-Franzens Universität Graz, 2011); A. Westermann, *Die vorderösterreichischen Montanregionen in der Frühen Neuzeit* (Stuttgart: Franz Steiner Verlag, 2009) describes an increase in the amount of coins in circulation likewise.

36. Hamilton, *American Treasure,* offers a general price index for Andalusia, Castile and Valencia for 1500–1650. Hamilton, *War and Prices*, offers only a price index for agricultural products in New Castile for 1650–1800. Furthermore, there are different basic years for the indices of the two price series, therefore the series are not fully compatible.

37. Pearce, *British Trade*.

38. M. Morineau, *Incroyable gazettes et fabuleux métaux: Les Retours des trésors américains d'après les gazettes hollandaises (16e–18e siècles)* (Paris and London: Cambridge University Press and Éditions de la Maison des Sciences de l'Homme, 1985), used these data as good proxy, but a comparison with the official Spanish documents shows the severe shortcomings. R. Pieper, *Die Vermittlung einer neuen Welt: Amerika im Nachrichtennetz des habsburgischen Imperiums 1493–1598* (Mainz: Philipp von Zabern, 2000).

39. For the hint to take Spanish quicksilver deliveries into consideration I would like to thank Philipp Lesiak. Rafael Dobado forwarded me his data on quicksilver in an Excel-file, published in Dobado, 'Las minas de Almadén', and tested in Dobado and Marrero, 'Role of the Spanish Imperial State', for their importance for Mexican silver production.

40. E. Flores Clair and C. Velasco Ávila, 'Los pasos de Alejandro de Humboldt por la minería novohispana', *Jahrbuch für Geschichte Lateinamerikas*, 42 (2005), pp. 47–58.

9 Giraldez, 'Cacao Beans in Colonial México'

1. A. von Humboldt, *Ensayo político sobre el Reino de la Nueva España*, 3 vols (México: Cia. General de Ediciones, 1953), vol. 3, p. 125.

2. J. Reglá, 'Edad moderna', in A. Ubieto, J. Reglá, J. M. Jover and C. Seco, *Introducción a la Historia de España*, (Barcelona: Teide, 1970), pp. 265–506, on pp. 273, 320.

3. Ibid., pp. 320, 334.

4.   E. J. Hamilton, *El Tesoro Americano y la Revolución de los Precios en España, 1501–1650* (Barcelona: Ariel, 1975), p. 89.

5.   G. Céspedes del Castillo, 'Las Indias durante los siglos XVI y XVII', in J. Vicens Vives (ed.), *Historia de España y América Social y Económica*, vol. 3: *Los Austrias: El Imperio Español en América* (Barcelona: Vicens-Vives, 1972), pp. 321–536, on pp. 350–1.

6.   T. Gage, *Travels in the New World,* (Norman, OK: University of Oklahoma Press, 1958), p. 330.

7.   Céspedes del Castillo, 'Las Indias durante los siglos XVI y XVII', p. 351.

8.   H. Tovar Pinzón, 'Remesas, situados y Real Hacienda en el siglo XVII', in A. M. Bernal (ed.), *Dinero moneda y crédito en la Monarquía Hispánica* (Madrid: Marcial Pons, Ediciones Historia, Fundación ICO, 1999), pp. 241–67, on p. 249.

9.   A. de Bethencourt Massieu, 'El comercio anglo-canario y la plata indiana (1580–1680)', ibid., pp. 293–306, on p. 305.

10. A. M. Bernal, 'Remesas de Indias: de "dinero político" al servicio del imperio a indicador monetario', ibid., pp. 353–84, on pp. 379–80.

11. S. D. Coe and M. D. Coe, *The True History of Chocolate* (London: Thames & Hudson, 2000), pp. 35, 39; R. F. Millon, 'When Money Grew on Trees. A Study of Cacao in Ancient Mesoamerica' (PhD dissertation, Columbia University, 1955), p. 282.

12. N. Bletter and D. C. Daly, 'Cacao and its Relatives in South America: An Overview of Taxonomy, Ecology, Biogeography, Chemistry and Ethnobotany', in C. L. McNeil (ed.), *Chocolate in Mesoamerica: A Cultural History of Cacao* (Gainesville, FL: University Press of Florida, 2006), pp. 31–67, on p. 47. Perhaps this absence explains why cacao was not consumed in South America, which is much better provided with such stimulants; and this region's inhabitants drank other beverages, such as *hierba mate*.

13. Ibid., p. 48.

14. Coe and Coe, *The True History of Chocolate*, p. 31.

15. W. R. Fowler, 'Cacao Production, Tribute, and Wealth in Sixteenth-Century Izalcos, El Salvador', in McNeil (ed.), *Chocolate in Mesoamerica*, on pp. 307–8.

16. Coe and Coe, *The True History of Chocolate*, pp. 19–20, 55.

17. M. León-Portilla, *Aztecas-Mexicas: Desarrollo de una civilización originaria* (Madrid: Algaba Ediciones, 2005), p. 119.

18. D. Duran, *The History of the Indies of New Spain* (Norman, OK, and London: University of Oklahoma Press, 1994), p. 342.

19. Ibid., p. 347.

20. Ibid., p. 380.

21. Coe and Coe, *The True History of Chocolate*, p. 71.

22. Millon, 'When Money Grew on Trees', p. 194.

23. A. de Ulloa, *Descripción geográfico-física de una parte de Nueva España*, in F. de Solano, *Antonio de Ulloa y la Nueva España* (Mexico: Universidad Nacional Autónoma de Mexico, 1979), p. 30.

24. Millon, 'When Money Grew on Trees', pp. 175, 215.

25. León-Portilla, *Aztecas-Mexicas*, p. 145.

26. B. Díaz del Castillo, *The Discovery and Conquest of Mexico* (London: George Routledge & Sons, 1928), p. 298.

27. F. S. Clavigero, *The History of Mexico,* 2 vols (New York and London: Garland Publishing, 1979), vol. 1, pp. 386–7.

28. A. M. Garibay, *Vida Económica de Tenochtitlan*, vol. 1: *Pocthecayotl (arte de traficar)* (México: Universidad Nacional Autónoma de México, 1995), p. 125; B. de Sahagún,

Florentine Codex: General History of the Things of New Spain, book 9: *The Merchants* (Santa Fe, NM: School of American Research and University of Utah, 1959), p. 48.

29. Relación de la Ciudad de Valladolid (1579), p. 338; D. de Landa and A. M. Tozzer, *Landa's relacion de las cosas de Yucatan: A Translation* (New York: Kraus, 1966), p. 324.

30. De Landa and Tozzer, *Landa's relacion de Yucatan*, pp. 324–5.

31. G. C. Vaillant, *Aztecs of Mexico Origin, Rise and Fall of the Aztec Nation* (New York: Doubleday, Doran & Co., 1941), p. 207.

32. T. de Motolinia, *History of the Indians of New Spain* (Washington, DC: Academy of American Franciscan History, 1951), p. 275.

33. Fowler, 'Cacao Production', p. 309.

34. Quoted in Coe and Coe, *The True History of Chocolate*, p. 99.

35. G. Fernández de Oviedo, *Historia general y natural de las Indias*, vol. 2 (Asunción: Editorial Guaraní, 1944), p. 247.

36. Coe and Coe, *The True History of Chocolate*, pp. 106–7.

37. Duran, *History of the Indies*, p. 500

38. Ibid., p. 509.

39. Coe and Coe, *The True History of Chocolate*, p. 97.

40. P. M. D' Anghera, *De Orbe Novo: The Eight Decades of Peter Martyr D'Anghera,* 2 vols (New York and London: G. P. Putnam's Sons, 1912), vol. 2, pp. 112–13.

41. P. M. De Anglería, *Cartas sobre el Nuevo Mundo* (Madrid: Ediciones Polifemo, 1990), p. 111.

42. Coe and Coe, *The True History of Chocolate*, p. 112.

43. Motolinia, *History of the Indians of New Spain*, p. 245.

44. J. de Acosta, *Natural and Moral History of the Indies* (Durham, NC, and London: Duke University Press, 2002), p. 210.

45. A. de Zorita, *Historia de la Nueva España* (Madrid: Librería General de Victoriano Suárez, 1909), p. 196.

46. Fowler, 'Cacao Production', pp. 309, 320.

47. C. Gibson, *The Aztecs under Spanish Rule: A History of the Indians of the Valley of Mexico 1519–1810* (Stanford, CA: Stanford University Press, 1995), p. 348.

48. J. I. Israel, *Race, Class and Politics in Colonial Mexico 1610–1670* (Oxford: Oxford University Press, 1975), p. 28.

49. Ulloa, *Descripción geográfico-física*, pp. 29–30. Soconusco's population figures for the colonial period indicated that they 'were at their lowest levels early in the eighteenth century'. Tribute paid in *cargas* of cacao fell dramatically during the same period and cacao trees were fewer. 'The late sixteenth century estimate for total trees under cultivation was approximately 1,500,000 whereas the figure for the early nineteenth century is fewer than 500,000'. This lower number presumably was the consequence of overall population decline. See J. Gasco, 'Soconusco Cacao Farmers Past and Present: Continuity and Change in an Ancient Way of Life', in McNeil (ed.), *Chocolate in Mesoamerica*, p. 329.

50. Humboldt, *Ensayo político*, vol. 1, p. 125.

51. Gage, *Travels in the New World* , p. 151.

52. Ibid., p. 239.

53. M. Aguilar-Moreno, 'The Good and Evil of Chocolate in Colonial Mexico', in McNeil (ed.), *Chocolate in Mesoamerica*, p. 276.

54. J. Lockhart, *The Nahuas after the Conquest: A Social and Cultural History of the Indians of Central Mexico, Sixteenth through Eighteenth Centuries* (Stanford, CA: Stanford University Press, 1992), p. 178.

55. A. J. Anderson, F. Berdan and J. Lockhart, *Beyond the Codices* (Berkeley-Los Angeles and London: University of California Press, 1976), p. 209.
56. *Testament of don Julián de la Rosa, Tlaxcala, 1566*, ibid., p. 51.
57. Fernández de Oviedo, *Historia general y natural de las Indias*, p. 246.
58. Lockhart, *The Nahuas after the Conquest*, pp. 178, 180.
59. Gibson, *The Aztecs under Spanish Rule*, pp. 205–6, 209.
60. Relación de Cotula y Tibulon, in *Landa's relaciones de Yucatan*, vol. 1, pp.101–2.
61. Provincia de Tabasco: Melchor Alfaro 1579, ibid., vol. 1, p. 326.
62. 'Los indios tributarios de la provincia de Tabasco y en quien están encomendados', ibid., vol. 1, pp. 327–41.
63. 'Relación de la Ciudad de Valladolid', ibid., vol. 2, p. 338.
64. Fowler, 'Cacao Production', p. 309.
65. Gasco, 'Soconusco Cacao Farmers Past and Present', in McNeil (ed.), *Chocolate in Mesoamerica*, p. 329.
66. I. Da Bergamo, *Daily Life in Colonial Mexico: The Journey of Friar Ilarione da Bergamo, 1761–1768* (Norman, OK: University of Oklahoma Press, 2000), p. 132.
67. M. Romero de Terreros, *Los tlacos coloniales: Ensayo numismatico* (Mexico: Regis, 1935), pp. 4–5.
68. Motolinia, *History of the Indians of New Spain*, p. 275.
69. Gibson, *The Aztecs under Spanish Rule*, p. 358.
70. The Anonymous Conqueror, *Narrative of Some Things of New Spain* (New York: The Cortes Society, 1917), p. 40; J. F. Gemelli Carreri, *Viaje a la Nueva España: México a fines del Siglo XVII*, 2 vols (Mexico: Ediciones Libro-Mex, 1955), vol. 1, p. 48.
71. J. de Acosta, *Natural and Moral History of the Indies* (Durham, NC, and London: Duke University Press, 2002), p. 166.
72. Hamilton, *War and Prices in Spain, 1651–1800* (Cambridge, MA: Harvard University Press, 1947), pp. 72–3.
73. H. Tovar Pinzón, 'Remesas, situados y Real Hacienda en el siglo XVII', in Bernal (ed.), *Dinero moneda*, pp. 241–67, on p. 262.
74. Reglá, 'Edad moderna', p. 403. In the US during the Geat Depression from 1929 to 1973, prices fell by only 28 per cent.
75. E. García Guerra, 'Las decisiones monetarias de la monarquía castellana del siglo XVII y su incidencia en el funcionamiento del crédito privado', in Bernal (ed.) *Dinero moneda*, pp. 576–92, on p. 579.
76. F. Serrano Mangas, 'El papel del vellón', ibid., pp. 567–73, on p. 569.
77. J. I. Israel, *Race, Class and Politics*, pp. 194–5.
78. Céspedes del Castillo, 'Las Indias durante los siglos XVI y XVII', p. 458.
79. Hamilton, *El tesoro americano*, p. 81.
80. R. Von Glahn, 'Foreign Silver Coins and Market Culture in Nineteenth Century China', in *Complementarity among Monies and Revision of Asian Monetary History* (Tokyo: University of Tokyo, 2006), pp. 85–108, p. 93.
81. Ibid., p. 108.
82. A. Kuroda, 'Complementarity Non-Integrable among Monies in History: Nature of Currency as Viscous, Non-Uniform and Separable Stream', ibid., pp. 3–11, on p. 10.

10 Deyell 'Precious Metals, Debasements and Cowrie Shells in the Medieval Indian Monetary Systems, *c.* 1200–1575'

1. '... in no year does India drain our empire of less than five hundred and fifty millions of sesterces, giving back her own wares in exchange, which are sold among us at fully one hundred times their prime cost'. Pliny, *Natural History*, VI.26, written in Rome *c.* 79 AD. Haider notes, 'Letters and legal documents of the Geniza collection [Cairo] reveal that the general movement of specie from the west ... to the east ... was a permanent feature of the India trade in the twelfth and thirteenth centuries': N. Haider, 'Coinage and the Silver Crisis', in I. Habib, *History of Science, Philosophy and Culture in Indian Civilization*, vol. 8, pt 1: *Economic History of Medieval India, 1200–1500* (New Delhi: Pearson Longman, 2011), p. 154. 'Wassaf, an early fourteenth-century Persian historian, saw India as the drain of gold which it had been in earlier and later centuries': S. Digby, 'The Currency System', in T. Raychaudhuri and I. Habib (eds), *The Cambridge Economic History of India*, vol. 1: *c. 1200–c. 1750* (Cambridge: Cambridge University Press, 1982), chs 3–4, p. 99. '... the precious metals are a commodity which it always has been, and still continues to be, extremely advantageous to carry from Europe to India. There is scarce any commodity that brings a better price there.' A. Smith, *The Wealth of Nations*, book 2 (1776), ed. A. Skinner (Harmondsworth: Penguin Classics, 1999), p. 311.

2. E.g. see D. MacDowall and A. Jha, *Foreign Coins Found in the Indian Sub-Continent* (Nasik: Indian Institute for Research in Numismatic Studies, 1995), which contains eight papers on Roman coins and three papers on Venetian coins found in India, both of which were imported in such numbers they became locally imitated. Seventh-century Iranian coins became so common in western India they gave rise to local imitations, the so-called Indo-Sasanian coins, which flourished for four centuries after the fall of the Sasanian empire. Fifteenth- and sixteenth-century silver larins (fish-hook money) of the Persian Gulf became so common on the Konkan coast that they gave rise to local imitations issued by the Adil Shahi rulers. The Mughal empire in the period 1556 to 1757 required all coins and bullion brought to India to be reminted into imperial coin; contemporary commentators and modern historians too numerous to mention have detailed the immense volumes of foreign silver absorbed by this system.

3. R. Shrivastava, *Mining and Metallurgy in Ancient India* (Delhi: Munshiram Manoharlal, 2006), pp. 7–37. Also 'Medieval India's Precious Metal Mineral Resources', appendix A in J. Deyell, *Living without Silver: the Monetary History of Early Medieval India* (New Delhi: Oxford University Press, 1990; repr. 1999), pp. 248–52. P. K. Chatterjee, *Annotated Index of Indian Mineral Occurrences*, part iii (Calcutta: Geological Survey of India, 1964), pp. 287–98.

4. Surface vein gold deposits are noted in Badakhshan, Kabul and Zabul: S. Coats, *The Potential for Gold* (Kabul: Afghanistan Geological Survey, n.d.), p. 3.

5. Ian Blanchard describes in detail a succession of Central Asian silver mining complexes beginning in the late fifth century and ending with their destruction by Genghis Khan in the early thirteenth century: 'The Central Asian Mining Complex, 480–1130 A.D', in I. Blanchard, *Mining, Metallurgy and Minting in the Middle Ages*, vol. 1: *Asiatic Supremacy 425–1125* (Stuttgart: Steiner, 2001), ch. 7, pp. 225–70. Of the Indo-Afghan borderlands, Le Strange says 'At the eastern source [of the Kabul River] are the celebrated silver mines, known to the Arabs as Banjahir (for Panjhir ...) from which large quantities of the precious metal were obtained, and Banjahir became a mint city under the Saffarid princes in the 3rd (9th) century ... Yakut gives us a long account of these silver mines with

their population of riotous miners … The ruin of the place was due to Changiz Khan; and when Ibn Batutah … came here in the 8th (14th) century, he found no silver mine, but only the disused tunnels of the former workings.' G. Le Strange, *Lands of the Eastern Caliphate* (Cambridge: Cambridge University Press, 1905), p. 350.

6. 'With the successive plunder of the Deccan kingdoms at the end of the thirteenth and beginning of the fourteenth centuries, which were more prosperous in the preceding centuries than northern India, a great quantity of precious metal came into the hands of the Delhi sultans …' Digby, 'The Currency System', p. 96. This has been demonstrated statistically by Shireen Moosvi using the Uttar Pradesh treasure trove hoards. She found that fully 63.2 per cent of the silver coins issued by the Delhi Sultanate in its first 200 years (thirteenth and fourteenth centuries) were struck in the name of one king, 'Alauddin Khalji (1296–1316). His career was launched by his conquest of the Yadava kingdom of Devagiri (in modern Maharashtra). S. Moosvi, 'Numismatic Evidence and the Economic History of the Delhi Sultanate', *Proceedings of the Indian History Congress* (Gorakhpur, 1991), pp. 209–10 (tables 1 and 2), cited by Haider, 'Coinage and the Silver Crisis', p. 150.

7. Wink has characterized these foreign ruling classes as 'post-nomadic elites who were immigrants from the arid zones … Converts to Islam, in India the nobility among them was referred to by the generic name of "Khurasanians"'. Drawing on Ibn Batuta, he further notes 'Whether they came from Anatolia (Rum), Iraq, Syria, Egypt, the Maghrib, Ghazna, Khwarazm, or, in effect, from Khurasan, all (elite) foreigners fell within the same category. Many of the Mongol amirs were included in it as well.' A. Wink, *Al-Hind: The Making of the Indo-Islamic World*, vol. 3: *Indo-Islamic Society, 14th–15th Centuries* (Leiden: Brill, 2004), pp. 125–6.

8. Overlay by the author. Base data ©2010 Google; © 2010 Tele Atlas; © 2010 Europa-Technologies; © 2010 Mapabc.com. Reproduction here is compliant with Google's 'Fair Use' policy available at http://www.google.com/permissions/geoguidelines. html#fairuse [accessed July 2010].

9. I recently reviewed the monetary interrelationships between these places in J. Deyell, 'Monetary and Financial Webs: The Regional and International Influence of Pre-Modern Bengali Coinage', in R. Mukherjee (ed.), *Pelagic Passageways: The Northern Bay of Bengal before Colonialism* (Delhi: Primus Books, 2011), pp. 289–99.

10. I. Habib, 'The Geographical Background', in Raychaudhuri and Habib (eds), *The Cambridge Economic History of India,* vol. 1, p. 6, later distilled in Habib, 'Forests, Deserts and Untilled Lands', in Habib, *Cambridge Economic History*, vol. 1, pp. 33–6. Also Wink, *Al-Hind*, vol. 3, p. 29.

11. 'The term dinnara and the monetary system of Kashmir', note 'H' in M. A. Stein (tr.), *Kalhana's Rajatarangini: A Chronicle of the Kings of Kashmir* (London: Constable & Co., 1900; repr. Delhi: Motilal Banarsidas, 1979), p. 328.

12. R. M. Eaton, *The Rise of Islam and the Bengal Frontier 1204–1760* (New Delhi: Oxford University Press, 1994), pp. 65–9, 97–102.

13. S. F. Dale, 'Empires and Emporia: Palace, Mosque, Market, and Tomb in Istanbul, Isfahan, Agra, and Delhi', *Journal of the Economic and Social History of the Orient,* 53 (2010), p. 212.

14. Unlike gold coins: hoards of regional sultanate gold coins, while small in volume, tend to contain the coins of many regional kingdoms, as far afield as Kashmir in the north and the Bahmanids in the south. I would attribute this to the preference for gold coins by Muslim officials, who often sought to better their position by service elsewhere, and

who would be keen to transfer their savings in a form at once discrete, portable and universally exchangeable.

15. Prakrit orginal: Thakkur Pheru Virachita, 'Prakritbhashabddha Dravyapariksha', *Indian Numismatic Chronicle*, 4:1 (1965), pp. 75–94. English tr. by V. S. Agrawala, 'Dravya Pariksha of Thakkura Pheru', *Indian Numismatic Chronicle*, 7:2 (1969), pp. 100–14.

16. I. Habib, 'The Price Regulations of 'Ala'uddin Khalji: A Defence of Zia' Barani', *Indian Economic and Social History Review*, 21:4 (1984), pp. 393–414, reprinted in S. Subrahmanyam, *Money and the Market in India 1100–1700* (New Delhi: Oxford University Press, 1994), pp. 85–111.

17. Note e.g. that fourteen of the twenty-nine research papers in the Indian History Congress's selection of annual congress presentations, concern agriculture and agricultural revenue: S. Chandra, (ed.), *Essays in Medieval Indian Economic History* (New Delhi: Munshiram Manoharlal, 1987).

18. 'The Military, the Economy, and Administrative Reform', ch. 12, in P. Jackson, *The Delhi Sultanate: A Political and Military History* (Cambridge: Cambridge University Press, 1999; repr. 2003), pp. 238–54.

19. Catalogued by H. N. Wright, *The Coinage and Chronology of the Sultans of Delhi* (Delhi: Oxford University Press, 1936; repr. New Delhi: Oriental Books, 1974), pp. 139–46 and discussed on pp. 166–7. Also see Digby, 'The Currency System', p. 97 and Jackson, *The Delhi Sultanate*, p. 262.

20. Md Bin Tughluq had some knowledge of the situation in contemporary China, for about this time he received an embassy from the Chinese emperor. In 1338 he dispatched the Moroccan traveller Ibn Batuta on a return embassy to the Yuan emperor. *The Rehla of Ibn Batuta*, tr. M . Husain (Baroda: Oriental Institute, 1976), pp. 150–1.

21. For a measured discussion see M. Husain, *Tughluq Dynasty* (Calcutta: Thacker, Spink & Co., 1963), pp. 185–90.

22. Digby, 'The Currency System', p. 97. Amir Timur related that when he seized the Delhi treasury in 1399, he found it to contain huge quantities of the 'Alauddin Khalji's gold tankas (issued almost a century earlier from the loot of the Deccani expeditions). *Malfuzat-I Timuri* or *Tuzak-I Timuri*, tr. Abu Talib, in H. M. Elliott and J. Dowson (eds), *The History of India as Told by its Own Historians* (London: Truebner & Co., 1867), vol. 3, p. 446.

23. J. F. Richards, 'The Economic History of the Lodi Period: 1451–1526', *Journal of the Economic and Social History of the Orient*, 8:1 (1965), pp. 47–67, repr. in Subrahmanyam, *Money and the Market*, pp. 137–55. More recently, see Jackson, *The Delhi Sultanate*, pp. 321–5 and Wink, *Al-Hind*, vol. 3, pp. 134–8.

24. See n. 6, above.

25. Haider, 'Coinage and the Silver Crisis', pp. 152, 158.

26. Wright, *The Coinage and Chronology*, appendix B1, 'Assays by Dr. S. W. Smith, C.B.E., Chief Assayer, the Royal Mint', pp. 403–8.

27. Both the Uttar Pradesh and Rajasthan treasure trove records show only modest volumes of *bahlolis*, especially in comparison with earlier and later series: A. K. Srivastava, *Coin Hoards of Uttar Pradesh 1882–1979* (Lucknow: State Museum, 1980); Rajasthan, http://www.ancientcoins.rajasthan.gov.in/. However large groups of *bahlolis* of both Delhi and Jaunpur occasionally appear in commercial channels, giving an impression of greater numbers than officially recorded.

28. As Moosvi notes, 'tax rates were maintained at constant levels in debased money'. S. Moosvi, 'The State and Economy', in Raychaudhuri and Habib, *The Cambridge Economic History of India*, vol. 1, p. 145.

29. Haider, referring to earlier work by Irfan Habib, discusses this issue in Haider, 'Coinage and the Silver Crisis', pp. 158–9.

30. Chilosi and Volckart note of contemporary Europe, 'The prevalence of fiscal debasements in princely territories was not necessarily a "scourge". They allowed princes to increase their revenues at short notice ...' D. Chilosi and O. Volckart, *Good Money or Bad? Debasement, Society and the State in the Late Medieval Ages*, Working Papers, 140/10 (London: London School of Economics, May 2010), p. 41. In Delhi, as in Europe, these debasements are noticeable in times of war.

31. Richards argued that there was no shortage of precious metals in the Lodi sultanate, rather a shortage of precious metals in the royal treasury, due to the alienation of the revenue-gathering system through feudal grants. This view relies too heavily on museum coin holdings, which over-represent the rare Lodi silver coinage and scarce Lodi gold coinage, and commensurately under-represent the relatively plentiful Lodi billon coinage. Richards, 'The Economic History of the Lodi Period', p. 153. More recently Wink has revisited this period, highlighting the Lodi's success in extending their Afghan tribal customs and values into their rulership of Delhi. He is of the view that they were able to leverage their close association with the horse trade into leadership of large bodies of cavalry recruited on promises of plunder rather than cash salaries. In examining this period of transition, however, his focus is on political rather than economic processes. Wink, *Al-Hind,* vol. 3, pp. 135–6.

32. Eaton, *The Rise of Islam*, pp. 194–5.

33. 'Economic Conditions', ch. 4 in M. R. Tarafdar, *Husain Shahi Bengal* (Dhaka: Asiatic Society, 1965), pp. 124–62.

34. More fully described in J. Deyell, 'Cowries and Coins: The Dual Monetary System of the Bengal Sultanate', *Indian Economic and Social History Review*, 47:1 (2010), pp. 63–106.

35. K. N. Dikshit, *Excavations at Paharpur, Bengal,* ASI Memoir 55 (Delhi: Archaeological Survey of India, 1938), p. 33.

36. 'Trade is carried on by means of *kauris*, which are the current money of the country'. Sulaiman, *Salsilat ut-Tawarikh,* in Elliott and Dowson (eds), *The History of India,* vol. 1, p. 5.

37. R. S. Wicks, *Money, Markets and Trade in Early Southeast Asia: The Development of Indigenous Monetary Systems to AD 1400* (Ithaca, NY: Cornell University/SEAP, 1992), fig. 3.7, p. 87; fig. 3.8, p. 91; fig. 4.3, p. 117.

38. Deyell, 'Cowries and Coins', pp. 73–4.

39. This has been aptly summarized by Heimann: 'Sources from the post-Gupta period [sixth century] up until the nineteenth century show that in this entire period there existed an ordered system of ratios between specific numbers of cowries and other forms of metallic currency. This stability was not only relevant in the market place but also to the state taxation system where, especially in Bengal, cowries were accepted as payment of revenues and taxes. Thus cowries functioned as money in all modern senses of the word – sensitive to changes in liquidity demands, supply, transaction and production costs and gross national product.' J. Heimann, 'Small Change and Ballast: Cowry Trade and Usage as an Example of India Ocean Economic History', *South Asia,* 3:1 (1980), pp. 56–7.

40. C. M. Cipolla, *Money, Prices and Civilization in the Mediterranean World* (New York: Gordian Press, 1967), p. 27.

41. Cowrie use in local markets in neighbouring Assam was described in some detail in 'Circulation of Cowrie Shells as Money', appendix A in N. Rhodes and S. K. Bose, *The Coinage of Assam,* vol. 1, *Pre-Ahom Period* (Kolkata: Mira Bose, 2003), pp. 57–64.

42. Source: Deyell, 'Cowries and Coins', fig. 3A, p. 82.

43. Eaton, *The Rise of Islam*, p. 96.

44. Chilosi and Volckart, *Good Money or Bad?*, p. 5.

45. See 'Mints with Known Dates', appendix B in S. E. Hussain, *The Bengal Sultanate: Politics, Economy and Coins (AD 1205–1576)* (Delhi: Manohar, 2003), pp. 330–5.

46. See Deyell, 'Cowries and Coins', table 2, pp. 83–4.

47. Ibid., table 3, p. 85.

48. S. H. Jahan, 'History of Cattagrama Port', in G. Bhattacharya et al. (eds), *Kalhar: Studies in Art, Iconography, Architecture and Archaeology of India and Bangladesh* (New Delhi: Kaveri Books, 2007), p. 28. Her reference was the account of Caesar Frederick in *Hakluytus Postumus*.

49. A. Cortesao (ed.), *The Suma Oriental of Tome Pires* (1515) (London: Hakluyt Society, 1944; repr. New Delhi: Asian Educational Services, 2005), p. 93.

50. E.g. von Glahn notes a collapse of silver production prior to the 1430s: R. von Glahn, *Fountain of Fortune: Money and Monetary Policy in China, 1000–1700* (Berkeley, CA: University of California Press, 1996), pp. 83, 113. Later the mines must have recovered; Bin Yang notes a doubling of silver mining taxes between 1458 and 1460: B. Yang, *Between Winds and Clouds: The Making of Yunnan (Second Century BCE to Twentieth Century CE)* (New York: Columbia University Press, 2008), p. 195.

51. R. von Glahn, 'Monies of Account and Monetary Transition in China, Twelfth to Fourteenth Centuries', *Journal of the Economic and Social History of the Orient*, 53 (2010), pp. 463–505.

52. 'The World of Islam: An Economic and Environmental Analysis', in Blanchard, *Mining, Metallurgy and Minting*, pp. 37–102.

53. J. Hogendorn and M. Johnson, *The Shell Money of the Slave Trade* (Cambridge: Cambridge University Press, 1986; repr. 2003), p. 11.

INDEX

Notes:

(1) The following terms, so commonly used in the essays in this volume, are not indexed: bullion, coins, credit, gold, silver, prices, inflation.

(2) The names of princes, kings, monarchs, dukes, popes, etc. are listed under their own proper names, and not by their titles (the titles are listed after their names).

(3) There are separate entries for:
   – Wars and Battles
   – Treaties (or Peace)

For Product Safety Concerns and Information please contact our EU
representative GPSR@taylorandfrancis.com
Taylor & Francis Verlag GmbH, Kaufingerstraße 24, 80331 München, Germany

www.ingramcontent.com/pod-product-compliance
Ingram Content Group UK Ltd.
Pitfield, Milton Keynes, MK11 3LW, UK
UKHW021614240425
457818UK00018B/547

*9 7 8 1 1 3 8 6 6 1 7 1 4 *